THE ART
OF PRESTIGE

A VOLUME IN THE SERIES

Studies in Print Culture and the History of the Book

Edited by

Greg Barnhisel

Robert A. Gross

Joan Shelley Rubin

Michael Winship

THE ART OF PRESTIGE

The Formative Years at Knopf,
1915–1929

Amy Root Clements

University of Massachusetts Press
Amherst & Boston

ISBN 978-1-62534-000-0

Designed by Jack Harrison
Set in Adobe Caslon Pro
Printed and bound by Sheridan Books, Inc.

Library of Congress Cataloging-in-Publication Data

Clements, Amy Root, 1967-
The art of prestige : the formative years at Knopf, 1915–1929 / Amy Root Clements.
    pages cm. — (Studies in print culture and the history of the book)
Includes bibliographical references and index.
ISBN 978-1-62534-092-4 (hardcover : alk. paper) — ISBN 978-1-62534-093-1 (pbk. : alk. paper)
1. Alfred A. Knopf, Inc.—History.   2. Knopf, Alfred A., 1892–1984.   3. Knopf, Blanche W.,
1894–1966.   4. Publishers and publishing—New York (State)—New York—History—20th
century.   5. Literature publishing—United States—History—20th century.
6. Authors and publishers—United States—History—20th century.   I. Title.
Z473.A48C58 2014
070.509747'10904—dc23
                          2013048750

British Library Cataloguing-in-Publication Data
A catalogue record for this book is available from the British Library.

PUBLICATION OF THIS BOOK

IS SUPPORTED BY A GRANT FROM

JEWISH FEDERATION OF GREATER HARTFORD

 CONTENTS

 ACKNOWLEDGMENTS

This book was inspired by conversations with my friend Stephen Pinson, who introduced me to the beauty of Vintage Books (Knopf's paperback line) when he was working at a bookstore as a college student. Two decades later, I visited the reading room at the Harry Ransom Humanities Research Center (HRC) on a quest to reconstruct the history of Vintage. I soon discovered that the truly uncharted territory was the early history of Knopf. My endeavor has been sustained by many wise souls, Michael Winship chiefly among them. His devotion to the history of the printed word is a gift to all who are fortunate enough to know him. The Bibliographical Society of America and its New Scholars Program generously gave me an opportunity to showcase my initial research on the production qualities of early Knopf books. These findings grew into chapter 5, "Distinctive by Design." Cathy Henderson and Richard Oram have dedicated much of their life's work to the Knopf archive at the HRC. I appreciate their guidance, their publications, and their tireless stewardship of the collection.

I am also immensely grateful to acquisitions editor Brian Halley and his colleagues at University of Massachusetts Press. Other key assistance was provided by copy editor and publishing maven Katherine Scheuer; Nancy Kuhl and her cohorts at the Beinecke Library; G. Thomas Tanselle; the Columbia University Archives staff, and Hana Crawford in the Columbia Center for Oral History; the staff of the New York Public Library's Manuscript and Archives Division; Alice Knopf; Anne Prescott; John Thornton; Sharon Nell, Lynn Rudloff, Mary Rist, and my other wonderfully supportive colleagues at St. Edward's University; Brian Bremen, Diane Davis, Linda Ferreira-Buckley, and Mark Smith at the University of Texas; Laurie Brown and Pat Johnson, who kindly arranged for my interview luncheon with a group of veteran Knopf staff members; Susan, John, Catherine, and Jennifer Stayton; Alison, John, and Travie Mitchell; Cecilia Clements; my five sisters, who have sustained me with a lifetime of ardent support: Carolyn Daugherty, Nikki Dowd, Mary Virginia Dowdle, Paula Mara, and Wendy Savage; and my artistic, articulate parents, who died many years ago but surely continue to guide my path.

Coining the term "becoming Borzoi," my beloved husband patiently assisted in the whelping of this book. Thank you, dear Andrew.

THE ART
OF PRESTIGE

INTRODUCTION

Books de Luxe

BORZOI BOOKS ARE BOOKS DE LUXE! In the refinement of the format—in the stability of the binding—in fact, in all those things that make a book worth while—its intellectual appeal, its ornamental appeal, and its appeal as a desirable permanent possession, Borzoi Books are Books de Luxe, equally a delight to the mind and an addition to the home!

1923 New York Times advertisement

IN JUNE 1915, twenty-two-year-old Alfred Knopf procured a desk in his father's advertising office on Manhattan's West Forty-Second Street and founded a publishing firm that would come to be regarded by many as the pinnacle of America's book trade. Knopf had recently been fired by publisher Mitchell Kennerley for poaching authors in anticipation of launching his own company. Knopf's first title, Émile Augier's *Four Plays*, debuted in October and was bound in pumpkin-orange paper over boards.[1] The most noticeable aspect of the binding is stamped in teal ink on the back cover, where the monogram AAK announces Knopf's arrival in 108-point type. Joining Knopf in this business venture was fellow bibliophile Blanche Wolf, whom he married the following spring. During their courtship, she suggested that a borzoi (a Russian wolfhound) might make a suitable emblem for the company. With a name derived from the Russian word for "swift," the borzoi appropriately made haste in becoming a sign of fine books produced under the direction of two young, dynamic arbiters of literary taste.

Now approaching its centennial, the Alfred A. Knopf publishing company continues to hold high status, having released works by thirty-four Nobel Prize winners (including Thomas Mann, Albert Camus, Gabriel García Márquez, and Toni Morrison), more than fifty Pulitzer Prize winners, and more than thirty National Book Award winners. Whether such prizes are a barometer of quality is a subjective matter, but two realities emerge: the literary tastes of the Knopfs and their editors match those of prize jurors, and the rise of the company paralleled the rise of literary prizes in the twentieth century. Knopf also enjoys frequent and fairly consistently favorable attention from book critics. When the *New York Times Book Review* published its annual list of the ten best books of the year in 2008, seven of those titles were published by Knopf.

Knopf books can easily be identified on store shelves because of the company's eye-catching logo, which depicts a borzoi leaping with vigor. "Borzoi Books" implies a special Knopf series, but the term has been used continuously by the company to refer to all its offerings. The line THIS IS A BORZOI BOOK now appears on the copyright page of every Knopf book, although it was not used in the book's interior pages in the initial years, when the line instead appeared on select jackets. The phrase "Borzoi Books," along with the wolfhound illustration, became a registered trademark in 1922.

This distinctive device reflects a spirit that led book historian John Tebbel to single out Knopf's launch in 1915 as "a turning point between the past and present of publishing history. [Alfred Knopf] retained some of the best qualities of former generations, yet he set new standards. . . . He introduced concepts of quality that had been all but forgotten in the rush to penetrate and, if possible, saturate the mass market."[2] Such comments underscore the enduring prominence of Borzoi Books as noble stalwarts against lowbrow publishing, reflecting a social tension that is a frequent focus in studies of literary modernism. The development of an award-winning roster of authors by a fledgling publisher during the collision of modernism and middle-class buying power in America raises questions that are fundamental to literary and cultural history, and the formation of Knopf offers particularly rich paths of inquiry because the company brought these questions to bear in such a visible way.

Tebbel rightly notes Knopf's impact on modern American publishing; Borzoi Books indeed brought prominence to an aesthetic movement in publishing history. Yet the history of Knopf's founding years reveals a narrative in which Blanche and Alfred did not *introduce* a higher standard of book production and content so much as they capitalized on standards already in varying degrees of use at several other houses (including Kennerley's), marketing and applying those standards with regularity. Tebbel might have more precisely referred to the Knopfs as publishers who *reintroduced* "concepts of quality." Furthermore, Alfred Knopf did not see himself as a gatekeeper between the intelligentsia and mass-market readers. Arguably, the gate was made irrelevant by affordable, beautifully bound classics in series such as the Modern Library. Instead, Blanche and Alfred were masters at branding the beauty of their books, creating a prestigious identity that was intended to capture the attention of a broad variety of audiences. Despite the air of exclusivity, each Borzoi Book would be marketed to the hilt in an attempt to reach a wide audience. The Knopfs permitted their branded identity to extend well beyond their professional lives, feeding their self-perceptions of social superiority.

In the publishing industry, prestige feeds off access to exclusive realms: an agent's access to editors who can grant contracts, a publicist's access to critics who can bestow media attention, a sales team's access to key buyers who can enhance the retail promotion of a book, an author's access to prize jurors who can bestow awards on a select few. *The Art of Prestige* reconstructs the initial years during which the Knopfs quickly gained access to these commercial and artistic circles and became power brokers in their own right, developing the ability to confer prestige (a manufactured value) on the authors who were chosen to be associated with Borzoi Books.

The transactions in such exchanges are aptly described as a struggle in James English's *The Economy of Prestige,* an exploration of the last century's profusion of prizes and awards for the arts whose stakeholders exemplify "the struggle for power to produce value, which means power to confer value on that which does not intrinsically possess it."[3] Unlike the legacy publishers at the helm of Harper's and Scribner's, the Knopfs were outsiders among the literati of their day. As unknowns, they had to take it upon themselves to carefully forge a prestigious identity for their firm and for their literature. In part, the Knopfs' prestige grew from an ability to declare their books to be worthy, in self-congratulatory yet charming sales copy. The image endured because it was reinforced by reality as Borzoi authors indeed received accolades, and the design of their books was often overseen by acclaimed figures in the emerging field of graphic arts.

Aspiring to not only join but to dominate key literary circles, the Knopfs also aspired to garner sufficient profit to feed their taste for luxury; therefore, they balanced these goals with the crafting of a brand designed to appeal, oddly enough, to a broad, sometimes economically middle-class (distinct from middlebrow) audience. Max Weber's theories of power-oriented prestige underscore the conundrum in which economic interests may require the expansion of a group, but the expansion has to be conducted in a way that doesn't tamper with the perception of exclusivity. "Selectness exists in associations of the most diverse kind," Weber writes. "[Clubs] as a rule admit nobody who is personally objectionable to the members. This very fact 'legitimizes' the new member toward the outside, far beyond the qualities that are important to the group's purpose." Anyone who seeks to join could potentially enlarge the group, but this is at odds with the benefits of existing members who enjoy "increasing their economic value through restriction to the smallest possible circle."[4] Borzoi Books' "club" of authors had a cultivated air of perceived exclusivity, often serving as informal agents and literary critics; access to that realm was publicly said to be tied to possessing quality, although the Knopfs' acquisition budget was an equally limiting factor. For the Borzoi's "club" of consumers (who quite literally had the option of joining one of several subscription book clubs run by the Knopfs' competitors), a message of exclusivity, real or perceived, attracted sales coast to coast.

This notion that mental influence—rather than empirically measured superior quality—drives prestige echoes the word's Latin origin, "praestigiae," referring to a conjuror's tricks. In Knopf's initial years, as the publishing world absorbed the young couple's claims of prestige, Blanche and Alfred seemingly conjured an elite aura for their unknown, upstart publishing house. Unlike tricksters, they delivered on their claims of excellence through a penchant for acquiring low-risk, venerable, prize-winning European imports and utilizing old-world design principles popularized by well-established artists.

The essential question "how did the Knopfs 'conjure' such stature so quickly, and what was the impact of their influence?" encompasses a range of factors, including the Knopfs' pantheon of luminary authors and teams of well-established experts in the fields of typography, design, and advertising who orchestrated the desired impact on readers' perceptions of the texts published under the Borzoi imprimatur. The question of economics (how did Borzoi Books achieve quick and enduring profitability, fulfilling Alfred's mandate to pay the bills promptly?) leads to answers that undermine the Knopfs' personae as daring purveyors of experimental titles. In fact, their early lists included a considerable number of highly accessible titles, from diet books to detective novels, and Alfred often proudly credited decidedly non-avant-garde Midwest booksellers with being his best initial retail outlets, in contrast to New York publishers who operated small bookstores meant to serve as gathering places for the intelligentsia, such as Albert and Charles Boni's Washington Square Bookshop, which was frequented by Greenwich Village radicals.⁵ The Knopfs' association with the fine-printing revival bears similar complexity. Their expensive limited editions (a concept that the Knopfs are sometimes erroneously credited with pioneering) were often abysmal individual financial failures, but they helped create the profitable illusion that all Borzoi Books were artifacts of old-world handicraft, evoking the aura of handmade paper, manual typesetting, and the hand press.

As a testament to Blanche and Alfred's extraordinary branding efforts, the Borzoi identity was not diminished when Knopf ceased to be an independent, family-owned house. After Blanche and Alfred sold their firm to Random House in 1960, the prominence of both Knopf and Random House only continued to grow, in part because the inimitable Borzoi image had been heavily reinforced by marketing throughout the company's first forty-five years, influencing the mindset of Blanche and Alfred's successor publishers as well. The growth of multi-house publishing conglomerates can dilute an imprint's brand identity (Dutton, Viking, and Putnam in many ways seem indistinguishable now under the Penguin umbrella), but Knopf's image among agents, authors, critics, booksellers, and prize committees has only become more prominent after decades of corporate absorption that continued with RCA's acquisition of Random House, Inc., in 1965; Advance Publications' acquisition of Random House in 1980; and the German media corporation Bertelsmann's acquisition of Random House, Inc., in 1998, at which time coast-to-coast media and trade publications referred to the Random House group of imprints as the crown jewel of American publishing, citing Knopf authors as evidence. This perception has not diminished in the face of yet another merger, this time between Bertelsmann and Penguin, finalized in 2013.

Tracing the origins of this cachet, *The Art of Prestige* examines a branding effort that was conceived by a loquacious, flamboyantly dressed Columbia University graduate who, with his equally youthful fiancée, managed to forge a corporate identity exuding elderly gravitas before reaching the age of thirty. Curiously, the third volume of John Tebbel's *History of Book Publishing in the United States* features a report on Alfred A. Knopf in both the section titled "The Old Publishers Continue" and "New Publishers of the Twenties," a decision Tebbel attributed to Knopf's role as "a transitional figure between the old and new. . . . Knopf came to be regarded with overwhelming respect, even awe, both in and out of the trade. In the twenties [less than a decade after the firm's inception] he was such an outsize figure that some of those who observed his progress hardly knew what to make of him."[6]

Other ironies include the fact that although the company is now associated with American literary lions and the discovery of new talent, ranging from John Updike to Sandra Cisneros and Cynthia Ozick, Knopf was founded on the premise that European writers are superior to American ones, with an initial publication list that predicted a modest future as a reprint house. Paradoxically, the Knopfs used modern promotional tactics to create an aura of Old World anti-commercialism for Borzoi Books. Raised by fathers who were salesmen, Blanche and Alfred learned to publicize themselves effectively, developing an image as highly affluent globetrotters who embraced European intellectualism and refinement while nonetheless becoming masters of the modern American marketing campaign (which was viewed as crass by old-guard publishers), using everything from billboards to street hawkers to promote their top sellers.

Cultural aspects of the Knopfs' identity are equally ironic. Their Jewish ancestry is noted by publishing historians who trace the courageous rise of Jewish American publishers during the early twentieth century in the face of resentment on the part of the publishing world's Protestant establishment. The

Knopfs were not immune to religious discrimination, but few seem to realize that they were decidedly secular. Alfred candidly recalled feasting at the Plaza Hotel on Yom Kippur when he was a child, rather than fasting on the Day of Atonement, and he avoided opportunities to find solidarity with other Jewish publishers who were on the rise in Manhattan. In his history of the Modern Library, Jay Satterfield describes the fact that the trade press tended to group Horace Liveright, Benjamin Huebsch, and the Knopfs together because they were Jewish, despite the very distinct motivations of those publishers. Liveright craved the limelight and reveled in the avant-garde literary community. Huebsch, with whom Knopf eventually forged a friendship, ran a small, discreet house that emphasized European concerns and did not measure success by sales figures. "The Knopfs," Satterfield observes, "while intellectually adventuresome, operated according to a finely calibrated calculus of prestige and profit."[7]

Blanche Knopf's powerful presence in the company is itself an anomaly that merits exploration, particularly because her accomplishments—including the acquisition of landmark, prize-winning international literature—defy conventional wisdom. Although she is often extolled as a pioneer who defeated gender discrimination in a male-dominated industry, she in fact had limited impact on opening career paths for women in publishing during her lifetime. As late as 1965 she was still barred from the Publishers' Lunch Club because of her gender, not to mention the permanent omission of her identity in the name—Alfred A. Knopf, Inc.—of the company she co-founded. She attempted to form a lunch club of women in publishing but "there were never enough of us to make it work."[8] When a women's college invited her to deliver a speech about the future of women in publishing, she declined the invitation "on the ground that there 'was no future worth mentioning.'"[9] Her obituary in the *New York Times* mentioned superficial attributes such as her weight ("Mrs. Knopf was petite and chic; she was once plump, but for the last 35 years of her life weighed no more than 100 pounds"), diminishing the credit given to her significant professional achievements elsewhere in the article and alluding to her oft-cited habit of nibbling dry toast while her gourmand husband savored multi-course meals.[10]

For all its contradictions, the house of Knopf is often described as the cohesive embodiment of modern American publishing. The early years of Borzoi Books illuminate a phase in the rise of modernism as Blanche and Alfred attempted to create a product that appeared rarefied yet was commercially viable. Modern literary publishing was never truly threatened by a mass-market groundswell during the Jazz Age, evidenced by the profitability of both realms throughout the 1920s; Borzoi Books perhaps narrowed the schism through advertising that celebrated elegant standards for design, manufacture, and content but invited readers from all corners of America to order Mr. Knopf's catalog and partake. His correspondence with individual consumers shows that he was eager to take on the role of personal bookseller for any fan of Borzoi Books. In a way, the brand signified the democratization—not the rarefaction—of literary works that the Knopfs deemed to be of merit. Satterfield succinctly captures the climate in which Knopf and other houses were able to achieve multi-strata success: "The redefinition of the term 'class' to describe a general state of good taste, combined with the development of a tiered hierarchy of taste, offered Americans a way to make social distinctions without adhering to an economic determinism they saw as undemocratic."[11]

Many of the overlooked cross-cultural networks of writers that formed as a result of the burgeoning Borzoi identity are also reconstructed in this history, facilitated by the fact that Knopf authors also served as book reviewers and literary scouts in an era when the professionalization of literary agents was in its early stages. The Borzoi's audience was composed of academics, critics, consumers, producers, and publishing competitors, and each of these groups contributed to the oscillation of the firm's modern and old-world identities. Ultimately, the company's history recasts Alfred Knopf as a prudent business-man who easily deferred to the will of censors and reveled in aesthetics less for art's sake than for profitable perceptions of prestige. He ran tongue-in-cheek advertising copy in which he called his products "books for the civilized minority," yet he also presented himself as a reassuring literary advisor for the majority—middle-class consumers.[12]

Because savvy rhetorical maneuvers lie at the core of the resulting Borzoi identity, rhetorical analysis enhances our understanding of the company's complex history. Kenneth Burke, a contemporary of the Knopfs who came to be known as the founder of modern rhetorical studies, approached such questions of identity as a social concept, offering a useful application for the local and international "societies" of readership with which the Knopfs interacted. In an essay comparing Burke's theories of identification to those proposed by Sigmund Freud, whom Burke simultaneously revered and sought to rival, Diane Davis writes that both theorists "describe identification as a social act that partially unifies discrete individuals." She then reminds us of Burke's assertion that "the primary aim of rhetoric is not to win an argument but to make a connection, shifting the imagery of the persuasive encounter from a duel to a 'courtship.'"[13] Applied to the stages of the Knopfs' publishing process, Burke's theory of identification reveals a kaleidoscopic range of "courtships," in which two newly married publishers sought to establish a literary identity by courting various communities within the bookselling world—especially those that could help them gain prestige and profit. The resulting Borzoi signification served as both a response and a call to authors, fellow publishers, consumers, visual artists, critics, and others concerned with the perception of written language in book form.

In this social dialogue, the act of publishing also became an act of authorship as the Knopfs attempted to shape how their authors' productions were received, in negotiations ranging from financial to aesthetic concerns. Burke's emphasis on "consubstantiality"—the quest between individuals to find elements (substances) of their own identities in one another—plays out repeatedly in this publishing story. As Burke predicts, the elements of identification that formed so much of the substance of Borzoi Books are sometimes contradictory but always symbolic: the Knopfs sought admission to a community they perceived as Anglophilic, gentrified, and intellectual, while writers and artists in turn sought admission to the prestigious Knopf list, which in turn set the stage for further recruitment to a newly minted symbol of exceptional literature: Borzoi Books.

Ninety-one-year-old Alfred Knopf and eighty-six-year-old Kenneth Burke, who had seldom interacted with each other previously, shared a stage at New York University in 1983, each receiving an Elmer Holmes Bobst Award in Arts and Letters for having "brought true distinction to the American literary scene."[14] Underscoring their dual performances of distinctive literary roles, the Bobst stage captured the fruition of Burke's most widely cited theoretical system—his pentad of dramatism (act, scene, agent, agency, and purpose). While the use of drama as a metaphor for human behavior has been taken up by scores of luminaries, Burke's components offer an opportunity to probe a variety of factors at play in human action. Whether they acknowledge it or not, the "act" for all publishing companies includes interceding in the rhetorical exchange between author and reader. Notably, the Knopfs' intercession commenced in an era defined by "making it new."

Blanche and Alfred Knopf were successful in identifying themselves as power brokers among modernist literati and performing the role of arbiters of good taste for mainstream American readers coast to coast, yet the Knopfs were equally concerned about the perception of their books among other key audiences—including agents, authors, reviewers, and scholars. Tracing the publishing of printed books, the chapters that follow consider these roles as they affected various stages of the Borzoi brand's evolution, beginning with the social and educational influences that informed Blanche and Alfred's opinion of literature, which offered models for them to imitate, followed by a report on the extensive literary networks (spawned by Knopf's Columbia University professors) that enabled the couple to acquire books by increasingly prestigious authors who also served as scouts to expand the Borzoi circle.

The equally important network of relationships with book designers is subsequently explored, demonstrating the ways in which Alfred Knopf's first forays in publishing as an apprentice to Frank Nelson Doubleday and Mitchell Kennerley led to alliances with leading typographers, illustrators, and designers (including Bruce Rogers, Frederic Goudy, Elmer Adler, and William Addison Dwiggins). Research for this chapter was greatly facilitated by the recent acquisition of G. Thomas Tanselle's Knopf collection by the Beinecke Library at Yale University. Although the Knopfs' personal library, now housed at the Harry Ransom Humanities Research Center (HRC), features a copy of nearly all early Knopf books, the Tanselle collection is arranged chronologically, which made it possible to efficiently chart the transitions of the visual rhetoric reflected in renowned Knopf design traits through an examination of 909 volumes, 302 of which are in dust jackets.

The Knopfs' masterly use of book production as book promotion forms the bridge to a discussion of early Borzoi marketing, spanning trade promotion and consumer advertising—for which they made innovative choices in terms of both copywriting and the use of media. The shifting college-textbook environment, on which Knopf's college sales department attempted to exert considerable influence, is addressed as well. This history culminates in a consideration of the impact of these early legacies on the Knopf identity in the twenty-first century.

Alfred Knopf's interest in college textbook adoptions and other affiliations with universities is particularly significant in relation to his concept of prestige. Beyond the financial benefits of strengthening a publisher's backlist through course adoptions, academia's power in canon formation is on par with that of prize committees. John Guillory's noted analyses of canonical literary status include his observation that the authority of the canon is often considered (incorrectly) to lie in the texts themselves, rather than in a cultural perception of elitism. In an examination of the works of T. S. Eliot and the critic Cleanth Brooks, Guillory makes a pragmatic proposal:

> The authority of the culture, what maintains it as both marginal and elite, is not to be distinguished from the authority of the canon. For *some* reason *some* literature is worth preserving. We would not expect this or any other conception of authority to have escaped the vicissitudes of social hierarchy, but this is just the claim of the canonical text, which is assumed to be *innately* superior. Indeed we refuse (and this refusal is grounded in much critical theory) to think of the literary work as good or bad for some extrinsic reason; such a possibility can be conceived only as propaganda or censorship.[15]

Guillory then dissects various ideologies that separate the intrinsic versus perceived prestige of literary works, but the role of publisher as contributor to the dialogue in even minute ways is never addressed. Yet the publisher as propagandist, angling for canonical status as a gateway to prestige, is clearly captured in the history of Knopf, whose books were explicitly touted as worth preserving, which served as a justification for well-made bindings. These realities underscore the appropriateness of a rhetorical lens in examining the Borzoi identity. While explorations of literary prestige often rest on a foundation of critical theory (Pierre Bourdieu's concepts of cultural capital are particularly prevalent, informing Guillory's work as well as Catherine Turner's *Marketing Modernism between the Two World Wars*, James English's *The Economy of Prestige*, Phillip Barrish's *American Literary Realism, Critical Theory, and Intellectual Prestige*, and numerous others), rhetorical theory rarely has been applied to the cultural components of bibliographical history. While the transactions of literary modernism captured in the founding narratives of Knopf provide copious specimens of symbolic capital, particularly as we see Blanche and Alfred vying for a level of privilege that transcended material wealth through their promotion of the intellectual superiority of select Borzoi Books, it was through persuasive acts that the Borzoi brand's symbolic identities were shaped and disseminated. These rhetorical interplays are at the root of the distinctions mapped in critical theory's hierarchies of prestige. The rhetorical aspects of Bourdieu's theories regarding literary power are less often examined, but they jibe with Burke's interests. In his analysis of Flaubert, Bourdieu describes the literary world as "a force-field acting on all those who enter it, and acting in a differential manner according to the position they occupy. . . . The generative and unifying principle of this 'system' is the struggle itself. . . . The principle of change in works resides in the field of cultural production and, more precisely, in the struggles among agents and institutions whose strategies depend on the interest they have—as a function of the position they occupy in the distribution of specific capital."[16]

One of the most recent studies of the modern publishing industry's use of marketing to create and distribute the capital of prestige, Catherine Turner's book offers groundbreaking analyses of book-promotion campaigns but is limited to just one case study of Knopf, charting the campaign for Thomas Mann's *Magic Mountain*. Surprisingly few other histories of the company have been published, and most of them report without an interpretive lens. The 2010 release of Cathy Henderson and Richard Oram's *The House of Knopf*, volume 355 in the Dictionary of Literary Biography series (and, at 589 pages, the lengthiest work in the series), is a boon to researchers, with a chronological scope that concludes in 1960, when Knopf was sold to Random House. The DLB volume reprints hundreds of gems from the HRC's Knopf archive, including correspondence, ephemera, and portions of Alfred Knopf's memoir, with chapters focusing on fifteen authors as well as special sections on Knopf's American historians and American poets. Grouped by decade, the artifacts are accompanied by commentary from Henderson and Oram.[17] *The House of Knopf*'s distribution will be fairly limited to institutional use; the retail price is more than three hundred dollars. A more accessible supplement is the exhibition catalog *The Company They Kept: Alfred A. and Blanche W. Knopf, Publishers.* Edited by Henderson and Oram, this volume accompanied the Knopf symposium hosted by the HRC in 1995.

In the late 1960s, the Pulitzer Prize–winning nonfiction writer Susan Sheehan began research for a Knopf biography, a project enthusiastically supported by Alfred, but the manuscript never came to fruition.[18] The *Newsweek* book critic and former E. P. Dutton editor Peter Prescott dedicated a number of years to working on a biography of the Knopfs, conducting crucial interviews with Alfred Knopf and with family members from Alfred's generation, but Prescott died in 2004 before the manuscript could be completed. His mammoth project has been taken up by the literary agent John Thornton, who describes the process of researching Knopf as reminiscent of biographer Lytton Strachey's tactics: "[Strachey] would look at the sources like someone rowing out over a great sea of information and lowering his bucket here and there and pulling up samples and examining them. So I think that's the best I can do: row my boat through the Knopf collections and see what turns up."[19]

Other efforts to capture the company's history are presented by the Knopfs themselves in *The Borzoi 1920* and *The Borzoi 1925* (commemorative books that collect essays written by their authors) and *Portrait of a Publisher,* a two-volume tribute published in conjunction with the company's fiftieth anniversary, collecting sentimental reminiscences from the publishing community and reprinting articles written by Alfred Knopf. Rather than illuminating the significant challenges faced by the fledgling publishing house, the commemorative volumes generally only reinforce a belief in the Knopfs' inherent literary nobility, reflecting Guillory's criticism and skirting the practical questions of how the company's backlist, and therefore its prestigious reputation, was built.

From the late 1950s through the 1970s, Alfred Knopf attempted to write a memoir, a dictation project carefully transcribed by assistants, Katherine Hourigan (who later became the company's managing editor) among them. Because of the breadth of the project, the result is a manuscript of more than one thousand disconnected, partially edited pages, which he dubbed "those damned reminiscences" and published only in segments. The memoir nonetheless brims with meticulous detail, though it is heavily reliant on its author's ability to recall or verify a multitude of facts, covering nearly all of Knopf's life as well as a corporate history during which at least five thousand new Borzoi titles were published. His memoir is an essential trove for any researcher of Knopf and is in many cases the only extant source on crucial topics in the company's early history, but Alfred Knopf's notes acknowledge the potential for factual error in any memoir.

The Art of Prestige is therefore the first close examination of the company's formative years, tracing the early influences and the company's inception in 1915, through the rapid development of an inimitable brand, culminating at the cusp of the Great Depression, when price-cutting measures marked a significant shift in the bookselling community and created a climate of austerity from which Knopf was not immune. The focus of this history—Knopf's rapidly achieved stature during the Jazz Age—reconstructs the origins of a publishing identity that both reflected and directed aspects of a modernism while adhering to old-world publishing traits. What emerges is a portrait of two publishers who managed their finances meticulously while feeding a reputation for extravagance, and who cultivated a circle of literary authors by artfully commercializing the company's supposed disdain for commercialism.

Crafting a history of the Borzoi community, the scenes (as Burke termed his rhetorical sites for dramatism) include a variety of locales, ranging from bohemian Greenwich Village to London's Bedford Square and continental Europe as the Knopfs repeatedly set sail on the *Mauretania* ocean liner searching for worthy literature abroad. The Borzoi's midtown offices also form an important stage for the performance of identity. In at least one instance, Knopf's promotional copy even used the Borzoi as a metaphor for theater, whimsically referring to it as a location where adventures (through books) were performed. A 1924 brochure for a novel about a mischievous New Orleans native reads, "*Sandoval: A Romance of Bad Manners* by Thomas Beer presented May 23 by Alfred A. Knopf at The Borzoi. . . . Seats for each and every performance of this great romance are $2.00 net. Everyone can have the best seat."[20] Other instances of the Knopfs' use of the Borzoi as a locale include Dr. Eugene Christian's 1916 *Eat and Be Well*, which opens with a letter touting the author's credentials, signed "Alfred A. Knopf, Publisher" and listing The Borzoi as a physical location in the space where a city and state customarily would have been typed.

This concept of a publisher's identity as a realm within and beyond the geographical space of the "house" is reflected in Sheryl Englund's examination of the Knopf translation and marketing of Simone de Beauvoir's *Second Sex*. Englund writes, "Those of us who love literature are prone to forget that in the publication of a new book—whether fictional or scholarly—the quality of a work's intellectual content cannot alone account fully for its public reception. Within a publishing house, the editors and the publicity department deliberately attempt to influence the public's perception of a work's text in order to increase sales of the book."[21] Even Foucault's deconstruction of literary roles in the now-canonical "What Is an Author?" fails to sufficiently acknowledge the publisher, emphasizing instead the social forces that influence an author, and the signification of authorial identities.[22] It is equally ironic that as a widely published author himself, Burke did not scrutinize the agency of publishers. Yet the application of his rhetorical concepts to bibliography yields an understanding of publishing that applies as easily to the twenty-first century as it does to the 1920s.

Underscoring Englund's notions in an op-ed piece for the *New York Times* regarding debates over e-publishing licensing, prestigious Farrar, Straus & Giroux president Jonathan Galassi recently outlined the role of good publishers: "An e-book version of Mr. Styron's *The Confessions of Nat Turner* will contain more than the author's original words. It will also comprise Mr. [Robert] Loomis's editing, as well as all the labor of copy editing, designing, and producing, not to mention marketing and sales, that went into making it a desirable candidate for e-book distribution. . . . A publisher—and I write as one—does far more than print and sell a book. It selects, nurtures, positions, and promotes the writer's work."[23] Published in January 2010, almost a century after Blanche and Alfred ventured into the field, Galassi's sentiments remind us of the aspects of creating literature that extend well beyond the rhetorical exchange between writer and reader.

Blanche and Alfred amplified the publisher's role in extraordinarily distinctive ways, both personal and corporate. As the Knopfs tried to make a name for themselves (albeit a difficult one to pronounce, as no letter in "Knopf" is silent, and Alfred said it with a schwa vowel sound—Knuhpf), the Borzoi identity became an extension of Blanche and Alfred's personae, while Borzoi Books evolved within a vibrant literary landscape of prestige on both sides of the Atlantic.

 CHAPTER ONE

Educating a Future Publisher

I did not grow up in a particularly bookish atmosphere, but my father was generous in the allowance he gave me. . . . I frequented the secondhand book shops in Harlem—especially one run by Cox—father and son. The old man looked rather like Mark Twain in a boiled shirt and long black bow tie, but the son, Carol, was not far from my age and sold me many bargains.

ALFRED KNOPF, speaking before the Grolier Club in 1948

WHEN ALFRED KNOPF LAUNCHED HIS FIRM, Booth Tarkington and Zane Grey were among America's most popular living novelists. Other fiction writers topping the *Publishers' Weekly* bestseller lists included Eleanor Porter, who continued a lucrative series that year with *Pollyanna Grows Up;* the Missouri native Winston Churchill, whose novel *A Far Country* scorned the affluence of Midwestern robber barons; and Mary Roberts Rinehart, the prolific mystery writer associated with the phrase "the butler did it."[1]

Though Alfred Knopf aspired to prosper as a fledgling publisher, he chose not to set his sights on accessible, formulaic works such as these. Instead, the first Knopf list announced in the *Publishers' Trade List Annual* (*PTLA*) reflects a disdain for commercial American publishing. The books featured in this 1915 record are *Four Plays* (Knopf's première) translated from the French of Émile Augier; *Homo Sapiens,* a novel translated from the Polish of Stanislaw Przybyszewski (pshay-buh-SHEV-skee); *Moyle Church-Town,* a novel by Englishman John Trevena (the pseudonym of Ernest George Henham); Claude Bragdon's *Projective Ornament,* a treatise on design theory; Guy de Maupassant's *Yvette (A Novelette) and Ten Stories;* the anarchist Prince Petr Kropotkin's *Ideals and Realities in Russian Literature;* and five translated works of Russian fiction, including Leonid Nikolaievich Andreyev's *The Little Angel and Other Stories,* Vsevolod Mikhailovich Garshin's *The Signal and Other Stories,* the novel *Taras Bulba* by Nikolai Vasilievich Gogol, *Chelkash and Other Stories* by Maxim Gorky (Aleksei Maksimovich Peshkov's nom de plume), and Mikhail Yuryevich Lermontov's novel *A Hero of Our Time*.[2] The only American author featured on Knopf's inaugural list is Claude Bragdon, an architect and set designer who would soon have an impact on the physical attributes of early Borzoi Books. Though his book was included in the 1915 announcement, the Knopfs grouped it with books released in 1916 when they compiled the commemorative volume *The Borzoi 1920*.

Published two years before the Bolshevik Revolution, these eleven titles emphasize popular literature from Eastern Europe, in several cases reviving the works of authors who had died in the nineteenth century. At this point in the firm's history, the most American aspect of the list was the publisher himself, and the modern traits of the firm's identity had yet to be seen. The origins of Alfred Knopf's literary taste shed light on why the Borzoi brand evolved as it did throughout the twenties. Understanding Alfred's literary education also solves the conundrum of the early Knopf image: how did the Borzoi brand simultaneously become associated with innovation and tradition? Alfred Knopf's sources of inspiration varied in the short years leading up to the launch of his company, but it is clear that they also influenced Blanche Wolf Knopf's taste. Though Alfred often referred to Blanche as a co-founder of the company, and her courtship correspondence with him indicates that she was enthusiastic about European literature well before the Knopf publishing company was conceived, she was unquestionably his apprentice at the outset.

Three elements shaped Alfred's approach to book acquisition and ideals of literary prestige: the elegant home library of his childhood, paid for by his father's career as an advertising executive; his coursework at Columbia, which immersed him in scholarly firestorms over academia and literature; and his stints as an employee of other publishing houses. Inevitably, Blanche Knopf's approach to book acquisition absorbed these influences as well. In later years, the couple would be notorious for their bitter office feuds, becoming near-rivals who lived in separate quarters. She preferred their Manhattan apartment, eventually choosing a midtown address within walking distance of the office, rather than a more heavily residential neighborhood in the city; he preferred their house in Westchester County. However, in this early phase of the company's history, Blanche and Alfred were collaborators.

The diverse cast at the helm of Alfred Knopf's literary education included a radical Columbia professor named Joel Elias Spingarn; the Nobel Prize–winning novelist John Galsworthy, whose friendship Knopf cultivated on a 1912 trip to England; two key figures in America's early twentieth-century publishing world (Frank Nelson Doubleday, conservative and prosperous; and Mitchell Kennerley, adventurous and perpetually broke); and Samuel Knopf, the publisher's father, who was both prosperous and always precariously living beyond his means. Knopf authors served as literary scouts and thereby exercised considerable influence in shaping the Borzoi circle, but that phenomenon did not gain momentum until after the company's cornerstones were formed. In fact, numerous factors shaped the house of Knopf before there was such a house.

Alfred Abraham Knopf's Youth

Although the atmosphere at home was not particularly "bookish," and Alfred was the only truly voracious reader in his family, his father sparked his childhood literary expectations by introducing him to the novels of Captain Frederick Marryat, an Englishman who had served in the navy and was a member of Charles Dickens's circle. Alfred's father also encouraged him to read detective stories by Émile Gaboriau.[3] Western European literature was readily available in the nineteenth-century United States, and the mass popularity of European authors often overshadowed the success of new American writers. Contrary to the optimistic predictions of those who favored American authors, the passage of the Platt-Simmonds Act in 1891, extending US copyright protection to the works of foreign authors, did little to quell the popularity of imports, perhaps because the Act granted copyright protection only to works that were manufactured in the United States. The less expensive option of importing preprinted sheets of a foreign edition continued to be popular, despite the fact that the book would be automatically cast into the public domain.[4]

The works of Marryat and Gaboriau introduced Alfred to imported fiction, but their style is not reflected in the eastern European authors who would dominate the first lists of Borzoi Books. Alfred never publicly professed a link between his Polish ancestry and the books that dominated his company's launch, but the obvious parallels deserve exploration. Clarifying Knopf's genealogy also serves a practical purpose, as members of Alfred's family were early investors in his company. Furthermore, Samuel Knopf was heavily involved in his son's publishing firm from its founding in 1915 to Samuel's death in 1932. A biographical and ancestral sketch of him establishes what Kenneth Burke would call the "substance" that linked father and son as the company's image was crafted.

In 1871, at the age of nine, Samuel Knopf emigrated from the village of Przemyśl, located in present-day southeastern Poland near the Russian border. The Knopf surname is the German word for "button" (related to the English word "knob"), and coincidentally he would begin his career in the clothing trade. However, his parents were academics. His father, Abraham, had taught English at the University of Warsaw, and Samuel's mother, Hannah, had earned a degree in chemistry there. Setting up household on Manhattan's Lower East Side, Abraham taught English to recent immigrants, while Hannah used her skills as a chemist to make daguerreotypes. Neither endeavor was particularly lucrative, but Abraham and Hannah enjoyed social status as professionals in fields that required advanced education. Their experiences were preserved in family lore for which young Alfred was an audience.[5]

Breaking from his parents' intellectual tradition, Samuel embarked on a career as a traveling salesman for clothing and furniture manufacturers. Assimilating in a new homeland at a young age, he reportedly spoke English without an accent and, because his father did not emphasize the Polish language at home, was fluent in German instead, perhaps informing Alfred's interest in German literature as a young adult. In 1888, Samuel married Ida Japhe, a twenty-five-year-old public school teacher whose ancestors had emigrated from a Baltic region that corresponds to the present-day Republic of Latvia.[6] She gave birth to Alfred at home, on Manhattan's Upper West Side, on 12 September 1892. The following month, Samuel became an American citizen.[7] Alfred's sister, Sophia, was born two years later.

Alfred would always emphasize his upbringing in New York City, but in 1894 Samuel moved his family to Cincinnati, where he opened Knopf & Co., a wholesale clothing and furniture business, with plans to bring garment manufacturing to Cincinnati. He advertised heavily and generated frequent publicity for his business achievements, introducing the city's first electric delivery wagon and running for director of the Chamber of Commerce in 1896.[8] However, negative publicity about a personal tragedy brought his time in Ohio to a close. In the summer of 1896, Samuel confronted Ida about rumors of her infidelity; she and Samuel subsequently separated, and she moved to Brooklyn with the children. In February 1897, shortly after Samuel filed for divorce, Ida committed suicide by ingesting carbolic acid. The *Cincinnati Enquirer* reported on these developments in detail, ultimately declaring that Ida "had atoned for her sins" by taking her own life and that "at Bath Beach and Bensonhurst, Mrs. Knopf was a leader in the Hebrew social life of those places." Samuel returned to New York, where he went to work as a sales representative for the *Cotton and Cotton Goods Journal,* his entry into advertising.[9]

Composed primarily in the 1960s, Alfred Knopf's memoir expresses uncertainty about the cause of his mother's death. Not until 1977 did he find copies of the *Enquirer* articles. Yet in interviews with Peter Prescott, he claimed to have retained troubling memories of the incident, which took place when he was four years old.[10] This aspect of his childhood narrative, marked by published scorn from a judgmental public, distinguished his identity from that of his young peers. In 1898, Samuel married a divorcée, Lillie Harris, and Alfred acquired a stepsister, Elizabeth. In 1899, Samuel and Lillie's son, Edwin, was born. As Alfred's half-brother, Edwin Knopf become a Borzoi Books editor and sales representative in his twenties, but he left the company after five years to pursue a successful career as a Hollywood producer, director, and screenwriter. Sophia's son (Alfred's nephew) Alvin Josephy characterized his step-grandmother Lillie, a future shareholder in Alfred A. Knopf, Inc., as kind-hearted and indulgent but "addlepated" and naïve. Alfred did not adopt her Brooklyn accent, which was marked by the intrusive "r" (oil pronounced as *earl*).[11]

Alfred moved houses several times as a child, possibly because of the well-documented fluctuations in his father's fortunes. After leaving Cincinnati, Samuel purchased a four-story house, complete with a well-stocked library, on Convent Avenue in a block that at that time formed part of the northern boundary of Harlem at 148th Street. White-collar Jewish residents, many of Russian ancestry, populated the neighborhood alongside Irish and German immigrants. By 1910, Eastern European Jews would outpace the latter two populations as Harlem's dominant ethnic group.[12] Samuel later moved his family thirty-three blocks north to a house in bucolic Fort Washington, where the George Washington Bridge now stands. Alvin Josephy described the home as being in a then-undeveloped part of the city, "on a wooded hill above the Hudson River near 181st Street . . . with a long white porch overlooking the river."[13] By the time he reached adolescence, the turbulence of Alfred Knopf's early life had subsided, and he settled into an aura of privilege that would form the underpinnings of his public biographical narrative for years to come, including recollections that his father employed an African American servant in Cincinnati and Irish American servants in New York.

The Knopf children were raised as Reformed Jews, though their affiliation was motivated by cultural identity rather than reverence for religious doctrine. As a child, Alfred attended Temple Israel of Harlem, but he was confirmed at Temple Beth-El on the Upper East Side, where he played rambunctious games with the rabbi's son. Eventually, the Knopfs joined Temple Emanu-El, which Alfred characterized as a pinnacle of social achievement.[14] Knopf described his home as one in which the high holy days were only nominally observed. On Yom Kippur, the Knopf children lunched at the Plaza Hotel rather than fasting throughout the day, a treat that Knopf said balanced the tedium he experienced during the services. The Plaza was one of many establishments where young Knopf received his epicurean training.

He also frequented his local public library, where he fed his hunger for Arthur Conan Doyle, and he attended local public schools. He was briefly enrolled at the prestigious Horace Mann School for Boys, a private academy in the Riverdale district of the Bronx, a stint that ended after he was caught stealing books—an act that could not be attributed to a lack of reading material at home, where books were not only abundant but beautiful. Knopf savored the design features of elaborately bound sets of works by Thackeray, Dickens, and Balzac purchased by his father, who also lined the shelves with Sir Richard Burton's translation of *The Arabian Nights* and the ten-volume *Anglo Saxon Review* alongside many books on Napoleon. Knopf's vivid memories include recollections of full-color plates and red morocco (goatskin) bindings.[15]

In addition to providing a lavish home library, Samuel Knopf would also shape his son's future by settling into a career that would have significance for Borzoi Books. Drawing on his experience in the garment trade, Samuel launched an advertising firm in the West Village, producing catalogs and other promotional material for this industry, hiring such artists as Walter Appleton Clark and John Wolcott Adams to illustrate them. Before long, this led to Samuel's position at Barron Collier's national advertising agency, which managed railway media in more than 700 cities, including New York and Boston, and also provided full-service marketing for international companies, including the British firm Ridgways Teas. Unlike legacy publishers whose identities would be echoed in the names of their father's firms, Alfred Knopf would develop his sense of self in the shadow of Samuel's career in consumerism, with a home library funded by hard-won, fluctuating affluence.

Samuel Knopf's affiliation with Barron Collier coincided with a move once again, in 1906. This time, the family settled into an impressive country estate, complete with tennis courts, in the village of Lawrence on Long Island's south shore. Living outside the city also called for the purchase of a motorcar, in this case a luxurious seven-passenger Packard. The family embarked on a chauffeur-driven summer tour of New England, but Knopf claimed to have spent the trip focused on the pages of *Tess of the D'Urbervilles*, unimpressed with the American scenery.

Alfred was uprooted a final time when his father decided to make him a boarder at the now-defunct Mackenzie School in Dobbs Ferry, north of New York City on the banks of the Hudson River. Depicting himself as a bookish outsider, Knopf seems to have admired the school's Scottish founder, James Cameron Mackenzie, and claimed to have had closer friendships with faculty members than with his classmates.[16] After just one year, Mackenzie declared that Knopf was sufficiently prepared for college, and in 1908, at the age of sixteen, Knopf entered Columbia University, which had dedicated a gleaming new campus just ten years earlier. The Morningside location, with an entrance at 116th Street, was not far from the Manhattan neighborhood of his childhood. Knopf continued to live on Long Island, embarking on a complex series of train rides with reading material in tow. He attributed this cumbersome commute to the belief of his stepmother, Lillie, that young men should not be coddled. (Alvin Josephy asserted that Samuel spoiled Lillie and Alfred's sister, who "usually appeared in public in expensive Cartier, Tiffany, and Dreicer jewelry.")[17] As Alfred described Samuel as living beyond his means, it is equally plausible that Samuel was simply not able to afford the dual luxuries of a Long Island estate and on-campus housing for his son. Memories of this occasional financial insecurity may have contributed to Alfred Knopf's insistence that his publishing house pay its vendors and authors all that they were owed, and pay them promptly—a practice that was not universally followed in early twentieth-century American publishing. Even the revered house of Harper & Brothers had entered the new century in receivership, nearly toppling under the burden of two million dollars of unsecured debt.[18] To Knopf, the inability to pay was an unforgivable sign of powerlessness that undermined any social prestige a publisher might have won.

The New Columbia and Its Literary Climate

When Knopf entered Columbia in 1908, the university was experiencing an identity crisis that would shape his own intellectual identity. Nicholas Murray Butler, who served as its president for more than forty years, had begun his reign in 1902. By the end of his second decade at the helm, financial gifts to Columbia topped thirty-four million dollars, an unprecedented level.[19] The university saw other forms of extraordinary growth, captured in an early campus map featuring more than thirty completed buildings for student housing, classrooms, library space, and other uses, spread across nine city blocks (the result of the migration from the cramped midtown campus) and in the number of resident students, which jumped from 4,440 in 1901 to 9,929 in 1913.[20] Some faculty members perceived this growth as an indication of commercialization in higher education, a trend they viewed with disdain. Among those who shared this view was Joel Elias Spingarn, the professor of comparative literature who sparked Knopf's desire to become a publisher of literary fiction. When Knopf entered Columbia, comparative literature and English were separate departments.

Spingarn equated Butler's changes with a vocational approach to education, decrying the new emphasis on overly "pragmatic" course offerings. Spingarn's sentiments were vividly captured by one of his biographers, Joyce Ross:

> In the wake of advancing science, [Spingarn] sought to encourage interest in the humanities by inaugurating annual prizes for the best undergraduate entries in belles-lettres. He received widespread publicity in the New York press by refusing to conduct his classes in a new $500,000 lecture hall, on the grounds

that the pure white plaster and shining new blackboards were incompatible with such a romantic subject as comparative literature.[21]

The field of college English experienced a variety of rifts during this period, including the departure of composition-studies researchers and speech teachers from the Modern Language Association, marked most notably by the creation of the National Council of Teachers of English in 1911.[22] Echoing the fine printing movement's interest in the aesthetic quality of books' physical traits, debates also erupted between philologists, who emphasized linguistic aspects of literature, and proponents of purely aesthetic literary appreciation. Butler succeeded in merging comparative literature studies with Columbia's English program, making Spingarn a subordinate member of the English faculty, a demotion that Knopf's professor very publicly derided.

A scholar of Italian literature, Spingarn also believed that the best models for academic literary publishing lay overseas, particularly in Italian journals. "Compared with them our publications seem vulgar and banal," he wrote in a letter to Fred Newton Scott, founder of the University of Michigan's rhetoric department.[23] Such Eurocentrism, together with a penchant for invective, would become a hallmark of Knopf's rhetorical style.

Though Lionel Trilling is often said to have been the first Jewish member of Columbia's English department to earn tenure, Joel Spingarn was the first Jewish *literature* instructor at Columbia to do so, becoming a full professor in 1908, the year of Knopf's arrival on campus, when English and comparative literature were separate departments. Despite Spingarn's advancement in rank and the university's graduation of several future publishers who were Jewish (Bennett Cerf, Richard Simon, Max Schuster, and Arthur Sulzberger, Sr., among them), it is difficult to determine the degree of anti-Semitism in place at Columbia at the time. Frederick Keppel's *Columbia*, published in 1914 by Oxford University Press, offers this anecdotal assessment from the era:

> One of the commonest references that one hears with regard to Columbia is that its position at the gateway of European immigration makes it socially uninviting to students who come from homes of refinement. The form which the inquiry takes in these days of slowly dying race prejudice is, "Isn't Columbia overrun with European Jews, who are most unpleasant persons socially?" The question is so often asked and so often answered in the affirmative by those who have made no effort to ascertain the facts that it will do no harm to speak frankly about it. In the first place, Columbia is not "overrun" with Jews any more than it is with Roman Catholics or Episcopalians. The University is open to any student of good moral character who can satisfy the entrance requirements, without limitation of race or creed, and it is hoped that this will always be so. No questions are asked and no records kept of the race or religion of incoming

students, but it is evident that the proportion of Jewish students is decreasing rather than increasing.[24]

Jerome Karabel, a professor of sociology at the University of California, Berkeley, asserts that non-academic admissions criteria were not instituted in the Ivy League until the 1920s, when "it had become clear that a system of selection focused solely on scholastic performance would lead to the admission of increasing numbers of Jewish students, most of them of eastern European background. This transformation was becoming visible at precisely the time that the nationwide movement to restrict immigration was gaining momentum. . . . The top administrators of the Big Three (and of other leading private colleges, such as Columbia and Dartmouth) recognized that relying solely on any single factor—especially one that could be measured, like academic excellence—would deny them control over the composition of the freshman class."[25] For Knopf, finding commonality with Spingarn, a non-Christian man of letters who defied stereotypical depictions of the striving Jewish salesman, may have influenced his own sense of identity and informed his subsequent career decisions.

In order to gain admission to Columbia, Knopf had to meet the minimum age requirement of fifteen, produce a letter of recommendation (preferably from a principal), and earn sufficient points on a series of entrance examinations. Knopf chose to embark on a generalist's bachelor of arts degree, requiring coursework in English; French or German; History; Latin or Greek; mathematics; philosophy; physical education; chemistry or physics; additional science courses chosen from a block with options ranging from botany to experimental psychology; and units chosen from another broad spectrum that included astronomy, physics, and anthropology.

Columbia's other entrance requirement was that the applicant be male. Female applicants were referred to Barnard College, founded in 1889. The implications for Blanche, who never attended college, are noteworthy. She would launch an esteemed career in literary publishing under the guidance of a man whose literature professors and classroom peers were all men, trained in a canon that emphasized male authors.[26]

When Knopf would later publicly credit Spingarn with shaping his literary taste, he was invoking a name that was associated with rebellion, captured in Spingarn's headline-making dismissal from Columbia. Knopf was a student in the last comparative literature course Spingarn taught at Columbia. The termination letter, dated 16 January 1911, establishes the following: President Butler merged the comparative literature department with the English department, making Spingarn subordinate to the new chairman of the Department of English and Comparative Literature, Ashley Horace Thorndike. Spingarn refused to acknowledge Thorndike's authority over him, Butler wrote, and the university could not afford to pay multiple professors of comparative literature. Therefore, Spingarn's position was to be discontinued at the close of the semester.[27]

However, from Spingarn's perspective, the situation was far more complex, unfolding in a scenario that illustrates the climate of Columbia during Knopf's time there. Spingarn made the longer narrative plain in *A Question of Academic Freedom: Being the Official Correspondence between Nicholas Murray Butler and J. E. Spingarn,* a monograph of more than fifty pages published by Spingarn and, according to the title page, "printed for distribution among the alumni." Thus, Spingarn responded to his termination by distributing copies of his philosophical duel with Butler, along with appendices featuring testimonials from former students, the parents of former students, and an international cadre of literary critics.

In *A Question of Academic Freedom,* Spingarn states that one month before his termination, he had made a motion in a meeting of philosophy faculty (English and comparative literature faculty were listed as members of the Faculty of Philosophy in the 1909–1910 catalog) proposing that the group publicly acknowledge the academic services of their colleague Harry Thurston Peck. In addition to being a professor of ancient languages, Harry Thurston Peck was also a noted literary critic and had served as editor-in-chief of *The Bookman,* launching what is often considered to be America's first bestseller list in 1895.[28] He had been the defendant in a widely publicized breach of promise suit brought against him by Esther Quinn, a stenographer who claimed that Peck had engaged in a long-term extramarital affair with her during which he promised to leave his wife and marry Quinn. The suit was dismissed, but Butler dismissed Peck before that outcome had been reached. Spingarn's motion was immediately tabled, but his support of Peck was perhaps viewed as insubordination. In a letter to Butler written two weeks after his termination, Spingarn asserted that he had established a good working relationship with Thorndike, despite his initial insistence that Thorndike was not academically qualified to oversee Spingarn's professional life, and that Butler had been made aware of the congenial reconciliation between the two. Spingarn also disputed the Board of Trustees' legal right to discontinue his professorship, rejecting the claim regarding the university's poverty. Knopf viewed Spingarn's actions as inspiring and heroic.

The confrontation with Butler became Spingarn's forum for asserting the importance of comparative literature, which he believed could combat narrow-minded nationalism. His argument likely echoed the charisma with which he captivated Knopf: "To abolish comparative literature (except as a mere name) is to abolish literary history. Instead of diminishing the number of professorships devoted to it, it would at least be more reasonable to suggest that one or more be added to every literary department in the University, in order that one or two scholars in every department should be able to see beyond its own national or parochial limits."[29]

Spingarn's name was well recognized beyond the gates of Columbia. Not only did the academic world know about the ensuing war of words, but all readers of the *New York Times* were exposed to it also. Spingarn's imbroglio was covered in a series of updates over several weeks during the spring of 1911. His departure from the university gave him a much wider stage, however, and in many ways he provided a model for Knopf's aspirations to become a literary impresario and country gentleman. In his memoir *Days of the Phoenix,* the literary historian Van Wyck Brooks devotes a full chapter to Joel Spingarn's circle, who flocked to the estate he and his wife inhabited near Amenia, in upstate New York. Having inherited his father's fortune, amassed in the wholesale tobacco trade before the Civil War, Spingarn did not need to pursue a career in beyond Columbia. Instead, he turned his eye toward creating a haven for writers and critics such as Lewis Mumford, Ernest Boyd, modern artists Walter and Magda Pach, and Geroid Tanquary Robinson, a contributor to *The Dial* who undertook doctoral research in the Soviet Union in the 1920s.[30]

His collection *Creative Criticism* best captures Spingarn's vision of the role of a public intellectual. The volume includes his revolutionary lecture, "The New Criticism," as well as its update, a "new manifesto" titled "The Younger Generation." The book has been described by a variety of scholars as a radical work that pitted him against elitist New Humanists such as Irving Babbitt. The rhetorical theorist James Berlin, for example, notes that Spingarn wanted no moral interpretation, no taxonomy of genres or forms, and certainly no investigation of the author's personal life when exploring poetry in the classroom or as a literary critic.[31] It is important to note the distinction between Spingarn's New Criticism and that of second-wave New Critics (the future Knopf author T. S. Eliot among them) who rejected Spingarn's affinity for romantic reading theories. Arnold Goldsmith describes Spingarn's notion of "new" as stemming from frustration with philological approaches to literature, with their insistence on compartmentalizing literary forms, historical criticism, psychological criticism, and dogmatic criticism of any kind.[32]

Seeking to purge criticism of morality debates, Spingarn wrote a satirical take on the seven liberal arts for the literary magazine *Seven Arts.* "To say that poetry is moral or immoral is as meaningless as to say that an equilateral triangle is moral and an isosceles triangle is immoral," he wrote. "Imagine these whiffs of conversation at a dinner table. 'This cauliflower would be excellent if it had only been prepared in accordance with international law.' 'Do you know why the cook's pastry is so good? He has never told a lie or seduced a woman.'"[33] It is easy to imagine Spingarn professing such attitudes while Knopf was still his student and protégé.

Spingarn's circles also coincided with Knopf's during the Harlem Renaissance. In a lifelong campaign to eradicate racism, Spingarn and his brother Arthur, a New York attorney, became members of the NAACP's executive committee in 1910. Literary appreciation created bonds between Spingarn and NAACP members Walter White and James Weldon Johnson, both of whom became Borzoi authors. On the national front, Spingarn led daring but generally unsuccessful campaigns to overturn segregationist laws throughout the South, integrate the federal workplace, ban the film *Birth of a Nation* (which depicts the Ku Klux Klan as heroic), and impose federal laws that would mandate harsh penalties on lynch mobs. He was nonetheless highly successful in generating numerous sizable bequests to the NAACP while making significant financial contributions himself.[34] Perhaps surprisingly, there is no evidence of Spingarn's attempting to spur African American enrollment at Columbia. "Theme for English B," the widely anthologized poem by the Harlem Renaissance poet and future Knopf author Langston Hughes, is often interpreted as expressing the isolation Hughes experienced when he briefly attended the predominantly white Columbia in 1921. Hughes ultimately graduated from Lincoln University, a historically black college in Pennsylvania.

Spingarn's influence on Knopf's emergence as a publisher extended beyond the abstract. On a practical level, Spingarn led Alfred to his first prestigious connections in the book business. Knopf published several reviews in *Columbia Monthly*, the undergraduate literary publication, but he was more successful as the publication's advertising manager, a triumph that he attributed to his father's work as an advertising executive. Yet in April 1911 he published a review of John Galsworthy's novel *The Patrician*, aspiring to submit a longer piece on Galsworthy for Spingarn's student-essay contest.

In years hence, Knopf would consider this to be the fateful turning point on his road to success.[35] Searching for additional biographical details about Galsworthy (a quest that was antithetical to Spingarn's New Criticism), Knopf wrote to the author in care of his publisher, the revered William Heinemann. Knopf did not win the prize, but he launched a friendship with Galsworthy, who in turn would introduce him to William Henry Hudson, whose novel *Green Mansions* would become Knopf's first lucrative title. Galsworthy never became a Knopf author, being published in the United States primarily by Charles Scribner's Sons, but he served as Borzoi Books' first impresario and contributed forewords to several Knopf books, including *Green Mansions*.

In approaching Galsworthy, the eighteen-year-old Knopf was not satisfied with a simple written interview. Instead, he wanted to place his professor and the venerable Englishman in conversation with each other. He relished the role of ringmaster, causing his literary circle to grow before he had even determined that he wanted to become a publisher. When Galsworthy dismissed scholars in a letter to Knopf, the young student responded by sending his correspondent a copy of Spingarn's *New Criticism* and printing the latter's reply in a subsequent issue of *Columbia Monthly*.[36] In June 1911, shortly after Spingarn's dismissal from Columbia, Knopf and his former instructor corresponded about the review, embarking on a friendship based on new roles as Spingarn enthusiastically debated questions of aestheticism.[37]

As secretary of the university's Peithologian Society, a Columbia literary organization formed in 1806 but on the wane by the 1920s, Knopf organized a tea for Spingarn in the aftermath of his turmoil with Butler, assuring the former professor that Peithologian members and comparative literature students remained his champions.[38] When Knopf neared graduation, he solicited a final essay for *Columbia Monthly* from the ousted Spingarn, who thought the request was courageous and agreed to submit a piece on New Criticism as his final "seminar" for the student literary publication. Knopf told his former professor that he would do anything for the cause of academic freedom.[39]

As a student in the last undergraduate course Spingarn taught, most likely Introduction to European Literature "from the Renaissance to the present day," Knopf would have read works "from Dante to Tennyson, and with the development of the main currents of literature in modern Europe."[40] He recalled that Spingarn would frequently sit at the back of the classroom, asking the students to hold forth. The course concluded with an examination essay that Knopf found tremendously difficult. He predicted that none of the students would pass. Yet they were each awarded an A because, Spingarn later told them, he wanted to give them something to remember him by. Knopf later discovered that Spingarn had asked a colleague, George C. D. Odell, to post the grades on his behalf, knowing this would provoke ire in traditionalist Odell.[41]

Spingarn imparted one particularly significant lesson to Knopf: the impact of a publisher's reputation. Knopf asserted that Spingarn was the first instructor he had encountered who described books from the perspective of a bibliographer, citing Macmillan as an example of excellence.[42] At a talk delivered to the Grolier Club in 1948, Knopf found this characterization of Macmillan to be outdated ("It amuses me nowadays to recall his statement"), but he reiterated Spingarn's role as a bibliophile, an influence that caused him even to appreciate the aesthetic features of his textbooks:

He was the first to talk to me about the virtues of different editions of classic authors, of typography and the appearance of books. . . . Also at college I was much impressed by the beautiful work done by Ginn and Company at their Athenaeum Press. I was told that in those days books like Robinson's histories were set by hand. I do not know whether this was the case, but they struck me as very beautiful books—bindings apart. And Holt's first edition of Hazen's *Europe since 1815* was a well-made book indeed.[43]

As public feuds were erupting between Spingarn and Butler, Knopf was savoring another course that would influence his early publishing decisions. The class was led by Bayard Boyesen, a poet who did not hold a degree beyond the A.B. Boyesen exalted Russian literature, though eastern Europe was not featured in any Columbia literature course title at the time. Also dismissed from Columbia, for reasons that remain unclear, Boyesen subsequently gave a lecture to art students at the Ferrer School in Greenwich Village, praising "philosophic anarchists" who had fallen on their swords in the name of creative freedom, including Euripides, James Fenimore Cooper (who was expelled from Yale), and Spingarn's mentor, George Woodberry, another ousted Columbia professor. After the lecture, Boyesen was quoted in the *New York Times* as encouraging his audience to "read the story of the Russian makers of literature. Except Tolstoy, of whom the Government was afraid, every one of them was put to death, sentenced to death, or exiled."[44]

Anarchism repulsed Knopf, but the seeds for his interest in the literature of Europe, particularly Russia, were sown. Knopf later regretted his decision to avoid the legendary Brander Matthews's American literature course, a rare offering in a department that otherwise tended to restrict its course of study to British authors. Knopf would later write that at the time he believed there was no such thing as American literature.[45] However, he did study drama under Matthews, whose title was professor of dramatic literature. This led Knopf to sometimes attend as many as three theatrical performances a week while in college, buying balcony seats for 75 cents and fostering an enthusiasm for dramaturgy that would lead him to publish more than thirty plays during his company's first decade, many of them packaged in distinctive checkerboard-patterned jackets and bindings within the Borzoi Plays series. While the concept of reading a play in book form has little appeal to most of today's book buyers, it was the early twentieth-century equivalent of buying a popular film on DVD or streaming it online for home use. Random House founder Bennett Cerf confirmed the lucrative aspect of hardcover plays (as opposed to paperback scripts, for performers) during this period, observing that such books were well advertised by the plays themselves. His firm's edition of Eugene O'Neill's *Ah, Wilderness!* reportedly sold more than 50,000 copies.[46]

Knopf's taste in theater meandered beyond Matthews's reading list, including a controversial play by the Irishman John Millington Synge in which the protagonist commits patricide, shows no remorse, and is admired by County Mayo villagers for it. Titled *The Playboy of the Western World,* the play sparked riots when it debuted in Dublin in 1907 and attracted hecklers to subsequent performances in New York.[47] In a profile of Synge published in Columbia's literary magazine, young Knopf expressed ebullient admiration for his Celtic literary hero and also revealed a flair for hyperbole, which would later inform the voice of advertising copy published under his signature. "Mr. Yeats has written beautiful verse but nothing in my opinion that can compare for sheer glory with the wonderful prose of Synge," the undergraduate Knopf wrote. "*The Playboy* is unique; nothing like it exists: it is a distinct and noble contribution to our literature. . . . His best works are well-nigh perfect specimens of theatric art." The only displeasure Knopf voiced regarding Synge's works was that the characters in *The Tinker's Wedding* too often used profanity and other slang, which Knopf disliked not on moral grounds but on elitist ones: "There is less beauty in this work than in the others—for it deals with coarser folk."[48] Nearly fifty years later, Synge would posthumously join the Knopf ranks in paperback.

Perhaps surprisingly, John Erskine—the Columbia professor closely associated with the great books movement—seems to have made only a minimal impression on Knopf. Erskine joined the faculty of Columbia in 1909 and rose from adjunct to associate professor status while Knopf was an undergraduate. During those years, Erskine taught composition and English literature of the sixteenth, seventeenth, and nineteenth centuries. Erskine's renowned "great books" course was not launched until 1920, under the title General Honors, emphasizing classical texts read in translation and discussed in small groups over a two-year period.[49] The course was renamed Colloquium in Important Books in 1932, three years before Erskine joined the roster of Knopf authors. In his memoir and in several interviews, Knopf recalled being a student in a summer composition course led by the illustrious Erskine, but he more often invoked the name of Joel Spingarn when questioned about his literary education.

The Graduate's Junket

Having developed a rich appreciation for all aspects of a book's value—intrinsic and extrinsic, binding as well as content—Knopf graduated from Columbia on 12 February 1912 with a bachelor of arts degree and embarked on a tour of the countries he had been trained to associate with superior literature.[50] At the time, Columbia conferred degrees at the October and February meetings of its University Council and on Commencement Day. Though always candid about his mediocre grades (he failed economics and earned a D in musical harmony), Knopf was equally candid about his motivation to complete the degree early: his father had promised him a trip abroad. His family had embarked on a European tour the preceding summer, but Knopf had stayed home. He preferred to make his transatlantic sojourn alone, after his studies had concluded.

Preparing for the trip, Knopf diligently attempted to arrange appointments with a variety of literary figures, ostensibly for the sole purpose of enriching his appreciation for books, not because he aspired to start a publishing house. Though several of the social engagements he enjoyed on this trip led to significant acquisitions after he became a publisher, including books by Alfred Ollivant, by all accounts Knopf intended to study international law at Harvard in the fall of 1912. The only entrance requirement for doing so was completion of an undergraduate degree. Without the obligation to prepare for an entrance examination or the need to find employment, Knopf was able to savor an itinerary driven by sheer pleasure. In his case, this especially meant spending time in theaters, concert halls, and bookstores.

The US State Department issued a travel certificate to him on 29 January 1912. The document describes Knopf as having a dark complexion and being five feet nine inches tall.[51] The other vital document he carried was a letter of credit for $1,500, sufficient for half a year's stay, from February through August, if he budgeted carefully.[52] His initial lodging had no running water.

His first destination was not England but Germany, where he was to meet with the novelist and teacher Hermann Krüger. Samuel Knopf was fluent in German, perhaps leading his son to study the language in college, and Rudolf Tombo, Knopf's German professor at Columbia, supplied a letter of introduction. Staying at a Hanover pension he had found through his *Baedeker,* he befriended a German professor who spoke no English. Knopf spent several hours with him in a beer hall, where his new acquaintance asked him whether he was Catholic or Protestant. When Knopf replied, "Jew," the professor asked if their boarding house provided kosher food, assuming that Knopf required an orthodox menu and forcing him to confront the question of identity as he presented himself on foreign territory for the first time. He could not deny that he would have to resolve the difference between what a Jewish identity meant in his own mind versus the assumptions made by non-Jewish Europeans. Throughout this leg of his trip, Knopf also was also exposed to a variety of interpretations of the American identity. These included sailing aboard the Hamburg America Line's *President Lincoln,* and spotting a portrait of William Jennings Bryan that hung in the boarding house, honoring the former presidential hopeful's time as a lodger there.

Immersing himself in European creative endeavors, he was in the audience for varied and numerous performances, including the controversial playwright Arthur Schnitzler's *Das Weite Land* (which Knopf declared "terrible"), a German performance of George Bernard Shaw's *Arms and the Man* ("excellent"), and Wagner's *Ring* cycle. Visiting many galleries, he professed a passion for Rubens. Traveling by third-class rail, he mapped out a tour that included Prague, Dresden, Berlin, Munich, Leipzig, Trieste, Mainz, Cologne, Heidelberg, and many other stops. In Bonn, he visited the house where Beethoven was born. In Budapest, he joined the Puccini craze and applauded opera performed in Hungarian. By April, he was in transit to Vienna, learning of the *Titanic* disaster while he was a passenger on the Orient Express.[53]

In May, he sent a letter to Joel Spingarn, who had urged his former student to tour Italy, home of Benedetto Croce, a literary critic Spingarn revered and a future Knopf author. With candor, Knopf expressed complete disdain for Italy, showing no hesitation in writing disparagingly of a country his mentor had loved. The young graduate said that Italy disgusted him so much that he wanted to leave soon and had no intention of ever returning.[54] With similar candor, he told his parents that Paris did not suit him either, rejecting the city that his future wife would consider a second home.[55] He was more content in Versailles and Chamonix, savoring *A Set of Six*, Joseph Conrad's stories for children, en route.

The Great War would prevent Knopf from returning to Europe for more than a decade, and he occasionally described the pending military crisis (albeit with a degree of naïveté) in letters to his family. He surmised that the Kaiser Wilhelm II was a dove in a country on the brink of civil war. As for the Ottoman conflicts, Knopf declared that Italy should have dedicated more resources to improving the water quality in Venetian canals rather than annexing Tripoli.[56]

Knopf felt decidedly more at home in England and Scotland than on the continent, though one of his most-anticipated events in Britain involved eastern Europeans. In 1912, Hungarian-born Artúr Nikisch became conductor of the London Symphony Orchestra with a debut performance featuring a widely publicized new symphony composed by Ignace Paderewski, who shared Knopf's Polish ancestry. Nonetheless, the remainder of his experiences in the United Kingdom reflected his Anglophilic tendencies, including an Edinburgh performance of John Galsworthy's play *The Pigeon* and Shakespeare at the Savoy under the direction of the renowned Harley Granville-Barker.

Knopf had solicited an essay from the English novelist Alfred Ollivant for the *Columbia Monthly*, an endeavor that produced considerable correspondence and enhanced Knopf's admiration for Ollivant's novel *Bob, Son of Battle*, whose protagonist is a dog. While in Europe, young Knopf telegraphed birthday greetings to Ollivant and boldly asked for an appointment.[57] This led to Knopf's introduction to the Savile Club, where he dined as Ollivant's guest, immersed in an aura of literary exclusivity derived both from the club's membership (ranging from Thomas Hardy to William Butler Yeats) and from the stately architecture of upper-class Mayfair.

During this first English sojourn, Knopf's most consequential hosts were John and Ada Galsworthy, who lived on a two-hundred-acre farm in Devonshire. Met by Mrs. Galsworthy with a team of horses, Knopf found their village of Manaton preferable to Oxford and Stratford, which he had discovered to be as overrun by tourists as Italy was.[58] That night, the Galsworthys would express surprise that Knopf had not heard of their friend W. H. Hudson or his novel *Green Mansions*. Knopf would read it before the summer was over, becoming enamored of the book's exotic tropical setting, and in 1916 it would become his company's first strong seller.

Knopf also met a bookseller who would play an important role in the future of Borzoi Books. In New York, he had frequented The Little Book-Shop Around the Corner, founded by his future employer Mitchell Kennerley. The store was managed by Laurence Gomme, an Englishman who would buy it in 1912.[59] Before his trip, Knopf received a letter of introduction from Gomme, providing a formal link with the London bookseller Dan Rider. The art critic, Aubrey Beardsley biographer, and future Knopf author Haldane Macfall described the shop as "where the young literary bloods, here and from America, were wont to forgather before the war—the 'lions' den,' where the young lions roared and the asses brayed on their way to becoming editors of limited editions . . . while Dan Rider's laugh, where he sat enthroned at the seat of custom— I never saw him sell a book,—rattled the windows of St. Martin's Lane."[60] Throughout the summer of 1912, Knopf spent considerable time at Rider's shop, meeting Macfall, the journalist and publisher Holbrook Jackson, and the social commentator Gerald Stanley Lee. The most significant introduction Knopf achieved there was to John Middleton Murry, the critic and Bloomsbury Group editor, who was often accompanied by Katherine Mansfield, his future first wife.[61] Books by both Murry and Mansfield would populate the Borzoi list over the next decade, though for unknown reasons the loquacious Knopf claims to have never spoken to Mansfield during those encounters in Rider's shop. If Knopf was reticent in Mansfield's presence, he was not shy with Rider, at one point even procuring an invitation to lunch with the bookseller and the Socialist leader Henry Halliday Sparling, former son-in-law of fine printer William Morris.[62]

Knopf's father had also supplied him with letters of introduction, though Samuel's associates had little to do with the literary world. Through his father,

Knopf was a guest at the home of Ridgway Tea executive Stanley Cooper, who took him to the Royal Ascot derby. As a guest of M.P. Cecil Harmsworth, Knopf watched a session in the House of Commons. Cognizant of the 23 September deadline for presenting his diploma to register for the law program at Harvard, Knopf could easily have spent his time in Europe fostering additional connections in mercantile fields and law. By the time he returned to the States, however, he had settled on publishing—a career that would allow him to immerse himself in his newfound passion for the humanities without sacrificing an interest in commercial enterprises. Reminiscent of the Harlem booksellers he recalled with affection, he would look for good books at bargain prices, maximizing his "allowance" throughout his career.

His motivation for pursuing publishing began in the shadow of his Columbia professor, but it emerged as a result of many factors from his upbringing. In *A Grammar of Motives,* Kenneth Burke observes that "each man's motivation is unique, since his situation is unique, which is particularly obvious when you recall that his situation also reflects the unique sequence of his past."[63] Spingarn stoked Knopf's motivation to develop an identity as an aficionado of European literature, providing both the agency for Knopf's affiliation with John Galsworthy and the academic credentials that Samuel Knopf lacked. Yet Samuel furnished funding and business connections, reminding his son of the economic credentials that were equally powerful in gaining access to prestigious "agents" and demonstrating another means to satisfy the universal motivation of winning admiration, respect, and access to gatekeepers. Letters of introduction provided Knopf with an especially tangible example of the social nature of identification, a symbol of courtship designed to unite individuals who met prescribed criteria.

For Spingarn at Columbia, the truly fulfilling act of "courtship" was to inspire students, who were the most accepting audience members in his widely publicized feuds with administrators. His motivation in continuing the correspondence with Knopf was not limited to a craving for student flattery, however. Knopf distinguished himself by becoming a student who not only wrote *about* literature but who also wrote *to* producers of literature, clearly wanting to be in dialogue with a prestigious literary scene, scheduling meetings with authors during his European tour and putting them in conversation with his professor. It was surely apparent to Spingarn that Knopf would eventually share a stage with him, rather than simply remaining an apprentice.

CHAPTER TWO

Apprenticeships and Partnerships

I couldn't have been a very bright boy, because some days passed before it
dawned on me that I was receiving no salary, only carfare and the promise of a
commission on any orders I secured.

ALFRED KNOPF on selling ads for the *New York Times*

IN THE SUMMER OF 1911, Samuel Knopf used his connections to get Alfred a
job as an advertising sales rep for the *New York Times.* Recalling the experience
more than forty years later in the *Atlantic Monthly*'s "My First Job" feature,
Knopf mused that he showed no early promise as a salesman. He called on a
variety of prospects, ranging from a varnish company in Newark to an haute
couture shop in Midtown, but he was turned away every time. Eventually,
Samuel's client Meyrowitz Opticians was willing to sign a sizable contract with
the *Times,* and eighteen-year-old Knopf was allowed to place the order. The
Times denied him a commission because the advertiser had previously bought
space in the paper. The indignant Knopf demanded to be paid, to no avail. The
Meyrowitz account provided his only sale that summer.[1]

The following year, when Knopf returned from his glorious European tour
eager to begin a literary career, his attempts to find employment in the book-
publishing industry were just as grueling as his attempts to sell ads. He reportedly called on every major house in the city, even meeting personally with
Arthur Scribner, but no one was willing to hire him. Conventional wisdom is
that his rejection was the result of anti-Semitism, though it should be noted
that among the publishers who refused to hire him was Benjamin Huebsch,
whose corporate logo was a menorah. The son of a rabbi, Huebsch launched
his firm in 1902 and became the publisher of an impressive list that included
Sherwood Anderson and Sinclair Lewis. In 1925, he merged his company with
Harold Guinzburg and George Oppenheimer's newly formed Viking Press,
and the candelabra was replaced by a Nordic ship drawn by Rockwell Kent.
Though Huebsch denied the young Alfred a job in 1912, he later became one of
the Knopfs' most trusted friends.

To gain his first book-publishing job, Alfred Knopf was forced to rely once again on his father's contacts, an array that included Long Island Rail Road president Ralph Peters. Doubleday, Page & Company had recently built an extraordinary facility on nearly forty acres in Garden City on Long Island, supplementing the firm's Manhattan headquarters. Frank Nelson Doubleday was lobbying the LIRR to establish a railway station at the new complex and paid heed when, in October 1912, Alfred Knopf presented a letter of introduction from Peters. The publisher's initials, F.N.D., had earned him the nickname Effendi, the Turkish word for "master." He agreed to meet with Knopf and listened to his young applicant's promise that he would gladly do anything—even set type—in order to join the company. Two weeks later, Knopf was interviewed by the treasurer, Samuel Everitt, and was assigned to the accounting department, a role that mirrored stereotypes equating Jews with financial prowess, despite the fact that Knopf's coursework and aspirations were better suited to an editorial role. Knowing that Doubleday imported a considerable number of books from the English publisher William Heinemann, Knopf carried a Heinemann edition of a Dostoyevsky novel with him to the interview. In subsequent commutes to his Garden City job, he passed the time by reading additional European works, including *War and Peace* and the ten-volume novel *Jean-Christophe*.[2] The train stop where he arrived to work is still called Country Life Press.

Doubleday and Kennerley Train Their Future Competitor

Working for Effendi placed Knopf in a company, and a facility, that embodied few aspects of literary modernism. Doubleday's Country Life Press was a marvel of industrial precision, yet it touted architecture that evoked the feeling of an old-world manor house. Opening its doors to employees in the autumn of 1910, barely four months after the cornerstone was laid by Theodore Roosevelt, the Country Life Press management boasted that "nothing should be omitted which would add to its efficiency. The power was to be conveyed to every machine by electric wires, and each, no matter how small, even the adding and invoicing machines, should have its own motor. Letters, also, are folded, the stamps put on the envelopes, and the envelope sealed—by a machine with its tiny motor giving it life."[3]

In essence, Knopf went to work in a book and magazine factory. When he joined Doubleday, the facility housed Lanston monotype equipment, a mammoth press room (to which paper was delivered directly from freight cars), and a bindery that by 1919 finished 20,000 cloth- and leather-bound books a day. True to its name, the Country Life Press was also home to elaborately landscaped grounds, featuring a rose garden, hundreds of tulips and lilies, a bowling green, a tennis court, seventy-foot-tall cedar trees leading to an Italianate pool, and a sundial emblazoned with a brass reproduction of two leaves from a Gutenberg Bible. The Press also offered workers onsite hospitalization and dental care.[4] The Garden City complex is still in use by a bookselling conglomerate, Bookspan, whose holdings include the Book-of-the-Month Club, founded in the 1920s. Coincidentally, Bookspan was owned in partnership by Knopf's parent company, Bertelsmann A.G., and Time, Inc., until it was sold to a private equity firm in 2008.[5]

While a core staff remained in a Manhattan office, the Long Island facility was created not only to provide Doubleday, Page with a centralized manufacturing plant but also to expand the company's magazine sector (including *The Garden Magazine, Country Life in America, World's Work,* and *Short Stories*), and to accommodate Frank Doubleday's enthusiasm for mass-produced, inexpensive reprints, in many cases produced, for a fee, on behalf of other publishing houses, including Grosset & Dunlap. Knopf made note of the handsome fees Grosset & Dunlap paid to publishers for the right to produce cheap hardcover reprints.[6] Though Knopf would work at the Country Life Press for only a year and a half, he would be dispatched to two key areas beyond accounting: production and marketing. This fundamental education would serve him well, and in time he would share the curriculum with Blanche.

He was surprised to discover the sometimes counterintuitive economies of scale that drive the book trade. In the accounting department, he encountered figures that continued to stun him fifty years later when he recalled Effendi's profit and loss card for an edition of Kipling's poems. The book's retail price was $1.80, with a royalty of 25 percent (steep by today's standards). Factoring in the firm's production expenses for laid paper, gold stamping on the spine, a high-quality cloth binding, and a gilt top, along with the bookstore discount, Knopf estimated that Doubleday barely broke even on a book whose costly features would make such editions even rarer over the next two decades.[7] It is also evidence that Doubleday, Page did not eliminate high-quality production standards for all its titles when becoming a purveyor of mass-produced works.

Knopf's recent travels to London proved useful to Doubleday in at least two instances. His familiarity with Harley Granville-Barker led him to solicit a contract for *Prunella, Or, Love in a Dutch Garden,* a play written with Laurence Housman. Granville-Barker scoffed at Knopf's offer of a 10 percent royalty, insisting that he earned 20 percent minimum from English publishers.[8] When Gerald Stanley Lee's obscure, quasi-sociological book *Crowds: A Moving-Picture of Democracy* became a top seller in Chicago thanks to regional publicity, Knopf reminded his employers that he knew Lee personally, having met him at Dan Rider's bookshop. Knopf was then dispatched to spend several days with Lee, enticing him to remain a Doubleday author even if his fame led to offers from other houses. Knopf's network would grow by the thousands over the course of his career because he learned to capitalize on connections, rather than trying to segregate the various components and phases of his life. He was a natural master at blending his personal and professional rosters.

Knopf took a special interest in the works of Doubleday author Joseph Conrad, who had befriended John Galsworthy during an 1893 South Sea voyage. When Knopf's duties included making binding selections in the production department, he chose to indulge in colored "extra cloth," a high-grade fabric, for Conrad's novel *Youth*. Because Conrad's books did not sell well, and would hence be printed in small quantities, Knopf was permitted to make slight upgrades in the production materials.[9] Again, today's production managers would find this approach counterintuitive: pricey packaging is reserved for books with high projected sales, not vice versa.

Knopf was also permitted to attend weekly editorial meetings and was allowed to take home the manuscript for Conrad's *Chance*, the novel that would finally garner American commercial success for the author. *Chance* is the only one of Conrad's novels to feature a female protagonist, inspiring Knopf to embark on a testimonial-driven marketing campaign promoting all of Conrad's works. He enlisted Galsworthy's assistance and soon received a lengthy letter from Conrad expressing gratitude to Knopf. Conrad made it clear that he had felt considerably neglected by Doubleday. He then outlined the details of numerous other American publishing agreements to which he had been a party, from Appleton to Harper & Brothers, reiterating the consistently strong media attention he had received and the consistently poor sales that accompanied it. He urged Knopf to reissue his autobiography, published by Harper's only a year prior, and to implement a grander marketing scheme for it.[10] Knopf's reply demonstrates his role as a bold novice, proposing the promotional booklet and offering terms of a 12.5 percent royalty, with an advance of forty pounds, even though Effendi was out of the office. In this correspondence, Knopf nonetheless acknowledges his own youth, telling Conrad that he is too young to continue being called "Mr."[11]

Knopf envisioned a sales booklet that contained both a biographical profile and testimonials from leading authors on both sides of the Atlantic. In response to his solicitation project, Conrad received eloquent praise from voices such as the poet Robert Service (dubbed the Bard of the Yukon) and the adventure writer Rex Beach, but the campaign was roundly perceived by others as being in bad taste. Knopf had tried to ward off accusations of poor etiquette by using his personal letterhead, rather than Doubleday's, ordering fine stationery for himself on handmade paper imported by the Japan Paper Company, adorned with the name of his father's Long Island estate: *Mon Terrace.*[12] Yet this personal touch seemed only to exacerbate the ire of the luminaries Knopf chose. Among the rebuffs that poured in was a letter from fiction writer and poet Margaret Deland, who observed that Conrad's books were too long to be popular with typical readers. William Dean Howells apparently received follow-up correspondence from Knopf when Howells ignored the first solicitation. He gruffly replied that he had ignored the initial request because he assumed it was common knowledge that he never provided promotional blurbs for books.[13]

Despite rejections such as these, the marketing brochure was issued, featuring Knopf's lengthy, sophisticated, and of course hyperbolic homage to Conrad. Knopf's text lists Conrad's given surname, Korzeniowski, and praises the author's rapid mastery of English despite an upbringing in the Ukraine. Knopf never publicly acknowledged that he shared an eastern European heritage with the author, preferring to focus on the achievements of assimilation (both Korzeniowski's and that of his own ancestors). Though Conrad's subsequent books sold well in the United States, perhaps because of Knopf's promotional prodding, Conrad would never become a Borzoi author. Nonetheless, he would later recommend that Knopf call on the *Baltimore Sun* columnist H. L. Mencken, who frequently praised Conrad's works. This introduction would lead to one of Borzoi Books' most significant early partnerships, and one of Knopf's most enduring friendships.

Knopf went to work in Manhattan in March 1914, easily turning his back on books by the likes of Booth Tarkington. He had accepted a job with a publisher whose office was less salubrious than the Garden City facility but whose wages were higher. Mitchell Kennerley offered to pay Knopf twenty-five dollars a week, compared to the twelve dollars he was earning at Doubleday, Page.[14] While Frank Doubleday provided Knopf with practical skills, Kennerley provided him with a pantheon of authors and designers, unwittingly building the creative bridge Knopf needed to launch a competing firm. The early look of Knopf books and the emphasis on imported highbrow titles owe much to Knopf's apprenticeship with Mitchell Kennerley, but equally significant was the fact that Knopf's duties included serving as a traveling salesman.[15]

Knopf often described his fourteen months spent working for Kennerley as a time when he honed his knowledge of how to import a title from overseas, how to alienate lucrative authors by failing to pay royalties, and how to underpromote a book, ensuring its lackluster success in the market. Fourteen years older than Knopf, Kennerley was born in England and exploited his transatlantic connections throughout his career in the United States. Like Blanche, he did not attend college, completing his formal schooling in his mid-teens. In London, he took a job in an antiquarian bookshop owned by John Lane, who also directed the Bodley Head publishing company and was publisher of the decadent *Yellow Book*. Lane sent Kennerley to New York in 1896 to launch the American branch, the John Lane Company. Initially setting his sights on American magazine publishing, Kennerley served as the business manager for a pre-Mencken version of *The Smart Set* and at age twenty-four founded a publication called *The Reader*, which emphasized literary criticism and poems. Yeats was among the contributors. Kennerley's book-publishing company was launched in 1906 in a building where the struggling typographer Frederic Goudy leased space. This led not only to collaboration on book design but also to Goudy's creation of a typeface bearing Kennerley's name. Other Kennerley designers who would later contribute to the Borzoi look included Thomas Cleland and Claude Bragdon, evidence that Knopf should not be thought of as *introducing* a superior standard of book production in America. In many ways, Borzoi Books simply improved the business and marketing efforts of a concept already established by Kennerley.

In 1910, Kennerley's publishing company created a highly unprofitable literary magazine called *The Forum*, which featured works by Ezra Pound, Robert Frost, Leo Tolstoy, H. L. Mencken, and Jack London. Despite the publication's low rate of financial return, Kennerley was rewarded by his proximity to a highbrow literary milieu. High-profile Kennerley authors included Upton Sinclair and D. H. Lawrence, represented by the literary agent Edward Garnett, who would become part of the Knopf roster along with his wife and son.[16] Other names appearing on both the Kennerley and Knopf lists include John Trevena (a pseudonym for Ernest George Henham), author of *Moyle Church-Town*, featured in the Borzoi's debut; and Joseph Hergesheimer, who with his wife became close personal friends of Blanche and Alfred. He was one of the few American writers Alfred had hoped to have on his inaugural list, but Hergesheimer was struggling with writer's block.[17] In 1917, the Knopfs released their first American novel: Hergesheimer's 408-page *Three Black Pennys*, a narrative in three parts—The Furnace, The Forge, and The Metal—whose protagonists are a family of Pennsylvania iron manufacturers with the surname Penny. The *New York Times* hailed it as "a notable achievement," and curiously downplayed the artistic merits of the writing while observing that "the background of furnace fires and glowing metal is always interesting. It is a book to arouse interest, inspire thought, and provoke discussion."[18] The book proved to be a top seller, sending the Knopfs back to press "immediately on publication."[19] Alfred then successfully negotiated to buy the plates of two other Hergesheimer novels from Kennerley.

Kennerley played a role in Knopf's insistence on paying all his bills on time; too often, he had seen Kennerley threatened with lawsuits for failing to pay royalties. Kennerley is said to have refused to pay royalties to the lucrative poet Vachel Lindsay because of Lindsay's "disgusting" table manners.[20] Edna St. Vincent Millay, for whom Kennerley professed great affection, complained that he would not release a penny of royalties. When he did attempt to pay authors their due, they had to cope with the risk that his check would bounce. At one point, Kennerley proposed to solve his chronic fiscal problems by selling his company to Samuel Knopf. Samuel, Alfred, and stepmother Lillie accepted an invitation to dine at the Kennerley home in Westchester County, but the overtures did not result in any negotiation for a sale. Knopf attributed this to his father's own precarious financial situation at the time, which led to the sale of the Lawrence estate. His family subsequently took up residence at 850 Park Avenue, on Manhattan's Upper East Side and approximately six blocks south of Blanche Wolf's home.

By 1920, the year after he became a US citizen, Kennerley was publishing just six books a year while Knopf's annual list topped seventy new titles. Knopf believed that Kennerley "had no real competition in distinguished books, especially by younger people" and was frustrated that Kennerley's titles were not being marketed to their potential. Knopf described him as "a man who had a very fine sense of typography and of sound conservative book-making" but who was "a damn bad publisher."[21] Convinced that he could succeed where Kennerley was poised to fail, Knopf set in motion the launch of his own company by poaching Kennerley's authors. The subsequent termination letter, dated 21 May 1915, oddly acknowledges Knopf's intent to resign:

> When you told me some weeks ago that you had decided to become a publisher, specializing in Russian literature, I felt that you had made a wise and fortunate decision. . . . I was quite willing that you should use my time and offices during the early stages of your preparations. . . . Some weeks ago when looking on your desk for a proof I came across a letter from Mr. Hergesheimer . . . and was shocked to find that you were negotiating with him for the publication by you of a book by him. . . . I am therefore going to ask you to resign your position with me to take effect immediately upon receipt of this letter.[22]

Knopf sought more than a publishing contract from Hergesheimer: he wanted to become the latter's mentee. In a letter dated only May 1915, handwritten on Mitchell Kennerley's letterhead, Knopf made plans for "Joe" to meet "Miss Wolf" over the summer and used his new friend as a sounding board for publishing ideas, particularly the potential demand for more Russian translations.[23]

The novelist Howard Vincent O'Brien also received a letter from the aspiring young publisher. Knopf asked O'Brien to consider the possibility that he might launch his own company at the end of Kennerley's spring 1915 selling season. Billing himself as a combination of Wannamaker, Machiavelli, and Savonarola (the latter reference surely reflecting an error on Knopf's part, as the fifteenth-century priest Savonarola was a zealous book burner), Knopf slyly asked to publish O'Brien's next book and requested that O'Brien maintain utmost secrecy regarding the proposed new publishing house.[24]

Knopf's apprenticeships took place in two quite different scenes: Garden City versus 32 West Fifty-Eighth Street, where Mitchell Kennerley's offices were located. Knopf's act of leaving the Country Life facility reflected his belief that blatantly "industrial" publishing should not become an aspect of his identity, yet his departure from Kennerley reflected his decision to embrace the pro-business traits of Frank Doubleday's identity. The result was a paradox. On one hand, the Borzoi brand identity exalted staid, un-experimental European literature over commercial American works. Yet Alfred himself conveyed a sufficient level of youthful exuberance and business acumen to impress such notable authors as W. H. Hudson.

Blanche and Alfred's Cornerstones

Throughout this period in Alfred's life, he was courting the woman who would become his partner in life and in business. He often claimed that his decision to abandon law school and pursue a publishing career was inspired in part by Blanche Wolf, a teenage girl he had met on Long Island the summer before his trip abroad. Returning to New York from Europe in late August 1912, he began thinking very tentatively of marrying her, deciding that law school would postpone the prospect of marriage for too long.[25] In a tribute to his wife published in *The Borzoi Quarterly* shortly after her death in 1966, Knopf stated that their mutual interest in books fostered their courtship. Though they had not corresponded while he was overseas, Blanche easily resumed their friendship, despite her parents' strong disapproval of Alfred. He was still living with his father and earned poor wages at his low-level publishing job.

Though much is known about Alfred Knopf's education, Blanche Wolf's life before the summer of 1911 is much less well documented, possibly because of her own silence on the matter. The notion of her family's higher social status recurs in many published anecdotes about the marriage, reflecting a reality of dissention at the time between American Jews with German or Austrian ancestry versus those from Eastern Europe, who represented a later immigration wave.[26] Blanche occasionally implied that her father was a well-established jeweler, which would have carried greater prestige than Samuel Knopf's fluctuating wealth derived from the burgeoning realm of advertising, still a field of dodgy respectability in some circles and occasionally associated with the stereotype of a *shtetl* peddler. When Blanche met Alfred for the first time, his family lived on Long Island year-round. Her family lived on Manhattan's Upper East Side, at 40 East 83rd Street, and kept a summer house on Long Island in Woodmere, which was an easy bike ride from Lawrence. After their initial encounter in 1911, Blanche nicknamed Alfred "the talker" and declared him "the crudest young man she had ever met."[27]

Her condescending demeanor was described by their nephew Alvin Josephy as "cold, tart, and contemptuous-looking, as if she was barely tolerating our presence."[28] She invented many aspects of the aristocratic identity that gave her the confidence to feel superior. During Blanche's lifetime, the *New York Times* ran no advertising for or articles about jewelry firms associated with her father's name, Julius Wolf, but a 1907 incorporation announcement lists Julius and Bertha Wolf as directors of the new Wolf Manufacturing Company, producers of caps.[29] A recent history of a Jewish congregation in Boston lists a watchmaker and jeweler named Julius Wolf attending synagogue in the 1850s, but neither Blanche nor her family members mentioned an ancestral connection to Boston.[30] Peter Prescott's interviews with Blanche's relatives and with Edwin Knopf substantiated the likelihood that Blanche created the story about her father's occupation because she was ashamed that his wealth was derived from as mundane an occupation as manufacturing infant apparel.[31]

Although her parents felt superior to the Knopfs, Blanche found her own family's narrative to be insufficient for attaining prestige in the literary world.[32] Relatives recalled that Blanche's mother was the daughter of a slaughter-house owner named Lehman Samuels, but Blanche was quiet about this fact, perhaps because the company went bankrupt after heavy involvement in the chilled-beef trade with Great Britain.[33] In addition, Blanche sometimes referred to herself as an only child, refusing to acknowledge that she had an older brother, Irving. He operated an Upper East Side automobile garage with his father, documented in trade publications such as *The Horseless Age*.[34] She appears to have been the only one in her immediate family to have pursued a creative field.

Biographical sketches frequently and correctly mention that Blanche's formal education concluded with the Gardner School, a finishing school whose student body was primarily composed of Jewish girls. Manhattan's most exclusive finishing school, Brearley, rarely admitted Jews. Blanche also attended the Ethical Culture School (now the Ethical Culture Fieldston School in the Riverdale area of The Bronx) founded in 1878 by Felix Adler as a progressive kindergarten for the working poor.[35] By the time Blanche enrolled, the school had moved to a stately building on Manhattan's Upper West Side, and the curriculum had been expanded to include all grades through high school. Blanche

Wolf would have made a strong candidate for Barnard College, but her only postsecondary degrees were honorary ones from Franklin and Marshall College (1962), Adelphi University (1966), and Western College for Women (1966). Alfred Knopf's interest in publishing, and his interest in sharing ideas about publishing with Blanche, presented her with an alternative form of higher education. He would also be her sole, lifelong employer.

Alfred wooed Blanche with books, and with gifts of laid writing paper imported from Italy. Though the lasting legacy of Blanche and Alfred's office behavior would include loud, bitter, frequent fights, their courtship was apparently steeped in tenderness, with only occasional evidence of discord. In Blanche Wolf's copious letters to Alfred, she thanks him for sending beautifully bound books to her, including a copy of Conrad's *Lord Jim,* and she apologizes for criticizing him and spurring spats. Notably, she encourages him in his work for publishing houses.[36] She also began signing the letters "V.V.," a lasting nickname given to her by Alfred after the publication of Henry Sydnor Harrison's 1913 novel *V. V.'s Eyes.*[37]

The cache of Blanche's messages to Alfred, dated between 1912 and 1915, captures her need to be in constant contact through notes addressed to him in Lawrence; at Doubleday, Page; at Mitchell Kennerley's office; and at his family's home on Park Avenue. In the spirit of twenty-first-century text messages between teenage lovers, she also sent telegrams to his office, often issuing them from Western Union desks in Manhattan that were sometimes just blocks away from where he was spending his days. When he began making sales calls on behalf of Kennerley, with jaunts to Philadelphia and his first trips to the Midwest, she wrote emotional notes to him in care of his hotel. Perhaps equally significant is the fact that Alfred preserved these letters for the rest of his days, giving them status equal to his correspondence with literary lions.

They became secretly engaged on 6 March 1915, and, after Blanche's persuasive appeals to her family, were married at the St. Regis Hotel on 4 April 1916.[38] Alexander Geismar, a city magistrate and former rabbi, officiated at the ceremony. His decision to enter a secular profession impressed Blanche and Alfred, who rejected the idea of a religious service.[39] For their honeymoon, they traveled to Washington, D.C., and to the Southern Pines, North Carolina.[40]

When Blanche pursued Alfred in defiance of her parents, she surely saw him as her gateway to a role in a literary life. Though she would not join the company full-time until 1918, he did not keep his professional life sequestered and instead wanted to immerse her in it. She was coming of age in an era and a city that created unprecedented opportunities for women; in 1918, Blanche received her first opportunity to vote, joining other New York women who had been granted the right to cast their ballots. Although the Nineteenth Amendment was not ratified until 1920, New York women were granted the right to vote in general elections two years earlier. *New York Times* coverage of the event declared "WOMEN CAST VOTES AS READILY AS MEN . . . EASY DAY FOR THE POLICE."[41]

In that spirit, Alfred rarely relegated Blanche to the role of audience member. Instead, he asked for her advice on a variety of matters relating to his career. Through a shared identification as bibliophiles, he showed respect for her intellect, acknowledging a facet of her identity that might have been discounted by other men, particularly in a culture in which the wisdom of women's suffrage was considered debatable. In return, through her mythic ancestry and stable affluence, she offered him a chance to rise in social status, bringing him closer to the aristocratic identity he idealized.

His personal life in order and his early publishing education complete, Knopf spent the summer of 1915 trying to create a plan for capitalizing on his affinity for European authors. It is noteworthy that the full extent of Knopf's military service also occurred during this period, when he enlisted in the New York National Guard ostensibly because he wished to learn horseback riding; maneuvers featured horse-drawn caissons in Central Park. Though the United States remained militarily neutral in the recently erupted "war of the ten nations" until April 1917, headlines published in the months preceding the Borzoi's debut conveyed American anxiety regarding these gruesome events, as well as the volatile situation in Russia.

Completing his service at the rank of corporal, Knopf served in the seventh infantry, Battery B, first field artillery. He remembered the experience primarily as a means for meeting other publishing men, including a future advertising salesman for the *Atlantic Monthly,* along with commercial artist Louis Fancher and Heyworth Campbell, future art editor of *Vogue.*[42] When the Selective Service system was implemented in June 1917, Knopf was classified as 4A, or among the most eligible, though he was never drafted.

Knopf's decision to publish Russian fiction in considerable numbers reflected not only his taste in literature but also the American public's interest in a war-torn locale that was making headlines regularly. British readers were particularly hungry for information about Russia, their dubious new ally, which inspired English publishing houses to release many translations of Russian classics. Blanche and Alfred believed that this specialty would provide cachet and help them distinguish themselves from other small presses. Unable to travel to Europe, Knopf contacted George Doran, a major American publisher whose British authors included Arthur Conan Doyle and Virginia Woolf, before the company was merged with Doubleday, Page in 1927. On Knopf's behalf, Doran agreed to negotiate with the English house Hodder and Stoughton to purchase sheets of many books on the initial Alfred A. Knopf list, including Garshin's *The Signal and Other Stories* and a short-story collection by Leonid Andreyev. The terms of credit for such arrangements were advantageous, with English publishers often offering payment terms of up to six months. In some cases, Knopf's early "imports" were available without any transatlantic shipping. He published Prince Kropotkin's *Ideals and Realities in Russian Literature*, for example, by contacting his former employers at Doubleday, Page, who sold Knopf the American rights and the American-made plates.

Living at home, Knopf had saved two thousand dollars, which his father supplemented for startup capital totaling five thousand dollars. Samuel also provided Borzoi Books with its first address, allowing his son to use a desk at his advertising firm in the Candler Building at 220 West 42nd Street. It was here that the ambitious young Knopf spent his first days as a publisher, laying the groundwork during the summer of 1915 in preparation for an official launch in October of that year. The first address for the house of Knopf was characteristically impressive.

Completed in 1914, the Candler was the city's tallest structure above 24th Street, surely appealing to Samuel's extravagant tendencies. The twenty-two-year-old publisher soon moved to his own two-room space on the nineteenth floor of the building, whose location would prove convenient for future Grand Central commuters Blanche and Alfred.[43] Reversing roles, Samuel permanently took a desk in his son's office in 1918, when the Alfred A. Knopf publishing company became incorporated and Samuel began serving as treasurer. Knopf employees reportedly called Samuel's office "the gymnasium" because of the gesticulations that accompanied his frequent, angry outbursts.[44] However, his grandson Alvin Josephy cherished Samuel, remembering him as a fun-loving, affectionate, generous man while describing Alfred as "more shy and reserved than [Blanche], but he too could kick up a violent storm. . . . Alfred often covered his shyness and fear of someone hurting him by hurting the other person first, usually with an outrageous and unexpectedly aggressive verbal assault that insulted his stunned victim. . . . Such episodes, which often seemed as if Alfred was copying the ruthless examples of his good friend H. L. Mencken, made him many enemies."[45]

A volatile but highly productive trio, Samuel, Alfred, and Blanche would remain in the Candler building until 1922, when they moved fifteen blocks uptown to the newly constructed Hecksher Building at 730 Fifth Avenue, at the intersection of bustling 57th Street. (Now called the Crown Building, this structure is not to be confused with an additional Hecksher building at Madison Avenue and 42nd Street completed in 1916. Both towers were constructed by the developer August Hecksher.) The move from the Candler in the 1920s gave the Knopfs easy access to the first home of New York's Museum of Modern Art, which opened its première gallery in the Hecksher in 1929. The Knopf offices remained on Fifth Avenue until 1937, when the firm relocated to 501 Madison Avenue.

Though Borzoi Books changed addresses, the logo developed into a stable symbol of prestigious publishing. Alfred consistently said that Heinemann's windmill had inspired him to use a branding device that was not obviously related to books, yet he credited Blanche with the idea of using a borzoi for the logo, conveniently forming alliteration with the word "book."[46] Perhaps she would have preferred that Borzoi Books become the name of the firm, not just a trademark. Instead, the name Alfred A. Knopf dominated every action they took as co-publishers.

The rise of Borzoi Books coincided with the Russian Revolution, and with Knopf's acquisition of many titles by Russian authors, during a time when the borzoi was associated with czars. This breed of dogs was therefore rejected by Bolsheviks, who routinely slaughtered the wolfhounds.[47] As an American branding device, the leaping borzoi communicated Knopf's dual identity—a threatened form of old-world aristocracy, paired with charm and vigor.

Knopf explained his interest in Russian literature in an April 1916 essay for the *New York Times Review of Books*, stating that he wished to capitalize on an American interest in Russia sparked by the Great War, and by amateur translations of Dostoyevsky and Tolstoy produced by Constance Garnett, wife of literary agent Edward Garnett. In these pre–Bolshevik Revolution months, Knopf claimed that he wanted to protect these books from being snapped up by American publishers who would not do a very good job of promoting them. In addition, he justified the absence of translators' names on several of the books, stating that the English publisher refused to reveal them. Knopf was candid about the practical aspects of this arrangement: "If copyright relations were established between the United States and Russia, the Russian author would be able to control his American publisher, but even so, the American and English publishers would have a free hand as regards the work published before the passing of a new law."[48] At the time Knopf launched his company, American copyright protection could not be extended to an author from a nation that maintained no reciprocal copyright legislation with the United States, unless the author lived in the United States at the time of publication.[49]

These details went unmentioned in the company's earliest media coverage. In a *Publishers' Weekly* article titled "New Publisher to Specialize in Russian Literature," appearing three months before the first Knopf book arrived from the bindery, the opening paragraph simply echoes his belief that American writers did not produce belles lettres. The reporter observed, "Certain it is that whereas we in America have produced no really great work of fiction, at least six such have come from Russia. Consequently the announcement that a new publisher is really 'going in for' the publication of Russian literature—not a subscription edition of all the classics, not stray books from a number of authors, but all of the novels of real value—is of more than passing interest."[50] An article published in the *New York Times Review of Books* that month describes similar plans and motivations.[51]

Cautionary Tales

Knopf acknowledged the influence of current events, Columbia coursework, and publishing apprenticeships in shaping his literary tastes; he also credited a memorable bookseller, Max Maisel, with opening his eyes to eastern European works.[52] A Jew of Russian ancestry, Maisel served as one of Knopf's earliest editorial resources at the shop on Grand Street on Manhattan's Lower East Side, where Knopf's grandparents had set up housekeeping. Maisel's shop stocked one of New York's largest selections of Judaica, much of it in the original Hebrew or Yiddish, as well as numerous works in Russian. Maisel was also an anarchist, and when Emma Goldman organized fellow anarchist Prince Petr Kropotkin's well-attended New York lecture series, Maisel set up a bookselling stall on-site.[53] He may have inspired Knopf to purchase the rights and plates for Kropotkin's *Ideals and Realities in Russian Literature* from Doubleday.

It was Maisel's idea for Knopf to commission a translation of *Homo Sapiens*, a novel in three parts that would lead the young publisher to his first tangle with censors. Sharing Abraham and Hannah Knopf's homeland, the novel's Polish author, Stanislaw Przybyszewski, had a following among Europe's avant-garde in the early twentieth century and was a key figure in the neoromantic "Young Poland" movement, although he was forty-seven when Knopf released the novel. At the time, Poland was under Russian rule, enabling Knopf to avoid royalty obligations to Przybyszewski. Thus, Knopf's only editorial fee was to the translator, Thomas Seltzer.[54] Knopf was surely encouraged by Little, Brown's extraordinary success with Polish novelist Henryk Sienkiewicz, whose 1895 *Quo Vadis [Where Are You Going?]: A Narrative of the Time of Nero* sold more than 750,000 copies in two years, becoming the house's top-selling trade book before 1921 and contributing to Sienkiewicz's winning the Nobel Prize in 1905.[55]

Failing to measure up to the achievements of *Quo Vadis*, Przybyszewski's novel garnered mediocre American reviews and sales. Nonetheless, it caught the attention of the New York Society for the Suppression of Vice, which considered the book to be pornographic and brought the case to court. The novel's protagonist, Eric Falk, is an alcoholic sadist who seduces a series of women, one of whom is thirteen years old when she begins her decade-long devotion to him. Knopf's attorney was his lifelong friend and fellow Columbia alumnus Osmond Fraenkel, who would later become widely recognized for his work on the board of directors for the American Civil Liberties Union. Fraenkel fought a losing battle on behalf of *Homo Sapiens*, however, and the charges were dropped only after the intervention of Samuel Knopf's attorney, William Tipple, who was a member of the New York Society for the Suppression of Vice. Knopf agreed to melt the plates for the book, and the Society's leader, John Sumner (successor to the deceased Anthony Comstock), agreed to drop the charges.

The case represents an important element of the early Borzoi identity. In subsequent years, the Knopfs would continue to take the path of least resistance on several potential encounters with censorship, most notably with D. H. Lawrence and Radclyffe Hall. During the 1920s, D. H. Lawrence appeared on Knopf's lists numerous times, with the release of *St. Mawr* in 1925, *David* and *The Plumed Serpent (Quetzalcoatl)* in 1926, *Mornings in Mexico* in 1927, *The Woman Who Rode Away* in 1928, and *Pansies* in 1929. Conspicuously absent from this list is *Lady Chatterley's Lover*, which Blanche had assured Lawrence she would publish, noting that he would only need to make minor revisions to accommodate American conventions.[56] Despite Blanche's optimism, the book was banned in Great Britain for more than thirty years, though an expurgated American edition was released in 1928 by Nelson Doubleday, an independent firm founded in 1912 by Frank Nelson Doubleday's son. *Lady Chatterley's Lover* never became a Borzoi Book.

In her correspondence with Radclyffe Hall, Blanche made plain the reasons for canceling the contract to publish *The Well of Loneliness*. Unlike *Lady Chatterley's Lover*, Hall's novel is not sexually explicit and does not contain profanity, but its sympathetic portrayal of a lesbian relationship resulted in the book's being banned in Britain. Though Blanche at first wrote to Hall as a cordial champion of the novel, asking for samples of the pre-publication pamphlet being prepared by the English publisher Jonathan Cape, in September 1928, she abruptly informed Hall that the contract would be canceled in light of the legal issues that were being raised in the UK.[57] The book was soon published in the United States on the debut list of Covici-Friede, a small house founded in 1928 by bookshop owner Pascal Covici, a Jewish Romanian American, and Donald Friede, who had worked as a stock clerk for Knopf. *The Well of Loneliness* proved to be a significant financial success for Covici-Friede, and the company prevailed in Manhattan courts when the book was seized by John Sumner.

Book historians correctly conclude that Jewish publishers were able to gain a foothold in American publishing during the early twentieth century because of a willingness to embrace risky but ultimately enduring works rejected by their WASP counterparts. Similarly accurate claims have been made about the rise of the film industry, documented in books such as Neal Gabler's *An Empire of Their Own: How the Jews Invented Hollywood*, and the concept has even been successfully applied to the rise of Jewish law firms that were willing to accept unpopular corporate-litigation cases during the mid-twentieth century.[58] However, the Knopfs clearly should be cast as an exception to this trend. Rather than taking on risky creative projects, they attempted to imitate the aura of establishment and tradition that permeated older American and British firms, favoring previously published classics over untested works in the initial seasons of Borzoi Books.

Nonetheless, the scholar George Bornstein's studies of the intersection between modernism and marginalization group Alfred Knopf with Benjamin Huebsch and Joel Spingarn (on the Harcourt, Brace board) as examples of Jewish men who were daring in their choice of publishing projects.[59] The Knopfs are often listed alongside other examples of the twentieth century's bold new publishers, such as Bennett Cerf, Horace Liveright, Harold Guinzburg, and George Oppenheimer, who briefly managed advertising and publicity for Knopf before departing in 1925 to found Viking Press, which would publish all of James Joyce's books except *Ulysses*. Yet including the Knopfs solely because they shared a Jewish identity with these pioneers overlooks the reality that Blanche and Alfred in fact distinguished themselves from their peers by avoiding controversial works. Bennett Cerf spoke candidly about the animosity between Liveright and Knopf: "Knopf had the one thing Liveright missed. Knopf had class." Cerf recalled, "Knopf was the fellow he wanted to beat. He didn't care about these old fogies he was competing with. It was Knopf he had his sights set on. By the same token Knopf hated Liveright." According to Cerf, "Everybody said, 'These are fresh young Jews,' and Knopf didn't want to be in that class at all, so he resented Liveright."[60]

Other scholars of modern American literature have linked the marginalization of Jewish publishers with their willingness to publish African American writers. In *The Harlem Renaissance in Black and White*, George Hutchinson includes Knopf in a characterization of America's publishing climate at the time: "The new publishers . . . were almost all Jewish and had been excluded from the inside circles of the established, Anglo-dominated industry even in New York. . . . They had nothing to lose by taking risks—no influential contacts, no contracts with established writers, no debts to the publishing establishment."[61] However, the few writers of color published by Knopf during the Harlem Renaissance were signed when the company had considerable assets to lose—including Eurocentric prestige—if a risky title didn't pan out. The

Knopfs decided to publish Langston Hughes's debut book, *The Weary Blues*, because of reassurances from their close friend and successful author Carl Van Vechten, who made the recommendation after Hughes's work was deemed suitable for publication (and therefore less risky) by the editors of *Vanity Fair.*

An erroneous categorization of the Knopfs was also echoed by Tom Dardis. In his definitive biography of Jewish publisher Horace Liveright, Dardis captures the pro-Bolshevik stance that led Liveright to eagerly publish Trotsky after the October revolution. Unlike Knopf, Liveright fought censorship attempts, defeating John Sumner in court for the right to publish the ancient *Satyricon* of Petronius. Without any assistance from established Christian publishers, Liveright defeated a local bill advocated by the Clean Books League. The bill required jury trials in censorship cases, rejected expert testimony regarding a book's merits, and gave the New York Society for the Suppression of Vice wide latitude in banning any books it deemed offensive. Dardis suggests that Liveright's lack of support from other houses may have been a ploy on the part of anti-Semitic publishers who wanted to let their Jewish competitors become legislated and litigated out of business. Offended by the indifference of the WASP publishing community after a courtroom victory that financially benefited them all, Liveright withdrew from the National Association of Book Publishers.[62] Though Dardis acknowledges Knopf's hesitation to fight censorship, he attributes it to Knopf's lack of money rather than to his cautious sensibilities, overlooking Knopf's eagerness to join clubs of established publishers.

Twenty-five years after the *Homo Sapiens* incident, Knopf issued a statement on censorship—a characteristically moderate one. His words reflect an unambiguous distaste for censorship, along with a distaste for distasteful literature: "Long experience with censors and much soul-searching has convinced me that the civilized and intelligent person can never be comfortable in any position other than that of unalterable opposition to any censorship of anything, anywhere, at any time," he writes, echoing a tenet often voiced by his former professor Joel Spingarn, in essays and lectures promoting literary criticism that was devoid of moral judgment. The remainder of the statement lacks Spingarn's verve. Instead, Knopf's preference is simply to have patience, to hope that social standards will change, and to trust the whims of the marketplace: "My own considered opinion is that you have to wait, however uncomfortably, for time and the taste of the public at large to do the censoring. You may find this position painful from time to time, but in the long run you can live with it . . . in the sure knowledge that what doesn't deserve to endure never does last very long."[63]

In light of Alfred's cautious approach to modern literature, it is easy to understand why the firm's première title was *Four Plays* by Émile Augier. It

FOUR PLAYS
By ÉMILE AUGIER

TRANSLATED WITH AN INTRODUCTION
By BARRETT H CLARK
WITH A PREFACE BY BRIEUX

NEW YORK · ALFRED A KNOPF · 1915

Title page for the first Knopf book

may seem contradictory that a company founded on the promise of distinctive publishing would be launched by a collection of works by a minor French playwright who had been dead for twenty-six years and whose storylines contained little of the exuberance of Broadway in 1915; Augier is described as having "always stood for the great middle classes" in the book's preface by Eugène Brieux.[64] Knopf met the translator, Barrett H. Clark, through mutual friends. At the time, Clark was actively involved in New York's theater scene as a translator and editor for Samuel French, Inc., a publisher and licensor of plays.[65] Brieux had held steady on the *Publishers' Weekly* nonfiction bestseller list in 1912 and 1913 with his own collection, *Three Plays,* which showcased themes of social justice. The bookseller Adolph Kroch summarized the three men thus: "Knopf's first book . . . was *Four Plays,* by Émile Augier, the realist with a sharp tongue and with no mercy for convention. The preface was by Brieux, whose *Red Robe* had stirred the conscience of France. The translator was Barrett H. Clark, a young dramatic critic who has since attained fame in drama-lore."[66] Though Knopf's debut book made nods to progressivism, it was a time-tested literary revival.

With *Four Plays* at the top of his inaugural list, Alfred Knopf began to educate his young wife in the process of developing literary prestige, while she educated him in the process of acquiring social prestige. Paradoxically, neither of them possessed any true prestige at this point, but they saw their potential for it and, through their publishing firm, began a performance of nobility that permeates the Borzoi brand to this day. It was fitting that Knopf selected a book of plays for his debut. He loved theater, both as a spectator and as a performer of grand impresario roles. With the publication of Augier in October 1915, his stage was set.

CHAPTER THREE

The Borzoi Abroad

The Russian barzoi [*sic*], or Siberian wolfhound, is one of the noblest of all dogs.
The Field magazine, 1887, quoted in the *Oxford English Dictionary*

BLANCHE AND ALFRED KNOPF's imported works became the cornerstone on which they built a reputation for being among the noblest of all American publishers. Authors and readers alike received the impression that the Borzoi roster was elite, and this image was enhanced by the company's emphasis on European works. However, we should not attribute these transatlantic acquisitions entirely to Blanche and Alfred's belief in European cachet. Alfred's financial prudence played an equal role as he calculated the benefits of buying previously launched books that had already been edited, typeset, printed, and tested in an English-speaking marketplace.

The Knopfs' list of authors eventually included a diverse array of American luminaries, but the initial transition was from eastern European authors to British poets and novelists. Rooted in Alfred's quest for favorable financial terms, the Knopfs' subsequent acquisition of books by Scandinavian authors, some of whom had been rejected by other American houses, provided a gateway to the Nobel Prize, which continues to contribute to the Borzoi's aura of nobility.

In almost all of the company's first fifteen years, the majority of Borzoi Books were written by authors born in Europe. The most significant exception is 1919 (the year after the armistice between the Allies and Germany was signed), when approximately 58 percent of Knopf's new releases were written by authors born in the United States. In 1917 and 1918, the ratio of European to American authors was roughly equal. Yet for the other twelve years, the percentage of American-born authors averaged only 31 percent. This reflects the criteria for "prestigious literature" of the era. University catalog offerings from the period, including those of Princeton and Columbia, underscore the fact that American literature was unlikely to be considered worthy of serious study. National pride was only slowly beginning to create momentum for American literature in academia. That momentum accelerated between 1917 and 1921, five years after Knopf's graduation, with the publication of the four-volume *Cambridge History of American Literature,* a project spearheaded by Columbia professors John Erskine, William Peterfield Trent, and Carl Van Doren.[1]

During the formative years at Knopf, the company's ties to Europe were strengthened by the emergence of a new breed of publishing professional: the literary agent.[2] The rights to books by lesser-known and celebrated European writers alike could be easily negotiated through up-and-coming agents, who made it their business to track and sell ever-expanding segments of a book's commercial potential. These segments included reprint rights for varying hardcover formats; international rights; magazine serialization; and motion picture rights. Kenneth Burke's use of the word "agent" in describing persuasive interactions neatly complements Knopf history at this juncture, providing a convenient summary of a human element in the process of publishing.

Although it was initially Alfred's vision to acquire books from overseas, Blanche's legacy became more closely tied to European authors, in part because of his later emphasis on the American West and books about American history. For these reasons, Blanche's immersion in publishing makes an apt beginning to the story of the Borzoi abroad. Her interest in publishing rose as her interest in family life waned, leading her to foster an international "family" of authors. Soon after their marriage, she and Alfred were melding their professional and personal lives in ways that made the couple memorable in transatlantic publishing circles. Their reputation abroad easily survived the demise of their ill-fated branch office in London. Despite the failure of that venture, the company's founding years created an enduring image of Borzoi Books as an international enterprise, with Blanche Knopf as its overseas matriarch.

A Woman's Place Is in the (Publishing) House

By the time Blanche was promoted to president of Alfred A. Knopf, Inc., in 1957 (when Alfred became chairman of the board), she had devoted more than four decades of her life to Borzoi Books, though as late as 1965 she was still barred from the Publishers' Lunch Club—and from other organizations to which Alfred belonged—because she was a woman.[3] Her rise to prominence began when she acquired difficult French works such as the future Nobel Prize winner André Gide's philosophical novel *Strait Is the Gate,* published by Knopf in 1924. Her ties to French publishing led to her being made a knight in the Legion of Honor in 1949, rising to the rank of officer in 1960.

Though she did not attend college and had no professional experience, Blanche made a remarkably rapid transition from uncertain novice to savvy businesswoman. When Alfred incorporated his firm in 1918, he named Blanche vice-president and director. This occurred not long after the birth of their only child, Alfred Abraham Knopf, Jr. (called Pat, a nickname she gave him when he was a newborn) on 17 July 1918.[4] Alfred's diary for that date blends notes about the birth with details of bookselling appointments.[5] He recorded the fact that Blanche awakened him at six o'clock in the morning and told him she was in pain, though she did not appear to be in labor. He was worried, but he nonetheless took the train to Grand Central Terminal and spent the morning meeting with Brentano's and Baker & Taylor. After lunch, he received a phone call announcing Pat's birth at White Plains Hospital. He left his office earlier than usual to meet his newborn son.[6]

At the time, Blanche was a conventional American housewife with a routine that included taking a trolley to shop at the White Plains Produce Market. Her household briefly included two borzois. This was the only time Blanche and Alfred tried to keep them as pets; they found the dogs to be unruly and disloyal, preferring their devoted mixed-breed bulldog named Pete.[7] Their subsequent dogs included poodles and Yorkies. The Knopfs were able to accommodate the large borzois because in 1916 they had bought a house twenty miles north of New York City in Hartsdale, near White Plains. The down payment was made with money from Blanche's family, and the seller tried unsuccessfully to renege on the contract when he discovered that Blanche and Alfred were Jewish.

Their time in Hartsdale was short-lived. Two weeks before Pat was born, Blanche signed a contract to sell the house because, according to Alfred, it was beyond their means. The departure from Westchester County marked the end of Blanche's tenure as a homemaker.[8] By the end of the summer of 1918, the Knopfs and their infant son had moved to Manhattan's Upper West Side, renting an apartment that was spacious enough to also accommodate their nanny. They would not own a home in Westchester again until 1928, when they would build the Tudor-style house they called The Hovel, which Alfred inhabited for the rest of his life. Blanche took a small apartment in midtown Manhattan, staying in the city most weeknights and joining Alfred in Westchester on weekends, when they would often host elegant dinner parties for authors.[9]

As a publisher, Blanche was known for her fierce independence and volatile temper, but in the company's earliest years she was utterly dependent on Alfred. She relied on him to hone her knowledge of European authors and counsel her on practical issues such as translators' fees. Her tutelage comes to light in the many letters she wrote to Alfred when he traveled on sales calls during the first months of their marriage. In these endearing missives, sometimes signed "woof woof," Blanche brims with romantic longing and expresses bewilderment over how to manage day-to-day affairs at the office. She often wrote to Alfred on company letterhead, her timid voice contrasting starkly with the assertive, all-capital letters of his name printed at the top of the stationery. Meek and deferential in her correspondence with him, she exuded few traits that would predict her future as an editor of Simone de Beauvoir and Albert Camus.[10] Yet by 1918, abandoning the suburban house for the publishing house, she had become a salaried, full-time partner in the company, emerging from her role as apprentice and demonstrating confident mastery of the publishing business. One of the fundamental business principles she learned from Alfred was that imported fiction offered an affordable way to foster a reputation as a highbrow publisher.

Her father-in-law, Samuel Knopf, held a dominant role in all aspects of Borzoi Books until his death in 1932, but company correspondence throughout the 1920s provides vivid evidence of Blanche's growing strength as a powerful decision maker. She relished this new life, making strides that were rare for women in the publishing industry, or any American industry for that matter. At the time, the only other women who held considerable status in a publishing house were Mary Norton and Ellen Knowles. Mary Norton assisted her husband, William Warder Norton, in publishing a series of educational lectures delivered at the Cooper Union. Combined with his adult-education efforts at The New School for Social Research, these endeavors led to the inception of their renowned trade and college textbook firm, W. W. Norton & Company (originally called the People's Institute Publishing Company), in 1923. Yet Mary never played as powerful a role as Blanche did, and Mary's involvement waned after her husband's death in 1945. Ellen Knowles became a director and stockholder at the young Harcourt, Brace & Company in 1920. She had served as Alfred Harcourt's assistant at Henry Holt & Company and later married him, but his business partner was always clearly Donald Brace, not Knowles. It's noteworthy that before he decided to launch his firm with Brace, Alfred Harcourt considered joining Blanche and Alfred's firm.[11]

Alfred welcomed and nurtured Blanche's interest in the firm, but it was through her own verve and initiative that she was able to propel herself to a level of authority that exceeded her female counterparts' roles in the industry. Over time, her progressive presence alongside Alfred greatly enhanced Borzoi Books' reputation for sophistication.

Becoming Importers

While Alfred Knopf had affection for the Lower East Side booksellers he had called on in his company's early days, especially the bookmen who recommended his Russian acquisitions, he remained very much an Anglophile, scouting for prospects by reading English reviews of European books, a

Birthplaces of Knopf Authors

Year	Number of Titles Issued	Authors Born in US	Authors Born in UK	Other
1915	12	0	8%	92%
1916	36	17%	22%	61%
1917	34	50%	29%	21%
1918	40	53%	28%	19%
1919	62	58%	30%	12%
1920	76	34%	50%	16%
1921	57	46%	33%	21%
1922	79	34%	35%	31%
1923	128	35%	31%	34%
1924	109	35%	34%	31%
1925	119	31%	35%	34%
1926	146	43%	33%	24%
1927	154	34%	40%	26%
1928	136	36%	34%	30%
1929	140	35%	30%	35%

technique that guided his acquisitions process throughout the 1920s. Between 1920 and 1929, the number of new Borzoi titles published annually nearly doubled, but books by American authors remained in the minority.[12]

Acquiring foreign books in pre-printed sheets allowed the young publishing company to enjoy favorable repayment terms, which suited the Knopfs' lean start-up budget. However, from an accounting standpoint, buying imported books on credit carries mixed risks. By buying sheets in small quantities as part of a British publisher's edition, the Knopfs avoided the cost of typesetting, proofreading, and printing, but they took the risk of having only a limited inventory of a book that might quickly become a top seller. On the other hand, if a publisher buys the rights to a foreign book, there is a risk associated with manufacturing unsold copies (particularly on credit) if the print run is set too high and the book fails to sell through. In 1915, as into the twenty-first century, a publisher could actually lose money on a bestseller because it is impossible to calculate with precision how many copies will ultimately sell, while printers, paper vendors, and binderies must be paid for all finished copies, regardless of the final sales numbers for a title. Setting a print run too low is equally risky; if a book becomes briefly popular, demand for it may wane by the time additional copies can be manufactured and shipped. Print-on-demand and e-book technologies are reducing this risk for today's houses, but for the Knopfs, the decision to import pre-printed sheets was a path of least peril.

One way in which the Knopfs balanced their options was to avoid importing more than 1,500 sets of sheets for any title.[13] For books that held a strong promise of sales beyond that number, Alfred and Blanche found it worthwhile to take the risk of paying for the typesetting and printing costs themselves. Only occasionally did they incur double costs, importing sheets for the initial release of a work and later investing in US typesetting and printing for subsequent copies when a foreign book proved to be popular. The two early Knopf editions of Thomas Mann's *Royal Highness: A Novel of German Court Life* provide an example of this approach.

Some have argued that foreign works from countries that did not recognize international copyright law were appealing because royalties would not have to be paid. Knopf liked the fact that Russian authors could exert no control over their US publishers, but he was not motivated by freedom from royalties.[14] In fact, royalties pose no risk to a publisher's finances because royalties are essentially a profit-sharing plan—an expense incurred only if a book is selling. However, the payment of advances does involve considerable risk, so it is not surprising that the Knopfs, like most of their contemporaries, paid advances rarely and grudgingly, reserving them only for authors who had already proved to be lucrative. The pervasiveness of advances for trade-book authors, now seen as a necessary sign of confidence in a new work, did not begin its gradual emergence in America until the mid-twentieth century, when agents began abandoning the etiquette of avoiding simultaneous submissions to multiple publishers.[15]

For the Knopfs, international copyright law—not royalties—had the greatest impact on their fiscal decisions regarding imported works. Understanding this legislation enhances our understanding of which books were popularized on both sides of the Atlantic during the turn of the last century. In his memoir, Knopf's tales of elegant teas at Claridge's Hotel and resurrected masterpieces of Russian literature are interwoven with pragmatic references to copyright law.

Until 1891, US copyright laws restricted protection to authors who were citizens or residents of the United States. Therefore, in most cases American publishers who wanted to reprint foreign texts could do so without any financial obligation to the author or original publisher. However, they risked being scorned within the industry if they failed to pay a courtesy fee to the original publisher. Publishers who participated in this "courtesy of the trade" could rest assured that if they paid the fee, other American houses would refrain from releasing a competing edition, which had significant consequences for the acquisition of foreign works that held special potential to become popular (and therefore lucrative) in the United States. Those who ignored the courtesy of the trade were labeled pirates, though they in fact broke no laws. That arrangement changed in 1891, when controversial new legislation provided a means for obtaining US copyright protection on foreign works. Under a clause favoring American labor, authors of foreign English-language books could achieve US copyright protection only when the book was manufactured by an American typesetter and/or printer. The law required the publisher to mail or hand-deliver two copies of the book to the Library of Congress no later than the day of the book's initial publication, regardless of whether that debut occurred in the United States or abroad. This prohibited US copyright from being gained in hindsight. In addition, foreign authors could secure US copyright only if they resided in a nation with a reciprocal copyright agreement.[16]

Under a 1909 provision, no copyright could be assigned retroactively to a work that was in the public domain. Any work published in the United States or elsewhere before the 1909 act went into effect was considered to be in the public domain unless it had been previously registered with the Library of Congress. Works that had been registered were granted an increased renewal term, raised from 14 years to 28, setting the maximum term for which a book could be excluded from the public domain at 56 years. The 1909 act also included a manufacturing clause that acknowledges the emergence of Linotype and Monotype technology, reiterating that the typesetting must be accomplished within the limits of the United States, "either by hand or by the aid of any kind of typesetting machine." A further provision required that the work be both printed *and* bound in the United States. In addition, authors from nations that had no reciprocal copyright law could now obtain US copyright if they lived in America at the time of the work's first publication.

One provision in particular made it considerably easier for an American publisher to complete a transatlantic acquisition: US copyright could be secured if one complete copy of an English-language book published abroad—before publication in the United States—was deposited in the copyright office within thirty days of overseas publication. This replaced the previous requirement of sending books on publication day, defined by these statutes as the day on which a book was made available for sale. Within that thirty-day interim, an authorized edition manufactured and published within the United States could be deposited as a "replacement" copy, gaining full-term US copyright protection.[17] Another change that would have affected the Knopfs was enacted in 1919, when the Great War caused the interim period to be extended to sixty days for books published abroad in English "on or after the date of the President's proclamation of peace."[18]

What did these evolving laws mean for the Knopfs? Borzoi Books printed from imported sheets did not qualify for copyright protection because they had not been manufactured in America. Therefore, if a competing house planned to issue the same work, the Knopfs had to find ways to add value to their edition, through lavish bindings, illustrations, or the inclusion of a copyrightable introduction, usually written as a testimonial by a literary luminary. Under the public domain provisions, the Knopfs were not able to secure a retroactive copyright on a previously published European work whose US copyright had not been secured within the required time constraints—even if the Knopfs manufactured the book in the United States rather than importing sheets. Essentially, the laws made it impossible for American publishers to hold copyright on a foreign English-language book unless the work was relatively new, manufactured domestically, and written by an author who either lived in the States at the time of publication or was a citizen of a country with which America shared reciprocal copyright laws.[19] Out of the approximately nine hundred early Knopf volumes I have examined, only sixty-five were printed abroad, all of them in the UK. This indicates that less than 10 percent of the Borzoi's early acquisitions were imported in sheets. This number tapers sharply after 1923, indicating that the young publishers began setting and printing imports themselves as soon as it was economically feasible to do so.

Green Mansions and the House of Knopf

The Knopfs' early acquisitions lists give the impression that Blanche and Alfred called on British houses frequently, but in fact they remained in the United States during the company's initial six years, conducting overseas transactions through correspondence or through agents in New York. Blanche and Alfred did not make the first of their legendary European tours until 1921. In the meantime, Alfred continued to reap the benefits of his 1912 visit abroad, using contacts from his college-graduation trip to help him procure foreign works. His friendship with John and Ada Galsworthy proved to be especially useful as they became the Borzoi's unofficial literary scouts abroad and nurtured Alfred's focus on British writers. Replacing Max Maisel as an editorial advisor to Knopf, Ada Galsworthy expressed dislike for Przybyszewski's *Homo Sapiens* after Alfred sent her a copy. She candidly told him that she found the book to be monotonous, with an overemphasis on sex.[20]

The Galsworthys earned modest fees from the Knopf firm—Ada as a translator and John as a writer of introductions—but no Galsworthy title ever became a Borzoi Book. Possibly, their interest in Blanche and Alfred was simply rooted in the pleasure of serving as mentors to the amusingly enthusiastic young publishers. Revered in England both as a playwright and a novelist (and best known today for his trilogy, *The Forsyte Saga*), John Galsworthy actively assisted other literary figures at home and abroad, an ambition that is preserved in the P.E.N. legacy. The P.E.N. American Center, whose acronym refers to poets, playwrights, essayists, editors, and novelists, was founded in New York City in 1922, but the organization originated with Galsworthy and a Cornish novelist, Catherine Amy Dawson-Scott, whose novels were published by Knopf on imported sheets. Galsworthy and Dawson-Scott founded the P.E.N. Club in London in 1921, hoping to foster an international writers' circle that could ease animosity between nations in the aftermath of the Great War. Galsworthy was awarded the Nobel Prize in 1932, a year before his death.[21]

During Alfred's solo trip to Europe, Galsworthy introduced the aspiring publisher to the novel that would become the first lucrative Borzoi Book, W. H. Hudson's *Green Mansions*. By the time Knopf produced his reissue in 1916, Hudson was 72 years old and hardly reflected modernist verve, though *Green Mansions* contains exotic elements.[22] Set in Venezuela and Guyana, the novel depicts a complex, doomed romance between an English-speaking traveler named Abel and an adolescent girl, Rima, who has never ventured beyond the jungle.

Hudson's clear focus is the heroism of Rima and her natural world; she loses her life because of Abel's intrusions on her community. Yet Knopf's advertising copy reduces the plot to a commercial romance and doesn't mention the novel's setting. Beneath a Borzoi Books banner, set in a point size equal to novel's title, the ad copy describes *Green Mansions* as "the story of a girl's slow and timid awakening to the meaning of love, and a man's passionate and chivalric devotion."[23] Other Knopf advertising copy applauds the foreword and says nothing about the novel: "This is the book which John Galsworthy would have every man, woman and child read. Read the first paragraph of his foreword at your bookshop. It will convince you."[24] However, Knopf did not believe that the Galsworthy introduction was suitable for the college market. When he published the novel in his new Students' Library of Contemporary Fiction series in 1926, he replaced Galsworthy's text with an introduction by Thomas Rankin, a professor of rhetoric at the University of Michigan.

Green Mansions placed Knopf and his Borzoi brand in the company of well-respected English writers, and it signaled his admiration for books from his parents' generation. Yet the book's praise of the noble native gave it a progressive air. It also gave Knopf an opportunity to prove that he was a better publisher than Putnam, a venerable firm that, Knopf believed, had botched its 1904 publication of the novel.

Knopf's publication of *Green Mansions* made little business sense. Putnam's edition had not sold well, and it had been issued in sheets imported from Hudson's long-term English publisher, Duckworth. This meant that all prospects for securing US copyright for the novel itself, then or in the future, had been negated. Nonetheless, Knopf had a new edition typeset and printed in the United States. The new foreword by Galsworthy at least qualified for copyright protection and explains why the book could carry the phrase "Copyright, 1916, by Alfred A. Knopf."[25]

Knopf's edition of *Green Mansions* attracted impressive advance orders, including a request from a Los Angeles bookseller, C. C. Parker (described by Knopf as old-fashioned), for one hundred copies. Though Knopf's records do not specify the number of copies ultimately printed or sold, the Parker order confirms the early establishment of a coast-to-coast Borzoi sales network.[26] By the end of the year, Knopf saw fit to increase the price from $1.50 to $1.75.

Knopf attributed the weak Putnam sales to a poor marketing pitch. In contrast to Knopf's sensational advertising tone, Putnam quoted a tame review from the highbrow English literary magazine *Athenaeum:* "The author presents with admirable picturesqueness . . . the natural surroundings and the characters of the South American Indians."[27] Knopf's determination to "educate" American audiences about European authors whom he admired became a theme of his marketing, an approach begun at Doubleday in his marketing campaign for Conrad.

Knopf's efforts to resurrect *Green Mansions* began as early as 1913, when Galsworthy sent a letter of introduction to his friend Hudson on Knopf's behalf. Knopf failed to persuade Doubleday editors or Mitchell Kennerley to publish the book. The grateful, aging Hudson remained politely skeptical that Knopf would succeed, telling his young correspondent that he did not believe American houses would be receptive to his works any longer and predicting that his poor health would prevent him from writing another book.[28] He needn't have been pessimistic. Under Knopf's guidance, Hudson's American career flourished, a gradual process captured in more than three dozen letters to Knopf written by Hudson over the next nine years, including a missive sent less than two weeks before his death in August 1922. A recurring theme is Hudson's effusive gratitude for the financial security Knopf brought him in those final years. Knopf presented himself to the public as a benevolent impresario of culture, while he presented himself privately to his authors as a benevolent master of finance.

Though he had devoted his life to naturalism and ornithology, far removed from the business world, Hudson was not shy about discussing money with Knopf, and he candidly compared the process of negotiating with his British publishers to warfare. This resentment was surely exacerbated by the fact that he usually sold his copyrights to his publishers.[29] Letters to Knopf from Hudson acknowledge receipt of royalty payments ranging from one hundred to nearly seven hundred dollars, paid directly to Hudson rather than to his copyright-holding publishers, and by March 1922 Hudson was suggesting that *Green Mansions* would be appropriate for the cinema, though no dramatic adaptation would appear until 1937 with the broadcast of a radio opera, followed by a film more than twenty years later.

Hudson's relationship with the house of Knopf demonstrates how difficult it was for the young publisher to compete against other American houses vying for European works. Because Knopf was able to transform *Green Mansions* into a top seller, he soon found himself trying to earn the privilege of becoming Hudson's sole American publisher, but he repeatedly lost out to the established house of E. P. Dutton, which had long-standing working relationships with Hudson's English publisher, J. M. Dent & Sons—a reality that Hudson mentioned more than once in letters to Knopf. Presumably, Knopf lost out because he failed to be the highest bidder. He had particularly hoped to publish Hudson's memoir, *Far Away and Long Ago*—one of the few opportunities to release a previously unpublished work by Hudson, securing an American copyright. Knopf offered to host Hudson as a houseguest in New York, giving the author a chance to see his mother's homeland for the first time; though Hudson had spent most of his adult life in England, his mother was American. Despite Knopf's attempt to establish a more personal connection, however, Hudson sold the copyright to Dent for £300 and apologetically informed Knopf that Dent had sold the memoir to Dutton because they were willing to pay more than any other American house.[30] Hudson was also pleased that Dutton had plans to publish *The Purple Land*, his narrative of South America, with a foreword by Theodore Roosevelt.[31]

Out of the seven Hudson titles published by Knopf (*Afoot in England, Birds and Man, Green Mansions, The Land's End, A Little Boy Lost, Ralph Herne,* and *Tales of the Pampas*), none was exclusively published in America as a Borzoi Book.[32] Knopf had to distinguish his editions through packaging or illustrations. He asked Hudson to write a foreword to appear in his 1917 reissue of *Little Boy Lost*, offering a royalty of 10 percent.[33] In his reply, Hudson regretfully claims that he doesn't remember what inspired him to write the book, though he goes on to reveal many details about the process by which the book came about. Knopf printed the letter verbatim as a postscript on the final pages of *Little Boy Lost*, including Hudson's conclusion that "children do not read forewords and introductions; they have to be addressed to adults who do not read children's books, so that in any case it would be thrown away. Still if a foreword you must have, and from me, I think you will have to get it out of this letter."[34]

The Agents

Moyle Church-Town, the first British novel Knopf acquired, taught him a great deal about the process of acquiring an import. The transaction was negotiated by Jean Wick, whose office was on Washington Square in Greenwich Village. Advertising in the *Dial*, she described herself as representing authors of short stories, books, and plays, and she touted her own book, *The Stories Editors Buy and Why*.[35] In July 1916, Knopf squabbled with Mills & Boon, the UK publisher of *Moyle Church-Town*, over damaged goods. His letter to the house sheds light on the agent's role. Knopf paid Wick directly, and, after deducting her $100 commission, she issued a payment to Mills & Boon. Complicating the transaction, Mills & Boon was represented by James Brand Pinker, one of the world's first professional literary agents, who requested a sample in order to determine whether the books in question were indeed damaged, which provoked Knopf's ire. He claimed that a sample proved nothing; the damaged books had been inspected by Wick, and this alone should be sufficient evidence for Mills & Boon to take the matter up with its printers and packers, recouping the damaged-goods deduction Knopf had given himself on his remaining balance with the publisher.[36]

The incident didn't deter Knopf from pursuing even more significant imports, eventually landing him a business relationship with the prestigious English agent Edward Garnett. Knopf first corresponded with Garnett during the Kennerley apprenticeship, after Galsworthy provided a letter of introduction, but until the success of *Green Mansions*, Garnett gave Knopf a lukewarm reception. In the summer of 1915, Knopf invited Garnett to write a book on the art of translation for the Borzoi's inaugural list. Garnett declined.[37] In subsequent correspondence, he expressed doubt about Knopf's judgment and went so far as to predict that Americans would not embrace *Green Mansions*.

However, in 1920, Knopf signed a contract for Garnett's new collection of literary essays called *Friday Nights*. By this time, Knopf possessed considerably more bargaining power, agreeing to publish the essays only if he could also have American rights to Garnett's biography of Ivan Turgenev. Knopf promised a royalty scale that was typical for his company (and for the industry) during this period: 10 percent on the first 2,500 copies; 12.5 percent on the next 2,500 copies; and 15 percent after 5,000 copies, with an advance of fifty pounds on publication.[38] An English publisher, Jonathan Cape, bought five hundred copies of *Friday Nights* in sheets from Knopf.[39] In further transatlantic community building, Knopf attempted (albeit unsuccessfully) to persuade the *New York Times Book Review* to publish John Galsworthy's review of *Friday Nights* after advance sales stalled.[40]

Garnett led the Knopfs to acquire books by numerous contemporary authors, including D. H. Lawrence; Katherine Mansfield; and Garnett's son, David, who co-founded the Nonesuch Press and was an award-winning Bloomsbury Group novelist. Again, despite the appearance that Blanche and Alfred immersed themselves in European travel during the launch of the firm, they did not meet Edward Garnett until 1921, on their first trip abroad as publishers. For this introduction, they hosted a tea also attended by W. H. Hudson.

While Garnett was reluctant to work with Knopf at first, James Brand Pinker was an early supporter of Borzoi Books, despite the squabble over the damaged copies of *Moyle Church-Town*. Knopf first encountered Pinker through Joseph Conrad and furthered the friendship when he went to work for Mitchell Kennerley. Pinker opened his firm in 1896 after working as a newspaper and magazine editor. Through his editorial work, he was able to attract a clientele that included H. G. Wells, Oscar Wilde, Stephen Crane, Henry James, and Ford Madox Ford.[41] Pinker was more encouraging than Garnett in responding to the young Knopf's queries during the summer of 1915. He told the aspiring publisher to invest in works by the prolific novelist Francis Brett Young, who indeed became a staple of the Borzoi lists during the 1920s. Through Pinker, Knopf was also able to publish numerous works by Walter de la Mare, author of highly imaginative books for adults and a key figure in the growth of Knopf's books for young readers. Pinker also brought the poet, novelist, and classical translator Robert Graves to Knopf, as well as the short-story writer Elizabeth Dashwood.

Mary Ann Gillies, in *The Professional Literary Agent in Britain, 1880–1920*, illustrates the ways in which Pinker served as much more than a hawker of copyrights or an administrator of intellectual properties. She shows that he clearly also served a patronage role in literary modernism, loaning money to experimental authors and giving them access to the services enjoyed by more marketable writers. By giving his time, effort, and other resources to risky projects, he shaped the agent's role into one that replaced the dying patronage systems of Europe's nobility. Gillies also considers the ways in which Pinker and other agents managed authors who publicly claimed that a true artist disdains wealth while privately engaging in heated financial feuds with their publishing houses. Agents were able to capitalize on modernist, anti-commercial writers who required arbitration from someone who didn't find fiscal discussions problematic. "Do get me some money, will you: I am at the end," D. H. Lawrence wrote to Pinker.[42]

Pinker's success was soon followed by the rise of agencies such as the firm founded in London in 1899 by Albert Curtis Brown. Like Pinker, he was a former newspaper staffer; he had served as an American correspondent from the

New York Press. Reflecting a typical source of income for literary agents at the time, Brown's first negotiated sale was to *Pall Mall Magazine*—notably not to a book publisher—where he placed an article by novelist John Oliver Hobbes.[43] In 1920, at the recommendation of Galsworthy, Knopf contacted Brown and bought the reprint rights for four novels by E. M. Forster: *Where Angels Fear to Tread, Howards End, The Longest Journey,* and *A Room with a View.* He also purchased the rights to a volume of Forster short stories and an essay collection. By 1923, the apparently impatient Forster was disgruntled by his sluggish sales as a Borzoi author, calling on Blanche and Alfred in their London hotel suite to inform them that his next novel, *A Passage to India,* would be published in the United States by Alfred Harcourt and Donald Brace. Knopf considered the loss of Forster to be a bitter lesson.[44]

Despite the disappointment over Forster, the Curtis Brown agency was involved in the negotiations for the Knopfs' first major bestseller, *Sorrell and Son*, Major Warwick Deeping's fictional portrait of a Great War veteran adjusting to civilian life. The novel was brought to Blanche and Alfred's attention by their London scout, the novelist Margaret "Storm" Jameson. As a Curtis Brown author, she may have enhanced the Knopfs' negotiating power. Published in 1926 as a Borzoi Book and in 1927 by Grosset & Dunlap, this acquisition also represented the house of Knopf's first windfall from the medium of motion pictures. Released in 1927 by United Artists, *Sorrell and Son* was directed by Herbert Brenon, whose work on the film earned him a nomination for an Academy Award during the Oscars' inaugural year.[45]

Grosset & Dunlap's edition of *Sorrell and Son* contained photographic stills from scenes of the United Artists photoplay, while Knopf promoted his finely packaged edition with billboard advertising on upper Broadway.[46] The typesetting for Grosset & Dunlap's edition reflects a desire to economize: the kerning and leading are tight, while the text in the Knopf edition is inviting to the reader's eye. Grosset & Dunlap's heavily illustrated, full-color jacket emphasizes the book's photographs and touts other titles in the house's photoplay series, *Uncle Tom's Cabin* and *The Jazz Singer* among them: "These Are the Books from which the Big Movies Were Made. . . . Your favorite pictures will mean so much more to you."[47] Perhaps to further differentiate his edition from that of Grosset & Dunlap, Knopf reissued the book in 1927 in a deluxe package, described in a lengthy back-of-the-book publisher's note that reveals six-figure sales:

> This entirely new edition of "Sorrell and Son" supersedes the original American trade edition, which is henceforth out of print. The occasion chosen for making "Sorrell and Son" available in this considerably improved format is a birthday—a relatively early birthday of the book itself. What is commemorated is the second anniversary of the original publication of "Sorrell and Son" in

America, which took place 19 February 1926. Few books can have spoken elo-quently enough, or to a wide enough public, to call for so special an observance. But this first of Mr. Deeping's books to bring the author world-wide fame has conveyed its meaning with the same directness and simplicity to the minds of exacting judges and to the hearts of all manner of readers everywhere. As, now, it enters simultaneously in America its third year and its third hundred thousand, its publishers have felt that to bring it out in a finer dress is at once the least that they can do, and the most fitting thing possible to devise. . . . The type chosen is Garamont [*sic*]. The edition has been set on the monotype, electrotyped, printed, and bound in imported sunfast on cloth, by the Plimpton Press, Norwood, Massachusetts. The paper, an eggshell finish, was made by the Ticonderoga Pulp and Paper Company, Ticonderoga, New York. The binding is after drawings by Mr. Percy Smith.[48]

Alfred understood that his market niche was composed of consumers who sought a highly readable edition with a binding that looked rarefied. The Gros-set & Dunlap edition was not meant to be competition for Knopf's. The pres-ence of a cheaper version only helped to underscore what a Borzoi Book was *not*, while the popular mass-market edition ensured a broad level of awareness for *Sorrell and Son* in all its forms.

Sorrell and Son also represents Curtis Brown's involvement in a contract arrangement that would be implemented many times in Borzoi Books' early years, responding to authors who accused their publishers of insufficient advertising. Though the Borzoi packaging was seemingly more refined than the Grosset & Dunlap edition, Deeping's contract with Knopf is an artifact of commercialism. The first Knopf title to sell more than a hundred thousand copies, *Sorrell and Son* was heavily advertised but at a slight cost to the author. Knopf agreed to spend a fixed advertising sum on every copy of the book that sold. In return, Deeping agreed to a lesser royalty of 10 percent. If advertising expenditures dipped below a predetermined amount, the royalty would revert to 15 percent.[49]

While expat Curtis Brown was particularly instrumental to the Knopfs in England, in continental Europe it was the American literary agent William Aspenwall Bradley—an expat in Paris—who guided Blanche through her first transactions in the French publishing scene. Her major publishing achieve-ments in France would not be accomplished until after World War II, when she would acquire works by Simone de Beauvoir, Jean-Paul Sartre, and Albert Camus, but by 1924 she had imported a sufficient number of Parisian books to justify advertising the Borzoi's French translations, including a two-page list-ing at the back of Henry Céard's novel *A Lovely Day (Une Belle Journée)*. Brad-ley's firm was relatively new when Blanche first contacted him; she was one of

ALFRED A. KNOPF
P U B L I S H E R
220 WEST FORTY-SECOND STREET, NEW YORK

BORZOI BOOKS YOU MUST HAVE

GREEN MANSIONS   By W. H. Hudson   Color Jacket $1.50

Introduction by John Galsworthy who says of this delightful South American Romance: "For of all living authors—now that Tolstoi has gone—I could least dispense with W. H. Hudson. . . . 'GREEN MANSIONS,' a story which immortalizes, I think as passionate a love of all beautiful things as ever was in the heart of man. . . . In form and spirit the book is unique, a simple romantic narrative transmuted by sheer glow of beauty into a prose poem. . . . I would that every man, woman and child in England were made to read him; and I would that you in America would take him to heart. . . . As a simple narrator he is well-nigh unsurpassed, as a stylist he has few, if any living equals."

THE BUFFOON   By Louis U. Wilkinson $1.50

A brilliantly entertaining novel of contemporary life. Of it John Cowper Powys, the lecturer says: "A powerful work animated by a shrewd and searching psychology. A masterly book." THE BUFFOON will appeal to all admirers of Mr. Powys.

THE MEMOIRS OF A PHYSICIAN   By Veressayev $1.50

One of the most famous and remarkable of all Russian books, this will interest anyone who has to do with the medical profession (and who has not?) Write for special circular showing complete contents.

EAT AND BE WELL   By Eugene Christian $1.00

Dr. Christian is probably the greatest food expert in America today, and this book summarizes the results of his life work. It consists largely of complete menus arranged according to season, your age, and your occupation. There are curative menus for about 90% of human illnesses.

GREAT RUSSIA   By Charles Sarolea $1.25

The best popular survey of Russia today—her geography, her politics, her problems, her literature.

IN THE RUSSIAN RANKS   By John Morse $1.50

Mr. Morse's tale of his adventures (his flight from Prussia over the Russian border in 1914, his varied service in the army of the Czar, his capture by the Germans and his thrilling escape) will hold spell-bound even the most surfeited of war-book readers. Picture jacket in 2 colors.

THE LITTLE DEMON: A Novel
THE OLD HOUSE and other stories
By Feodor Sologub $1.50 each

These two books, by one of the most noted of the younger Russians, are now published in English for the first time. The translations are authorized. *The Egoist* calls "The Little Demon" "the finest Russian novel since Dostoevsky and Tolstoy and already considered a classic, although first published in 1907."

BIRDS AND MAN
By W. H. Hudson $2.25

John Galsworthy calls Hudson "about the greatest living English stylist . . . the finest living observer of Nature in her moods." This book represents the author of GREEN MANSIONS at his best. Color jacket.

A HERO OF OUR TIME
By M. Y. Lermontov $1.40

One of the great Russian novels, now published in America for the first time.

OTHERS: An anthology of the New Verse $1.50

No lover of poetry or of American literature can afford to overlook this first exclusive collection of poems gathered from the free verse movement for with the exception of a few English contributors, OTHERS is exclusively an American achievement. There are thirty-five contributors.

FOUR DIMENSIONAL VISTAS
By Claude Bragdon $1.25

An original and important contribution to the literature of the fourth dimension and of Theosophy, written in so charming a manner that the intelligent reader cannot fail to be interested.

A PRONOUNCING DICTIONARY OF RUSSIAN NAMES
By Thomas Seltzer $.50

There have been many inquiries for such a little book as this. It is exactly what its title implies and will tell readers of the Russians how to pronounce correctly the long and difficult names they are always meeting.

Publishers' Weekly advertisement emphasizing imported Knopf titles, 1916 his earliest correspondents. He arrived in Europe as a scout for Harcourt, Brace & Company, which helped him to master the details of selling translation and import rights. Like Alfred's, his wife was also his business partner. Together, William and Jenny Bradley created a literary salon that counted major modernist figures, from James Joyce to Gertrude Stein, among its members.

In the 1920s, the Knopfs were eager to sell French translation rights for American authors, but the Bradleys were interested in few of their manuscripts. In turn, Bradley tried to place articles by his authors in *The American Mercury* and offered the Knopfs deals on lesser-known nonfiction works, for which Alfred frequently asserted that he wanted full control over the English rights.[50] André Gide was one of the few consistently lucrative backlist authors who signed with Knopf through the Bradleys. Although it was through William Bradley that Blanche met Gide, this did not preclude her from meeting personally with Gide's editor, Alfred Vallette at the house of Mercure de France, to finalize the contract for *Strait Is the Gate*.[51] Twenty-four years later, Gide would receive the Nobel Prize. Gide's Borzoi works also include his literary criticism of Dostoyevsky as well as the novels *The Immoralist* and *The School for Wives*. Through Bradley, the Knopfs also published books on French literary history and culture, including Jean de Pierrefeu's *Plutarch Lied*, which criticized military leaders in the recent war, and René Lalou's *Contemporary French Literature*.

Keeping Company with Publishers

Because the literary agents' profession was relatively new, the Knopfs were under no pressure to negotiate contracts through agencies, as today's trade publishers generally are. In many cases, the Knopfs dealt directly with English publishers such as William Heinemann, whose successor and business partner, Sydney Pawling, called on Blanche and Alfred in New York throughout the company's early years.

Yet the English publisher who had perhaps the greatest influence on Knopf was not the venerable Heinemann but the relatively young Martin Secker, a contemporary of Knopf's who launched his own firm in London in 1910. Secker soon developed a reputation as a fashionable publisher of new talent, including Franz Kafka, D. H. Lawrence, and Thomas Mann. Through Secker, Knopf acquired more than a dozen works by Welsh novelist Arthur Machen, who was known for the fantastical, and Frank Swinnerton's anonymously published spoof titled *Women*. A member of the Galsworthy set, critic and novelist Swinnerton had written *Women* as a treat for Secker. Knopf often credited Secker with partly inspiring the look of Borzoi books, encouraging his use of stained tops—dyeing the thin upper edge of the pages in a color that complements the binding or stamping.[52]

In addition, Alfred was often led to English publishers simply by reading UK newspapers. Such was the case with Borzoi Books' most prolific British author, J. S. Fletcher, who wrote more than forty detective novels published by Knopf. Alfred first read about Fletcher in the *Westminster Gazette* and decided to approach Ward Lock & Co. to arrange for the US publication of *The Middle Temple Murder*. Knopf manufactured his own editions and paid royalties directly to Ward Lock, at one point unsuccessfully negotiating to buy the US rights to all of Fletcher's works in a single transaction. In a memo to Knopf staff member Saul Salzberg, Samuel Knopf noted with exasperation that the royalties on the Fletcher titles sometimes ran as high as 18 to 24 percent.[53] Though the royalties posed no financial risk, because they did not have to be paid unless copies actually sold, they exceeded Knopf's customary terms. Fletcher's sales figures were waning by the time Samuel Knopf sent this memo in 1932, three years before Fletcher's death at age seventy-two. Nonetheless, *The Middle Temple Murder* had marked a lucrative US debut for the author in 1919, enhanced by media reports that Woodrow Wilson was reading the novel while recovering from a cold. This testimonial was of course touted in Knopf advertising.[54]

To acquire works by continental European authors, the Knopfs used a similar process involving publishers as well as agents. The Borzoi's few Spanish translations were purchased through American agent John Garrett Underhill, a representative of the Society of Spanish Authors, whom Alfred Knopf met through Joel Spingarn.[55] With the exception of W. H. Hudson, who was born in Buenos Aires, books by authors born in South America did not become a significant part of the Knopfs' publishing plan until World War II, when Blanche traveled there in light of limited travel options in Europe.[56]

Alfred and Blanche made their first traveling tour as publishers in 1921. Using letters of introduction provided by Englishman Herman Bang, Heinemann's editor in charge of foreign and translation rights, they arranged for meetings in France, Germany, and Scandinavia.[57] The primary achievement of their time in France was the previously mentioned introduction to William Aspenwall Bradley, who led them to Gide's publishing house, Mercure de France. Unassisted by agents in Germany and Scandinavia, they nonetheless forged lasting relationships there with houses of great prestige.

One of the Knopfs' most significant meetings on the continent occurred at S. Fischer Verlag, the Berlin publisher of Thomas Mann, who would win the Nobel Prize in Literature in 1929. Knopf commissioned Kenneth Burke to produce a 1925 English translation of Mann's *Death in Venice and Other Stories*, a work that is notoriously difficult to translate. Five years later, Knopf released a different translation that he had commissioned from Helen Lowe-Porter in the UK. She was introduced to the Knopfs through Heinemann's firm.[58]

Knopf's first Mann title was *Royal Highness,* published in 1916 in sheets purchased from Sidgwick & Jackson. Alfred acquired the book because he wanted to broaden the European representation on his heavily Russian list—not because he predicted Mann's future in the canon of modern fiction. Through literary agents Brandt & Brandt, Knopf was able to negotiate additional reprint rights and issue a 1926 edition of *Royal Highness* that was manufactured in the United States and printed with the line "Copyright, 1909, S. Fischer, Verlag," clarifying that Knopf merely paid a reprint fee to Fischer and was not able to hold US copyright despite the fact that he had overseen the translation and manufacturing.[59] One of the ways he recouped part of his investment was to make an arrangement with Grosset & Dunlap for the latter to publish a cheaper edition using plates rented from Knopf.

Other Lowe-Porter translations of Mann issued by Knopf include *Buddenbrooks* in 1924, for which Blanche secured the rights for $500, and *The Magic Mountain* in 1927 (called *The Enchanted Mountain* in early correspondence, from the German *Der Zauberberg*).[60] Mann did not believe that a woman would be up to the job of translating the book, but he relented after meeting Lowe-Porter.[61] Partly because of shrewd advertising that made these esoteric works seem accessible, Knopf gradually succeeded with Mann's books, capitalizing on a bargain that would become a boon when Mann won the Nobel Prize.[62] Knopf observed that momentum for *The Magic Mountain* built slowly on both sides of the Atlantic, especially for the UK publisher Martin Secker, who apparently shared the cost of Lowe-Porter's translation fees with Knopf.[63]

In July 1928, Blanche received a letter from Mann expressing concern that Secker's version was being described in the German press as a cheap edition. Mann also asked Blanche to confirm that he was to receive an author's royalty on all English editions, which in turn confirms that the Knopfs had become the managers of Mann's English-language rights.[64] In later years, Alfred often touted his payment of royalties to Mann on these translations as evidence of his unusual generosity as a publisher.

On their initial tour of Europe, one of the Knopfs' most fruitful destinations proved to be Scandinavia. In Copenhagen, the Knopfs formed important ties with the house of Gyldendal, purchasing reprint rights for books by Knut Hamsun, who almost immediately became the Knopfs' first Nobel Prize–winning author. Hamsun was best known for his philosophical novel *Hunger,* originally published in the late nineteenth century, in which an unnamed protagonist traverses the city of Kristiania (now Oslo), unable to feed his physical and intellectual cravings. The novel reflected a stylistic departure for Borzoi Books, but Gyldendal's publisher managed to convince Knopf that it was an enduring masterpiece. Hamsun would later become a vocal Nazi sympathizer, despite the financial rewards he reaped after being published by Jews in America.

With candor, Knopf admitted that other American publishers weren't interested in the Gyldendal offerings. His acquisition of Hamsun's 1917 novel *Growth of the Soil*, which runs more than six hundred pages in length, was a particularly dodgy prospect. Published by Knopf in two volumes and priced at five dollars, the book nonetheless was described by Alfred as a gamble that paid off handsomely.[65] Steeped in themes of self-sufficiency, anti-modernity, and the quest for a peaceful existence, the book would become a staple of the Knopf backlist. In *My Reading Life*, the novelist Pat Conroy describes the day he received a copy of *Growth of the Soil* from bookseller Norman Berg, who told Conroy, "It's an essential book. A necessary one. . . . It's the most important book I've ever read. I named my farm Sallanraa in honor of Isak, the man who builds his home and raises a family out of nothing. . . . You don't just read this book, you must enter in. Live it. It contains the great truth. . . . Everything of virtue springs from the soil. Civilization always comes along to ruin it. But you can always find the truth if it comes from the earth."[66]

Despite the book's decidedly anti-commercial message, its author and publisher would enjoy considerable financial gain from it; *Growth of the Soil* was released in the months leading up to Hamsun's receipt of the Nobel Prize. For Knopf, the rewards of Hamsun's prize extended well beyond money. Though the Nobel Prize had existed for only twenty years when it was awarded to Hamsun in 1920, it conveyed an image of old-world aristocracy despite the reality of Alfred Nobel's life as an industrial magnate. In a similar vein, the prize gave Blanche and Alfred an opportunity to project an image that offset their mundane heritage; to this day, the king of Sweden personally bestows the medals.

Describing the cultural peculiarities of the Nobel Prize in Literature, James English notes that it was "founded in a thoroughly modern way, by a wealthy industrialist whose private foundation, bearing his name, would serve as the prize's perpetual sponsor, gradually laundering his economic fortune and symbolic reputation through a series of cleansing cultural transactions . . . yet [it is] deeply rooted in the bureaucratic traditions of early modern royal and national societies." The magnitude of the Nobel's cash award, the massive scale of international competition, and the grandeur of the award ceremony combine to bestow status not only on authors but also on their publishers around the world. For a fledgling house such as Knopf, this carried priceless benefits.[67] America's Pulitzer Prize, first awarded in 1917, had a similar impact on Knopf when *One of Ours,* Willa Cather's novel of the Great War, won it in 1923. Funded by a bequest from the Hungarian-American journalist Joseph Pulitzer, the prize can have an impact on American publishers even when no one emerges as the winner in a particular category. In 2012, when the Pulitzer Board announced that no prize would be awarded for fiction that year, many in the publishing industry reacted with anger, seeing the act as a snub of trends in contemporary American fiction. Sig Gissler, administrator of the prizes, explained that the decision was simply a result of the mandatory procedure; among the three novels nominated as finalists by a prize jury, none was able to achieve the required majority of votes from the board. The finalists included the Knopf novel *Swamplandia!,* about a family that runs a theme park in the Florida Everglades. Despite the literary community's uproar over the absence of a winner, Knopf Publicity Director Paul Bogaards told the *New York Times* that "since this year there was not a winner and there's much conversation about the finalists, this may be an opportunity and a catalyst for sales," underscoring the power and prestige of any media attention attracted by a major literary prize.[68]

Despite the impact of the Pulitzer, in Knopf's initial years most of the company's connections to prestigious prize winners were gained through European publishing houses. In initial negotiations, Gyldendal also persuaded Knopf to buy the rights to *Jenny,* a novel by Norwegian Sigrid Undset, another future Nobel Laureate (1928). Lengthy promotional copy, using the word "greatest" multiple times, announced the debut of Borzoi-Gyldendal books. The 1921 edition of *Grim: The Story of a Pike* by children's-book author Svend Fleuron, opens with a message in which Knopf aligns his identity with that of distinguished European publishing traditions:

> The firm of Gyldendal (Gyldendalske Boghandel Nordisk Forlag) is the oldest and greatest publishing house in Scandinavia, and has been responsible, since its inception in 1770, for giving the world some of the greatest Danish and Norwegian writers of three centuries. Among them are such names as Ibsen, Pontoppidan, Brandes, . . . Hans Christian Andersen and Knut Hamsun, the Nobel Prize winner for 1920, whose works I am publishing in America. It is therefore with particular satisfaction that I announce the completion of arrangements whereby I shall bring out in this country certain of the publications in this foremost house.[69]

The fact that Alfred and Blanche acquired numerous books by authors who later won the Nobel (which Alfred pronounced NO-buhl) is often attributed to the young publishers' good taste, but luck clearly played a role as well. When in 1933 Ivan Bunin became the first Russian author to win the prize, ten years after Knopf had issued three of his books, Blanche reportedly exclaimed,

"What in the world did *he* win it for?"[70] During the company's first fifteen years, the Knopfs published a total of nine authors who had won or would win a Nobel Prize. These authors comprise 26 percent of Knopf's complete roster of Nobel-winning authors. This includes T. S. Eliot, who won the prize in 1948 but was only briefly a Borzoi author. His relationship with the house of Knopf is described in chapter 4, "Producing American Literature," because his Borzoi Books appeared before he became a British subject. During the 1920s, in addition to Hamsun, Undset, Mann, Bunin, and Eliot, Knopf's Nobel stable included André Gide (who would win in 1947), Johannes Jensen (the 1944 winner), Carl Gustaf Verner von Heidenstam (who joined the Borzoi list in 1925, nine years after receiving his award), and Wladyslaw Stanislaw Reymont, who shared Knopf's eastern European ancestry. Reymont signed a contract with Knopf in December 1923 for the publication of *The Peasants*, a tetralogy spanning the four seasons. G. P. Putnam had canceled its agreement with Reymont over concerns about the length of the four-volume work. Reymont won the Nobel Prize a year after signing with Knopf.[71] Alfred Knopf was subsequently made a Cavalier of the Order of Polonia Restituta, receiving the Officers' Cross from the Polish Minister to the United States in a 1928 ceremony hosted by the Polish Legation in Washington, D.C.[72]

Many of the company's early publishing projects reflected an international image that was not tied to an author's nationality. A brainchild of Carl Van Vechten, Knopf's Blue Jade Library series housed a number of such titles. Selections ranged from Scotsman C. K. Moncrieff's translation of the letters of Abelard and Héloïse to English military veteran Haldane Macfall's *The Wooing of Jezebel Pettyfer*, a "comedy of negro manners" re-released in 1925 after its debut thirty years prior.[73] Set in the West Indies, the novel features long passages of Creole dialogue. Other examples of English authors who brought exoticism to the Blue Jade Library—usually through the lens of colonial imperialism— include (Mohammed) Marmaduke Pickthall, a London scholar and translator of the Koran who converted to Islam at midlife and traveled throughout the Middle East. Knopf published three of Pickthall's works during the 1920s: a children's book, *Saïd the Fisherman* (1925); a novel, *The Valley of the Kings* (1926); and a travelogue, *Oriental Encounters* (1929).

The Blue Jade Library was not Knopf's only vehicle for publishing "global" literature without having to travel beyond Europe to recruit authors. In addition to W. H. Hudson's *Green Mansions*, a prime example of this is the introduction of Bloomsbury resident Arthur Waley to the Borzoi list in 1921. Waley had been mentored by Ezra Pound, with whom he shared an interest in Orientalism, and he had served in the Oriental Prints and Manuscripts division of the British Museum. Waley's translations for the Borzoi list include three collections of Chinese poems and *The Nō Plays of Japan*, applauded in a *New York Times* review that praised Waley for preserving "so exquisitely the poetry, the delicate imagery, and the fastidious reticence" of these spare medieval dramas.[74]

Despite Blanche's enthusiasm for Paris, Alfred seems to have especially relished their time in Britain, amassing a list that featured works by Bloomsbury feminist Dorothy Richardson (one of the first women published by Knopf), Somerset Maugham, Gladys Bronwyn Stern, and all three Sitwell siblings (Osbert, Edith, and Sacheverell), reflecting a broad range of approaches to modern literature.[75] Eventually, Knopf became convinced that he was capable of being more than just a purveyor of British works. He aspired to become a British publisher himself, launching an overseas branch to acquire and sell books in the UK marketplace. The endeavor never measured up to his aspirations; it only proved that his popularity among London publishers was primarily due to his status as a good customer—an importer who paid them promptly.

The London Office

As he began envisioning a London branch, Alfred's initial impulse was to offer to buy Martin Secker's company.[76] Though his offer was turned down, leaving the Knopfs to strike out on their own, Secker's firm provided the inspiration for the Borzoi's London office.[77]

On trips abroad, Alfred was occasionally given a desk in Heinemann's office, as a courtesy. When he launched Alfred A. Knopf Ltd. in January 1926, he leased an office on Heinemann's street, at 38 Bedford Square. A year and a half later, Knopf optimistically signed an extended lease on the five-story building next door, at 37 Bedford Square.[78] Located in the fashionable Bloomsbury district, the square is composed of eighteenth-century townhouses surrounding an expansive, idyllic private garden. British publisher Jonathan Cape had chosen 30 Bedford Square for his headquarters in 1919.

The English novelist Storm Jameson, whose first job had been in advertising, was placed at the helm of Alfred A. Knopf Ltd. As early as 1923, she had corresponded with Blanche to negotiate imports, including several of her own books. A 1927 royalty statement lists a payment of $852.80 from the New York office to Jameson for her novel *The Lovely Ship*, after a $3,000 advance and editorial charges.[79] In 1926, on her first visit to the United States, she told *New York Times* essayist R. Le Clerc Phillips that she believed "modern American novels are not generally understood in England. . . . Personally, I think [Sinclair Lewis's] *Arrowsmith* [is] the best novel written since the war."[80] She was joined in the Knopf Ltd. endeavor by Guy Chapman, a history professor, editor, and war hero whom she married a month after the formation of the company, despite her being quoted in the *Times* interview as saying, "Marriage is a 100 per cent job. So is a career. Either the marriage or the career is bound to suffer when a woman tries to combine both." Her first book as a Knopf author had been *The Pitiful Wife*, published in 1923.

The Knopfs accepted Chapman grudgingly, but company letterhead listed Jameson and Chapman as co-managers of the firm.[81] The newlyweds were responsible for developing the company into a full-service publishing house, yet the task of acquiring British books not as imports but as commodities for sale to British audiences met with little success. Many opportunities for co-publication were lost due to poor communication with the New York office, lack of autonomy and authority among the London office's top personnel, and competitive situations in which Knopf Ltd. found itself ironically vying against other UK houses for the right to publish a variety of Knopf's American works.

For example, Alfred A. Knopf, Inc., became Willa Cather's American publisher of choice in 1920, but throughout the following decade the UK editions of her books were released by other houses, most commonly Heinemann. She was represented by Paul Revere Reynolds, considered by many to be the first person in America to formally launch a literary agency. His firm was established in 1893. Reynolds and Knopf shared such a high degree of mutual respect that Reynolds described Alfred Knopf as having the potential to become an American incarnation of William Heinemann, while Knopf claimed that Reynolds never brought him an unprofitable manuscript.[82] Nonetheless, neither this friendship nor Knopf's ability to sell Cather well in America seems to have mattered in securing the British rights to Cather's works, most likely because Knopf Ltd. failed to be the highest British bidder in negotiations with Reynolds.

The fact that Knopf Ltd. had yet to prove itself overseas surely created another conundrum in acquisitions. Writing to a London staff member, A. S. Lowy, in 1928, Alfred reported that he had recently signed up three novels by Isa Glenn, a native of Atlanta. Yet Glenn's agents (Brandt & Brandt in America, A. M. Heath in the UK) doubted that Knopf Ltd. could generate the highest possible UK income for the author. The agents were only willing to sell Knopf Ltd. the rights to the first novel, on a trial basis, before deciding where to place UK rights for the other two books. In addition, the agents sought an advance of fifty to a hundred pounds with a royalty that would increase from 10 to 20 percent if sales increased sufficiently over time.[83]

Compounding the challenge of establishing a reputation for excellence, London office staffers were frequently unsure about whether they had the authority to approve the acquisition of American rights for titles.[84] Their correspondence indicates that all aspects of the overseas operation received continual scrutiny and frequently sharp criticism, both in person and from overseas, from all three Knopfs—Samuel, Alfred, and Blanche—including decisions regarding sales calls, print runs, advertising schedules, and publicity campaigns. Even seemingly straightforward co-publication agreements, through which the London office purchased sheets from the New York office, required clarification. In 1928, fraught with illness, Blanche spent several months in Baden Baden, Germany, convalescing at Dr. Franz Dengler's renowned sanatorium. Despite her exhaustion, throughout her time there she continued co-managing all aspects of the London office.[85]

The confusion over levels of authority was captured in Knopf Ltd.'s letterhead, which was printed in two versions, one for each side of the Atlantic. Jameson and Chapman were listed as managers on one version of Knopf Ltd. letterhead, without any mention of Alfred and Blanche. The alternate version lists the Knopfs and an investor thus: "Alfred A. Knopf, Chairman, U.S.A.; Blanche W. Knopf, Managing Director, U.S.A.; Ira V. Morris, Resident Director, U.S.A.; Samuel Knopf, Director, U.S.A. (Polish Origin)."

Blanche and Alfred frequently deferred to Samuel on publishing matters, and the London office was no exception. Samuel's memoranda, some of which were composed aboard the S.S. *Mauretania* and the S.S. *Bremen* en route to England, indicate the extent to which his role as treasurer gave him control over editorial decisions, salaries, and other matters. He complains to Guy Chapman about the lack of regular updates on Knopf Ltd.'s financial status, claiming that Chapman ignores his requests for basic information such as the bank-account balance.[86] However, in keeping with his habit of lavish spending on creature comforts, Samuel launched a costly, extensive renovation of the Bedford Street building, claiming to give Chapman free rein while simultaneously micromanaging the process.[87] Part of the renovation expense was related to converting the building from residential to commercial use and bringing the structure into compliance with codes, such as the installation of a mandatory fire escape, but many of the modifications were purely ornamental in nature.[88]

The elder Knopf was certain that his son's company in London would flourish; he asked Chapman to make sure that the spacious new building would be furnished in such a way that staff would not feel cramped as the company experienced future growth. Despite that optimism, one of Samuel's last significant business duties before his death in June 1932 was to oversee the winding up of the London branch.[89]

Though the surviving London records do not include sales figures, the final inventory of Knopf Ltd. shows a balance between American and non-American authors spanning a diverse range of books. During the liquidation,

Heinemann bought the rights to several novels by Joseph Hergesheimer and Dashiell Hammett, as well as works by Sigrid Undset and Guy de Maupassant. George Allen & Unwin, Ltd. took practical nonfiction (*Improve Your Card Play, How to Bid at Contract Bridge, Restaurants of London*) as well as literary works, including Langston Hughes's first novel, *Not Without Laughter,* and James Weldon Johnson's *Black Manhattan,* in addition to selections by Knut Hamsun and Claude Bragdon. Reviews and advertisements for Knopf Ltd. in the *Times Literary Supplement* (*TLS*) provide additional evidence of the Borzoi's diversity, ranging from P. T. Barnum's two-volume autobiography to *Brimstone and Chili,* an account of the American journalist Carleton Beals's travels in the Southwest and Mexico. The firm's many translated works also included Marcel Proust's *Cities of the Plain* and André Gide's *Lafcadio's Adventures* (originally published as *The Vatican Cellars*).

British authors were in the minority on the Borzoi's London lists. Perhaps to rectify this, the Knopfs solicited un-agented manuscripts from the general public. The jacket copy for *A Book of Other Wines Than French* by Englishman Philip Morton Shand reads, "Alfred A. Knopf invite the submission of manuscripts, which will receive most careful consideration" beneath the publisher's address, along with an offer to be added to the Borzoi catalog mailing list. While this message conveys Knopf's quintessentially personal approach, which became a hallmark of his American marketing efforts, Knopf advertising in the *TLS* is devoid of such a voice.

In that vein of erudition, the Knopfs also attempted to create a viable textbook division abroad, albeit unsuccessfully. The dispensation records underscore Knopf's extensive efforts to support a British educational department, which released such titles as *England in the Middle Ages, Grammar of the English Sentence,* and *Some Implications of Social Psychology.* Knopf Ltd. even conducted a survey of English educators to determine their perceptions of the problems with "modern" educational books.[90] Scholars who received *TLS* review attention by contributing to Knopf Ltd.'s trade list included Maynard Shipley, founder of the Science League of America, which promoted scientific freedom in the face of controversies over evolution, and Yale historian Samuel Flagg Bemis, author of the multi-volume *American Secretaries of State and Their Diplomacies.*

Knopf Ltd.'s retail accounts were as diverse as the Borzoi Books they attempted to sell. A listing of the firm's receivables at the end of 1931 includes London-based Hamleys toy store, the venerable Goulden & Curry bookstore in Kent, and foreign accounts such as the Oxford Book and Stationery Company of Calcutta and New Delhi.[91] While America's economy was booming, many British retailers were struggling in a financial climate fraught by war debt, global competition for exports, and rising unemployment. In the end, the Borzoi's stint abroad amounted to a loss of $98,675. Ira Nelson Morris (father of the Ira V. Morris listed on the letterhead and one of Samuel Knopf's longtime friends) lost approximately 75 percent of his $25,000 investment. In 1923, Knopf had published his memoir of his tenure as America's minister to Sweden; perhaps this courtesy offset the disappointment he surely felt over the demise of Knopf Ltd.[92]

Alfred Knopf linked the business climate of Britain in the 1920s to anti-American sentiment because of demands that Britain repay its war debts immediately.[93] Though Alfred and his otherwise shrewd father had originally seen the British market as a viable opportunity for Borzoi Books, Alfred ultimately attributed the failure to resentment on the part of English publishers and their perception of the Knopfs as intruders.[94] Stephen Haden Guest, a staff member and translator, confirmed this theory when he sent Blanche a negative review for *The Road to Heaven: A Romance of Morals*, written by Iowa native Thomas Beer. The review had run in the *Daily Express*, which Guest claimed was anti-American because it reflected the views of its owner, the Canadian-born newspaper magnate Max Aitken, Lord Beaverbrook. Guest suggested smaller literary publications for the Knopfs' review list, including the *Fortnightly Review* and the *Cornhill Magazine*, which would not have garnered the wide readership necessary for a momentous publicity campaign.[95]

While the failure of Knopf Ltd. was surely related to a combination of cultural, economic, and management conflicts, an empirical analysis of Knopf's review coverage in the *Times Literary Supplement* refutes the notion that Borzoi Books were routinely snubbed. In my tabulations, only 21 percent of the Borzoi's *TLS* reviews were wholly negative, while 48 percent were wholly positive, 24 percent were mixed, and 7 percent were neutral summaries. From 1926 through 1929, the firm received multiple *TLS* reviews almost every month. On the other hand, the reviews that were negative often attributed the book's poor quality to an American sensibility. Isaac Goldberg's English version of Pío Baroja's "Struggle for Life" trilogy, set in the slums of Madrid, was deemed to be a "rather pedestrian translation with its American colouring."[96] Katherine Anthony's translation of a memoir by Catherine the Great was panned with the observation that "it is to be regretted that the present version is so lacking in literary quality: further, it is full of Americanisms which might be excused, or even defended, in a work published in the United States, but might have been modified for one published in London."[97] Nonetheless, Carl Van Vechten's novels received a favorable reception as entertaining trifles, while James Weldon Johnson was hailed for his "rare gift for storytelling."[98]

Knopf continually spent advertising dollars on the pages of the *TLS*, branding Borzoi Books but not "Mr. Knopf" in some twenty ads per year in 1927, 1928, and 1929. When the firm's *TLS* review coverage doubled in 1928, Borzoi advertising did not follow suit. The design of the ads looks striking on the mundane, un-illustrated pages because Knopf almost always used a frame pattern in which wolfhounds form a vine. However, the copy is usually limited to simple line listings and praise from regional papers, magazines, and literary reviews, ranging from the *Glasgow Herald* and the *Manchester Guardian* to the *Spectator* and the *Outlook*. One of the few provocative uses of a headline occurs in an advertisement for Carl Van Vechten's novel *Nigger Heaven,* in which Knopf invites readers to "COME TO HARLEM AND SEE LIFE IN THE RAW."⁹⁹ A similar ad for the novel ran almost simultaneously in the *New Yorker.* The book appears to have been a success for Knopf Ltd., as subsequent ads tout additional printings. A few of the firm's *TLS* ads are artifacts of cultural gaffes, including Knopf Ltd.'s first attempt at a holiday promotion in England. The headline "Alfred A. Knopf Christmas Gifts" appears above the title *The House of Satan,* a collection of George Jean Nathan's acerbic observations about the east coast theater scene. Other gift suggestions featured in the ad include *The Natural History of Ants,* published from a French archival manuscript, and *Crime and the Criminal* by sociologist Philip Parsons.¹⁰⁰

Despite the blunders, financial success and literary prestige were inextricably linked motives in Blanche, Alfred, and Samuel's early overseas efforts. In *A Grammar of Motives,* Kenneth Burke acknowledges that although financial exchanges seem impersonal, "money itself in its role as a medium or agency contains the humanistic or the personalistic ingredients that we have discerned at the very source of agency."¹⁰¹ Aesthetes and modernists opposed commercialism, but for the young Knopfs, financial exchanges often determined which "humanistic" circles of authors their firm would be able to attract and retain. What Burke might define as the "Borzoi constitution" was a private effort to succeed in the marketplace and maintain a healthy balance sheet while publicly appearing to scoff at those who viewed literature as anything other than a means to intellectual growth.¹⁰² In America, these acts were generally successful for the Knopfs. From their midtown Manhattan office, they prospered by performing the role of global sophisticates. Yet the identity of the Knopfs as quasi-Europeans failed—financially and otherwise—when performed on the authentically European stage of Bedford Square.

 CHAPTER FOUR

Producing American Literature

When a native author of any genuine force and originality appears in the United States he is almost invariably found to be under strong foreign influence, either English or Continental.

H. L. MENCKEN, "Foreign Poisons"

PREDICTABLY, TWO OF KNOPF's earliest top-selling American authors—Philadelphia native Joseph Hergesheimer and H. L. Mencken of Baltimore—were referred to him by Englishmen. Knopf first met with Mencken at the urging of Joseph Conrad, whom Mencken frequently praised in his book reviews for the *Baltimore Sun*. As discussed in chapter 2, Knopf met Hergesheimer through Mitchell Kennerley, who had published his debut novel, *The Lay Anthony: A Romance*, in 1914. Over the years, Hergesheimer and Knopf, and their wives, seamlessly merged a business relationship with an enduring friendship, and Mencken was a member of this set as well, giving Hergesheimer editorial suggestions while participating in the group's frequent revelry.

Two other key figures in the development of the Borzoi's American list, Carl Van Vechten and Willa Cather, also became members of the Knopfs' circle of personal friends, attracted by the reputation of Borzoi Books. In significant ways, these four writers contributed to the transition of the Knopfs' identity as they evolved from being thought of as a European reprint house. In their new roles as impresarios of American publishing, the Knopfs capitalized on previously unpublished titles written by rising stars whose work gained notice without making waves.

Charter Members

Knopf was eager to publish Joseph Hergesheimer, initiating their partnership with *The Three Black Pennys*, though writer's block kept the book from being released until 1917.[1] Under Knopf's imprimatur, Hergesheimer would publish more than a dozen additional books, many with international settings that included Cuba and Mexico. Though Alfred was the one who lured Hergesheimer from Mitchell Kennerley, the author's career was eventually shepherded by Blanche. Her copious correspondence with him describes contract negotiations, requests for autographed blank sheets to be tipped into special copies of his books for retailers, and other details of the publishing process. Hergesheimer's affectionate replies include a 1927 description of his unnamed, forthcoming "modern novel" as "a Blanche and Alfred and Dorothy and Joe book," most likely referring to *The Party Dress*, published in 1930.[2] The work he published in the interim, *Swords and Roses*, is a collection of historical vignettes that pay homage to the antebellum South. The book bears a cryptic dedication to Blanche: "Here is a book of swords, now wholly discarded, and of old-fashioned dark roses—vanished objects and flowers we both regard with an especial deeply personal regret. Well, they have existed for us only in imagination; unhappily we have been delivered to very different and far less engaging realities; and so we must write books, we must publish books and read them, in order to return, and only for a little while, to the simpler loveliness of the past. To Blanche W. Knopf."

A painter trained at the Pennsylvania Academy of Fine Arts, Hergesheimer approached fiction as an opportunity to demonstrate aesthetic sensitivity while capturing internal worlds of emotion. His autobiography, *The Presbyterian*

New York Times advertisement touting American authors, 1920

Distinguished Borzoi Books by Americans

SAN CRISTOBAL DE LA HABANA
By Joseph Hergesheimer

THE record of a happy impression of a city elusively lovely, an affair of marble whiteness under the formal greenery of royal palms on a sea reaching fantastically blue from its promenade wall and parks.

❧ Printed on Warren's India Tint Olde style paper, bound in Chinese orange-and-gold boards with gold label and black silk back stamped in gold.
$3.50 net

MOON-CALF
FLOYD DELL'S fine novel has sprung into a sudden and deserved popularity.

(1) "Drop whatever you are doing and read MOON-CALF...We'll say it's some novel."—Heywood Broun in the *New York Tribune*.

(2) "A great book, and an author full fledged, assured by this one book of a permanent place in the literature of America."—Harry Hansen in the *Chicago Daily News*.

(3) "Definitely puts Mr. Dell well to the fore among our few serious novelists."—Llewellyn Jones in the *Chicago Evening Post*. $2.50 net

YOUTH AND THE BRIGHT MEDUSA
By Willa Cather

"A VERITABLE Koh-i-noor among the rhinestone and paste tiara of contemporary literature . . . so dazzling that delight in its gleam swept the reviewer away. Decidedly a literary event which no lover of the best fiction will want to miss."—*New York Times*.

"One of the truest as well as one of the most poetical interpretations of American life that we possess."
—*The Nation*.

❧ A great American writer at the top of her art. $2.50 net

"*THE BORZOI 1920*" contains original, interesting contributions by *Willa Cather, Joseph Hergesheimer, H. L. Mencken, H. M. Tomlinson and many others, together with a Who's Who of Borzoi authors and much useful information to book lovers—profusely illustrated. A unique publication:* $1.00

ALFRED A. KNOPF, Publisher, 220 W. 42d Street, NEW YORK

Child, recalls his austere grandparents and a childhood marked by illness and introversion. Mencken's identity in this literary circle contrasted sharply with Hergesheimer's. While Hergesheimer painstakingly emphasized the art of fiction as a means to a quiet exploration of society and history, Mencken was a no-holds-barred satirist whose sometimes scathing sense of humor was unleashed on essentially everyone. Contemporary critics have particular difficulty reconciling his deep friendship with Alfred Knopf with allegations of his anti-Semitism. Ranging from Mencken's use of the word "kike" multiple times in his diary, which was made public for the first time as a Borzoi Book in 1989, to his statement in *Treatise on the Gods* that "the Jews could be put down very plausibly as the most unpleasant race ever heard of," the evidence presents a paradox because so much of his work comprised self-described satirical "buffooneries." The quoted comment about Jews is followed by additional invective, curiously leading up to overblown praise: "As commonly encountered, they lack many of the qualities that mark the civilized man: courage, dignity, incorruptibility, ease, confidence. They have vanity without pride, voluptuousness without taste, and learning without wisdom. Their fortitude, such as it is, is wasted upon puerile objects, and their charity is mainly only a form of display. Yet these same Jews, from time immemorial, have been the chief dreamers of the human race, and beyond all comparison its greatest poets."[3]

In his *Baltimore Sun* column, called "The Free Lance" (also the name of a Knopf series edited by Mencken), he used well-honed, deadpan humor to assail a variety of cultural conventions, including all forms of Protestant Christianity and piety in general. "[Mencken's] most important bolts of lightning were reserved for the Baltimore scene, its prominent citizens, its crooked reformers, its 'honorary pallbearers,' as he called them," writes newspaper historian George Douglas. "He also attacked bureaucracy, Christian Science, chiropractic science, blue laws, the Anti-Saloon league, and the Rotary. The 'good' people were against prostitution, so he was for it; they were against woman's suffrage, so he was for it . . . [supporting] quixotic ideas that were disarming to the reader."[4]

Mencken had to perform an about-face on several occasions when his humor was misinterpreted by the "booboisie" (his term for the dimwitted masses), such as the time he refused to allow a Chicago correspondent to reprint extracts from *Treatise on the Gods* because he feared that they would be inappropriately used in propaganda against Jews. Knopf approached the topic of Mencken's attitude toward Jews with nonchalance, believing that Mencken's anti-Semitic words were meant to spoof anti-Semites themselves and expressing exasperation with anyone who, in Knopf's opinion, was too small-minded to get the joke.[5]

Attacking Zionists and Klansmen with equally sharp invective, Mencken shared Knopf's dislike of any form of extremism. Mencken's *Prejudices,* a series of six books featuring expanded versions of his newspaper and magazine articles, expresses prejudice on a seemingly limitless number of topics, including his disdain for prejudiced people. The Scopes Trial provided particularly rich fodder for him, as did political conventions. Mencken arranged for Knopf to travel with him to the 1928 Republican Convention, securing a photojournalist's badge for the perpetually camera-toting Knopf, who relished this time on the road with someone he considered to be one of his closest friends.[6]

Mencken was also an accomplished translator, applying his knowledge of his ancestral German to Nietzsche's *Antichrist* published by Knopf as part of the Free-Lance series. With the Jewish drama critic George Jean Nathan, Mencken also served as co-editor of the highbrow *Smart Set* from 1914 to 1923, and the two founded *The American Mercury,* a mainstream literary enterprise, in 1924. Though Mencken and Nathan's friendship ended after bitter arguments over the editorial direction of *The American Mercury* (Mencken feared it was on the verge of becoming trivial and formulaic), Nathan's books were also a staple of the Borzoi's American lists during the 1920s. Samuel Knopf, with Blanche and Alfred, made several unsuccessful attempts to negotiate reconciliation between the two men.[7]

Mencken's magazines brought him in contact with Kenneth Burke's circle, ultimately leaving the two men at odds with each other for the remainder of their careers. *The American Mercury*'s inaugural issue carried a spoof written by the critic Ernest Boyd, who delivered a scathing lampoon of Burke's circle of "Greenwich Village aesthetes."[8] The essay, titled "Aesthete: Model 1924," describes a pseudo-intellectual, hypocritical, naïve *poseur* who "has evolved an ingenious style, florid, pedantic, technical, full of phrases so incomprehensible or rhetorical that they almost persuade the reader that they must have a meaning. . . . He will sweep aside the finest writers in French as lumber, launch into ecstasies over some Dadaist, and head the article with a French phrase which is grammatically incorrect, and entirely superfluous."[9]

The essay contains many references to dilettante editors of little magazines, details that easily matched aspects of Burke's life. Migrating to New York from Pennsylvania in 1915, Burke had immersed himself in cottage publishing industries whose mercurial nature mirrored the unpredictability of the lower-Manhattan bohemians who contributed to them. Burke's early works of literary criticism reflect his admiration for modernists, including his friends Man Ray and E. E. Cummings, whose experimentalism was mocked by Boyd and Mencken. In retaliation for the *American Mercury* spoof, a group of Dadaists hurled stink bombs at Boyd as he tried to leave his apartment, keeping him stranded in his home for three days. Lobbing an additional volley, Burke wrote a mock advertisement for the new magazine *Aesthete* in which he called on readers to join the "Mencken Promotion Society" and "Menckenize" their lives. The ad asks such questions as "Can't you understand modern art? Let Mencken show you the absurdity of the Ku Klux Klan. Can't you follow modern philosophy? Let Mencken snigger with you at Williams Jennings Bryan. Did you flunk Trig? Let Mencken ridicule professors for you." As with many of his philosophies, Burke held contradictory attitudes toward higher education. This is reflected in his decision to forgo a college degree, though he took classes at Ohio State and Columbia and later served on the faculty of several colleges.[10]

Verbal skirmishes such as the ones that erupted between Mencken and Burke demonstrate a climate in which the printed page itself created distance, despite the fact that the various factions often shared similar literary sensibilities. Regarding the *American Mercury* incident, Malcolm Cowley quipped that Boyd was simply behaving "like a cigarette manufacturer spreading the rumor that another cigarette manufacturer mixed alfalfa with his product."[11] In the realm of satire, the goal was to demonstrate not only intellectual superiority but also a superior ability to entertain. Regardless of the genre, these authors engaged in acts that reflected an attitude of elitism in a quest to court readership. While the authors and their readers might have viewed themselves as the power brokers in these interactions, the publisher in fact controlled the textual "scene," whether it be a little magazine, a *Times* review, or a book.

For Knopf, controlling this scene meant providing the financial backing for *The American Mercury* and serving as its publisher until 1935. It was Knopf's only foray into periodical publishing, unlike mammoth American houses such as Harper's, Scribner's, and Doubleday, all of which maintained healthy magazine divisions. *The American Mercury* was heavily promoted on the dust jackets of Borzoi books, and a promotional Borzoi Broadside in turn appeared in the *Mercury*. Fine printer Elmer Adler was entrusted with the layout. Mencken described the design as "'whorish,' which indicated his approval," and praised the magazine's direct-mail announcements for their "fancy whorehouse typography," which was of course an elegant, traditional approach that identified the publication as anti-experimental (and therefore anti-Dadaist).[12] It's worth noting that Knopf was not the only book publisher who touted the aesthetic appeal of his firm's magazine. A *New York Times* advertisement that ran on New Year's Day in 1928 announces that the new Scribner's magazine features "new cover—new type—best fiction. . . . A new cover, with a series of decorative motives [*sic*] by Rockwell Kent; a new type face, Granjon Old Face; a new method of illustration; special eggshell paper, making the printed page easy to read."

In addition to being a Borzoi author, Mencken served as a scout and manu-script reader for the Knopfs, urging them to buy Thomas Mann's *Buddenbrooks* and recruiting many authors who bolstered Americana in the Borzoi identity, including the short-story writer Ruth Suckow (an Iowa native whose work he published in *Smart Set*), the acerbic Midwestern editor E. W. Howe, and a literary editor from Virginia named Emily Clark, whose *Stuffed Peacocks* (sketches of her native Virginia) Knopf published in 1923. With Carl Van Vechten, Mencken also led the Knopfs to publish James Weldon Johnson.[13]

Mencken is sometimes credited with introducing the Knopfs to Willa Cather, whose fame as a fiction writer was widespread when they published her story collection *Youth and the Bright Medusa* in 1920. However, Alvin Josephy recalls that Mencken "did not particularly like Cather, whom he called derisively, 'a one hundred percent American.'"[14] Cather became a Knopf author through her own volition, but an advertorial appearing in the *New York Times Book Review* may have led to the erroneous claims that Mencken had served as her liaison. With a reference to Sinclair Lewis (nicknamed Red), who had become one of Cather's most ardent advocates but was never a Knopf author, the ad contains an excerpt from a poem attributed to "The Periscope" column written by *Chicago Daily News* critic Keith Preston:

> *Blithe Mencken he sat on his Baltimore stoop,*
> *Singing, "Willa, git Willa! git Willa!*
> *The red-headed Lewis joined in with a whoop,*
> *Singing, "Willa, git Willa! git Willa!"*
> *They woke every bird from the Bronx to the loop*
> *Singing, "Willa, git Willa! git Willa!"*
> *So we, willy nilly, got Willa and read*
> *And Willa proved all that the booster birds said.*[15]

Because of the company's lean budget, Blanche was staffing the switchboard at lunchtime when Willa Cather first approached the firm for consideration, calling to ask for an appointment with "Mr. Knopf." Blanche handled the call with nervous excitement and scheduled the meeting for that afternoon.[16] The first contract between Cather and Knopf was signed in 1920, for the short-story collection *Youth and the Bright Medusa* rather than a novel, perhaps because Cather wanted to work with the Knopfs on a trial basis.[17] The collection featured several of the canonical stories—"Paul's Case," "The Sculptor's Funeral," and "A Wagner Matinée"—that are today anthologized in textbooks, a form of reprint she abhorred.

Editors in subsequent generations, such as Jason Epstein of Random House and Doubleday, mourn the lost days of author loyalty, when a publisher would provide for an author's personal needs and authors in turn would not shop for better terms.[18] Cather is clearly an exception to that ideal, boldly complaining to Ferris Greenslet, her editor at Houghton Mifflin, and ultimately deciding to leave the publisher who had helped to launch her career. In 1919, Cather voiced exasperation to Greenslet about all aspects of her publishing experience with him, ranging from excessive charges for proof corrections to his failure to market her backlist. She directly compared Houghton's promotion of her books to Knopf's superior promotion of Hergesheimer, and without mentioning names she claimed that three other publishers had offered her more money, promising to increase her royalties and pay advances of between $1,000 and $1,500.[19]

After signing with Knopf, she was impressed by the sales figures the firm was able to achieve for her books, and she developed sincere friendships with Alfred, Blanche, and Samuel, who shipped an Oliver typewriter to her when she was in Europe.[20] Her correspondence with them is rife with letters of deep appreciation for the dozens of other carefully selected gifts they sent to her over the years, ranging from Italian cruets to a tortoise-shell fan, a dressing gown, and a "Chinese" blouse.[21] Perhaps their greatest gift to her was that they patiently incorporated her continual ideas regarding all aspects of publishing, from typography to the choice of quotes used in advertising.[22] Her involvement increased after her second Knopf book, a novel of the Great War titled *One of Ours,* was awarded the Pulitzer Prize in 1923, placing her among the most lucrative authors on the Borzoi roster. She had wanted to call the novel *Claude,* after its protagonist. Although Alfred tried to persuade her to change it, he did not force the issue and was surely relieved when *Chicago Tribune* book critic Fanny Butcher convinced her that *One of Ours* would be a better choice.[23]

Though Cather claimed to scorn commercialism, declining high-dollar offers for film rights and insisting on keeping her works out of the hands of publishers who produced cheap editions for mass audiences, she monitored her sales figures carefully and endured the exposure of mass-market publicity, including a 3 August 1931 profile in *Time* featuring her on the cover.

She is widely associated with novels inspired by her upbringing on the Great Plains of Nebraska, but her "prairie trilogy" (*O Pioneers!, The Song of the Lark,* and *My Ántonia*) was published before her move to Knopf. Among Cather's Borzoi Books are those that celebrate settings other than the Midwest, including *Death Comes for the Archbishop* and *The Professor's House* (both set in Cather's beloved New Mexico), *My Mortal Enemy* (New York and San Francisco), and *Shadows on the Rock* (seventeenth-century French Canada). Like the Knopfs, she felt at home in New York City and Europe, while her prestige captured the attention of mainstream American readers in a singular way.

The Borzoi in Harlem

An equally significant member of the Borzoi's exiled Midwestern authors was the music critic, *New York Times* correspondent, and novelist Carl Van Vechten, an Iowa native who found most of Cather's works to be intolerably limited and lacking in glamour.[24] Knopf's affiliation with Van Vechten was rooted in their shared enthusiasm for classical music. Knopf read Van Vechten's first book, *Music after the Great War*, soon after it was published in 1915 and summoned the thirty-five-year-old author to his one-room office on 42nd Street. In 1916, Van Vechten's *Music and Bad Manners* was released as a Borzoi Book, followed by several other works of music criticism, seven novels, and two books about cats (*The Tiger in the House* and *Lords of the Housetops*).

Yet Van Vechten's bestselling 1926 novel, *Nigger Heaven,* reflects perhaps his most noteworthy contribution to Borzoi Books because it captures his immersion in the Harlem Renaissance. Deriving its title from a slang term for the upper balcony of segregated theaters, the roman à clef features easily identifiable members of the black intelligentsia who populated Harlem's jazz clubs and speakeasies. Van Vechten was heavily involved in the packaging of his books, with a preference for calico cloth bindings. During the production process for *Nigger Heaven,* he told the Knopfs that he had found fabric he particularly liked for use on "tall paper" editions of the novel (perhaps referring to a special format used for promotional purposes). He recommended that Blanche and Alfred act quickly before someone else bought the bolt, which he informed them could be found for 25 cents a yard on the third floor of McCutcheon's, a fashionable purveyor of linens and other housewares.[25]

Controversial within the circles it depicts, the novel was defended by James Weldon Johnson, who (through Van Vechten, after Mencken's earlier recommendation) soon permitted his *Autobiography of an Ex-Coloured Man* to be revived by Knopf. Issued in 1927, Knopf's edition applied a British spelling to the word "coloured," perhaps with an eye toward the European import market; the London office had recently opened its doors, and this was indeed one of the early works Knopf Ltd. promoted. Confirming Van Vechten's role as the Knopfs' impresario to Harlem, *The Autobiography of an Ex-Coloured Man* had been published anonymously in 1912 by the small Boston house Sherman, French & Company, which failed to achieve strong sales for the novel. At Van Vechten's urging, Knopf released it as part of the new Blue Jade Library line, a reprint series launched in 1925 and described in marketing copy as resurrecting "those semi-classic, semi-curious books which for one reason or another have enjoyed great celebrity but little distribution."[26] The series was Van Vechten's invention and spanned a gamut of authors from well beyond Harlem.[27]

In 1926, the same year as the release of *Nigger Heaven,* Langston Hughes's first book, *The Weary Blues,* was published by Knopf with a striking cover illustration of a blues musician created by Miguel Covarrubias. Like Hughes, Covarrubias had gained the favor of *Vanity Fair* editors. The Knopfs' acquisition of *The Weary Blues* was the result of a chance meeting between the young poet and Carl Van Vechten in Harlem at a benefit party for the NAACP. Their second encounter occurred at a poetry contest and dinner sponsored by *Opportunity* magazine, published by the National Urban League. Hughes took first place, and Van Vechten formally introduced himself. The widely circulated story that Hughes was "discovered" by the poet Vachel Lindsay after bus boy Hughes laid three of his poems on Lindsay's table at Washington D.C.'s Wardman Park Hotel is true, but Lindsay was not responsible for leading Hughes to his first experience with book publishing. Lindsay did respond enthusiastically to the poems, leaving a trove of poetry volumes as a gift for Hughes and inscribing one volume with a multi-page letter of encouragement. This generated considerable publicity for Hughes, who had to cope with embarrassment when "the head waiter would call me to come and stand before some table whose curious guests wished to see what a Negro bus boy poet looked like."[28] Yet it was Van Vechten who led to Hughes's affiliation with the editors of *Vanity Fair,* and with the Knopfs.

In his master's thesis, the cultural historian Randolph Lewis characterized the Knopfs' decision to publish Langston Hughes as "more than a response to a fad. . . . After making room for themselves as Jews in the Anglo-Saxon publishing world, the Knopfs provided a niche for other alternative voices."[29] However, as with all Borzoi decisions, potential profit was surely also a factor in the Knopfs' motivations in backing Hughes, and the early Borzoi list contains few "alternative voices." Early correspondence between the poet and the Knopfs underscores the publishers' hesitance to explore segments of book publishing they knew little about.

Marketing *The Weary Blues* (or any Knopf title) to the white intelligentsia was second nature to the Knopfs, but correspondence between Hughes and Blanche captures her education regarding the promotion of books to a subculture with which she had scant familiarity. In 1926, Hughes recommended black media outlets for advertising, citing the circulation of *The Chicago Defender* (201,572) and reminding her that, like *The Saturday Evening Post,* it had a national distribution. Indeed, the *Defender* was the nation's bestselling newspaper edited by and for African Americans.[30] Blanche told him, as she told many authors, that the advertising budget was limited, and she assured him that the company was running sufficient advertising in mainstream newspapers.

In Washington, D.C., he took it upon himself to call on three small retailers, reporting to Blanche the quantities that would be purchased on a consignment basis by Timgad, Maxwell's, and Gertrude's Gift Shop. Anticipating that the Wardman Park Hotel might be a good venue for capitalizing on its "Negro bus boy poet," Hughes personally investigated the procedure for stocking books there, reporting to Blanche that the manager would allow Hughes to sell his own copies at the stall. In exchange, Blanche granted him the newsstand discount, which was higher than the author's two-fifths discount he was typically granted.[31] Hughes seems to have made tireless efforts to build grassroots sales while the Knopfs set their sights on a far broader plan that included the sale of foreign rights, leading a staffer to tell Hughes that he was vying with Kahlil Gibran for the distinction of becoming Knopf's most translated author.[32]

A year after the release of *The Weary Blues,* Knopf published Hughes's second collection, *Fine Clothes to the Jew.* Lewis asserts that the Knopfs "flinched" at the title.[33] In his memoir, Hughes concedes "it was a bad title, because it was confusing and many Jewish people did not like it," but he claims that his publishers remained silent on the subject: "I do not know why the Knopfs let me use it, since they were very helpful in their advice about sorting out the bad poems from the good, but they said nothing about the title." The collection invokes African American folksong forms and takes its title from Harlem slang that equated pawn brokers with Jews. The poems are populated by impoverished black New Yorkers, "people up today and down tomorrow, working this week and fired the next, beaten and baffled, but determined not to be wholly beaten, buying furniture on the installment plan, filling the house with roomers to help pay the rent, hoping to get a new suit for Easter—and pawning that suit before the Fourth of July."[34] Hughes's explanation only amplifies the bigotry of the title, perpetuating a stereotype of Jews as being so greedy that they are willing to exploit the clothes off the back of a desperate co-minority. Ironically, the phrase also reflects cultural transitions in the neighborhood where Alfred Knopf had spent his boyhood.

The poems themselves were panned by Hughes's peers, many of whom disapproved of his use of black vernacular. "Langston Hughes's Book of Poems Trash," proclaimed a headline in the *Pittsburgh Courier,* an influential black newspaper. "Langston Hughes—the Sewer Dweller," announced Harlem's *New York Amsterdam News.*[35] His next book, *The Negro Mother and Other Dramatic Recitations,* would not be published until 1931.

Van Vechten received full credit from Alfred for the Borzoi's affiliation with the Harlem Renaissance, but Alfred hyperbolically speculated that *Nigger Heaven* was the most successful book to arise in response to this literary movement. The Knopfs' immersion in the Harlem Renaissance was nonetheless a rewarding one for them, professionally and personally. In addition to

James Weldon Johnson and Hughes, they published Nella Larsen, Rudolph Fisher, and Walter White, all of whom were frequent visitors at Van Vechten's apartment on West Fifty-Fifth Street. The Knopfs' apartment was the scene of musical performances by Johnson's brother Rosamond (accompanied by Taylor Gordon), and Paul Robeson and his wife also visited the Knopfs at home.[36] The legacy would eventually lead to Knopf's acquisition of James Baldwin's *Go Tell It on the Mountain* in 1953, but significant luminaries in the movement and its aftermath were initially published elsewhere, including Zora Neale Hurston (J. B. Lippincott and Company), Countee Cullen and Richard Wright (Harper & Brothers), and Ralph Ellison (Random House).

Access to the Knopfs' prestigious brand, with its beautiful packaging and eloquent sales copy, helped to confirm the quality of the small circle of Harlem Renaissance authors invited to join the Borzoi. Though the Knopfs had little familiarity with marketing to subcultures, the Harlem Renaissance works blended seamlessly with the informed, educated, and often artistic fabric of the Borzoi's audience, contributing to a rhetorical performance that courted readers who saw themselves as enlightened and progressive.

Expanding the American Circles of Influence

The late 1920s also marked the Knopfs' acquisition of a book that would forge their relationship with a quintessential modern American storyteller, Dashiell Hammett, whose *Red Harvest* was released in 1929. The manuscript had been submitted without an agent, under the title *Poisonville*. *The Dain Curse* was published soon after, in the same year, featuring another installment of the anonymous detective called the Continental Op. A former Pinkerton's National Detective Agency operative, the San Franciscan Hammett represents a shift in the Borzoi's focus from the east coast to the west coast, and from the seemingly quaint mysteries of Englishman J. S. Fletcher to the grittier realism of hard-boiled American works. In addition, Hammett's success is proof of Blanche's maturity as a publisher who matched and perhaps surpassed her husband's acumen. Nonetheless, the salutation in Hammett's first letter to Alfred A. Knopf, Inc., is of course "gentlemen."[37] In return, Blanche's correspondence with Hammett was signed not "Blanche W. Knopf" but, as was customary, "Mrs. Alfred A. Knopf."

At the time of his debut as a novelist, Hammett was not new to elite literary circles. His work had appeared in Mencken and Nathan's *Smart Set*, a fact that he mentioned in his initial query letter. He also insisted on experimentation and novelty, with a particular interest in using soliloquy to enhance the voice of his fiction. Preparing to write *The Maltese Falcon*, which marked the debut of Sam Spade, he told Blanche that he very much wanted to apply stream-of-consciousness techniques, hoping to merge literary realms with detective writing and asserting that Ford Madox Ford's *The Good Soldier* could have made a fine detective novel. In the same letter, Hammett readily agrees to eliminate much of the violence from *Red Harvest*, as Blanche had requested.[38] Blanche was abroad when it was time to edit *The Maltese Falcon*. She turned the task over to editor Harry Block, who asked Hammett to eliminate homoerotic scenes, which Hammett politely refused to do on the grounds that they added novelty to the detective genre.[39]

Less than two months after Hammett's initial query, the manuscript for *Red Harvest* had been revised, and Blanche had sent a contract to him with a letter that reveals the Knopfs' attempts to be perceived as treating authors fairly. The boilerplate contract, Blanche told Hammett, was written by the attorney for the Authors' League.[40] As is true with most early Knopf authors, Hammett initially received no advance but began asking for one soon into his relationship with the firm, in contrast to H. L. Mencken, who gained favor with Knopf by notoriously never asking for an advance.[41] By the end of 1929, Block had extended a new three-book contract to Hammett, offering an advance of $1,000. In the same letter in which he refused to eliminate the homoeroticism from *The Maltese Falcon*, Hammett objected to Block's offer, asking instead for $2,500. Success had given him increased financial and editorial leverage; the same was true for his publishers as their company approached a new decade.

Hammett's influence on the American detective-novel genre exemplifies the Borzoi literary aura: compelling storylines that avoided the formulaic predictability of dime novels, accessible but unique characters who defied stereotypes, artfully drawn realism whose occasional grit was not gratuitous. Hammett's heir in the hard-boiled literary genre, California resident Raymond Chandler, easily perpetuated the legacy, joining Knopf's roster in the 1930s with novels that included *The Big Sleep*. Perhaps the most significant departure from Knopf's Fletcher series, however, was the fact that Blanche was the one who truly discovered Hammett and his approach to storytelling. She launched the spectacular career of an unknown novelist who, unlike Fletcher, had no reassuring British track record to ease the decision to publish. After publishing *The Thin Man* with Knopf, Hammett demanded ever-greater advances to no avail. Despite warnings from Alfred to Bennett Cerf, who had learned that Alfred and Hammett had finally cut all ties with each other, Random House wooed Hammett with an advance of $5,000 on a novel that he ultimately never wrote. *The Thin Man* proved to be his last.[42]

In today's publishing climate, such transactions would be overseen by an agent who would capitalize on a disgruntled Hammett or Cather. During the early days of Knopf, the agent's role was a work in progress; Cather was often represented by Paul Reynolds, but apparently a majority of his efforts involved placing her short stories in magazines and overseeing foreign sales rather than attempting to gain bigger advances or higher royalties. For the Hammetts and Cathers of the era, paying an agent a cut of the proceeds from such significant transactions surely seemed like an unnecessary expense. Today, agents usually secure a perpetual commission for themselves on each copy sold, making agents and publishers equally vested in developing strong backlists. In his chapter on agents featured in the 1929 primer *The Building of a Book,* Carl Brandt emphasizes the tasks of managing author royalties, subsidiary rights, and diplomacy, but he barely mentions the possibility of bargaining for ever-higher advances.[43]

Kahlil Gibran, whose books represent the most enduring source of profitability at Knopf, was published without an agent. He is associated with Middle Eastern mysticism, though he spent nearly all his life in the United States and was raised as a Maronite Christian. Born in 1883 in the town of Bshaari, in the segment of the Ottoman Empire now known as Lebanon, Gibran emigrated with his family as a child and was raised in poverty in Boston's South End. An artist and poet, he arrived in New York in 1911 at the age of 28. Written in Arabic, his initial books of stories and aphorisms gave him a following within Arab American communities. Knopf met him in 1918 through a network of authors who reflected the young publisher's circle at the time. Knopf recalled that a group of friends invited him to lunch in Greenwich Village in order to introduce him to Gibran. The diverse guest list included Witter Bynner, a gay playwright and translator of Chinese poetry whom Knopf had met while working for Mitchell Kennerley; James Oppenheim, a Jungian poet and novelist, and the founding editor of *The Seven Arts;* and Pierre de Lanux, future director of the Paris office of the League of Nations.[44]

Gibran's first book with Knopf was *The Madman: His Parables and Poems* (1918) followed by *The Forerunner: His Parables and Poems* (1920). Combining the form of a novella with the tone of mystic wisdom, *The Prophet* was released in 1923 sans subtitle and received lukewarm reviews, nonetheless becoming a bible of modernist countercultures and their redux in the 1960s. The absence of a subtitle appears to have been the author's choice; manuscript pages published by a collector in 1991 show no traces of any title other than simply THE PROPHET.[45] Although Gibran died in 1931, less than a decade after *The Prophet*'s publication, the book possessed enduring appeal and has sold more than nine million copies in the United States alone.[46] Under the terms of Gibran's will, all royalties are paid to his hometown of Bshaari.

Another way in which the New York office broadened its list was through

American literary agents living abroad. As discussed in the previous chapter, William Aspenwall Bradley was one of the most influential expat agents in Paris, where he and his wife, Jenny, dedicated their lives to building a prestigious agency that for many years served as a vortex of modernism.[47] The American authors they represented included Ernest Hemingway, Gertrude Stein, Scott Fitzgerald, and later Richard Wright. Though Bradley and Blanche negotiated many deals together, the Knopfs brought none of those bestselling authors to their list. Stein named Carl Van Vechten the executor of her literary estate, but their friendship did not lead Knopf to recruit her to his roster. Instead, the list of American houses that published her work included New Directions, Random House, and Harcourt, Brace. Blanche attempted to recruit Scott Fitzgerald directly while they were both in Paris. He declined her invitations but once responded with a handwritten letter that includes an amusing Prohibition-era grammar exercise in which he conjugates the verb "to cocktail."[48] Blanche also wanted to bring Ernest Hemingway to the Borzoi circles, not through New York connections but through the London office. In this futile quest, she asked the UK staff member and translator Stephen Haden Guest to ask Ira Morris, a Knopf investor and friend of Samuel, to do his best to secure a contract with the rising star overseas.[49]

It is not clear whether Bradley offered Ford Madox Ford's *The Good Soldier* to the Knopfs, but he definitely offered them Ford's biography of Joseph Conrad. Alfred Knopf rejected the book, predicting that Ford's name would not endure.[50] Bradley's circle also extended to Knopf author Walter White. The NAACP activist wrote for Parisian magazines and befriended André Gide, who had become a Knopf author in 1921. Illustrating the transatlantic aspects of the Borzoi network, it was the Frenchman Gide who introduced White to fellow American Bradley.

The other American "agent" who facilitated significant overseas transactions for the Knopfs was attorney John Quinn, whose anti-Semitism is well documented in his business correspondence. Nonetheless, Knopf never expressed any belief that he was being snubbed by Quinn; he even praised the way the powerhouse agent treated him during their first encounter. When young Knopf was embarking on the marketing campaign for Conrad at Doubleday in 1913, Conrad recommended that Knopf contact Quinn (who had purchased many Conrad manuscripts) for information that might help with an American promotional campaign. In his typically unabashed manner, Knopf consulted a New York telephone directory, found the John Quinn he was looking for, and was soon granted full access to the Conrad papers.[51]

Knopf encountered Quinn again in 1915 through Mitchell Kennerley, and ultimately Quinn was responsible for bringing expatriate American authors

Wyndham Lewis, Ezra Pound, and T. S. Eliot to the Borzoi list, though the relationships of the latter two with Knopf were short-lived. Through Quinn, in 1918 Knopf reissued Lewis's *Tarr,* an autobiographical novel of life in Paris before the war.[52] Lewis in turn had befriended Quinn client Ezra Pound, who had published twice with Knopf, first in 1917 with an introduction to the classical stage of Japan (elucidating Arthur Waley's translations) and in 1918 with *Pavannes and Divisions,* a collection of prose, including mystical short fiction, Socratic dialogues, and a manifesto defending free verse.

T. S. Eliot's first book of criticism, *Ezra Pound: His Metric and Poetry,* became a Borzoi Book in 1917. However, negotiating the terms for T. S. Eliot's *Poems* in 1920, Quinn granted Knopf only a ten-year license. Full copyright would have afforded him a term of fifty-six years.[53] Knopf suspected that the abbreviated terms were Eliot's idea, a realistic speculation in light of letters between Eliot and Quinn regarding arrangements with Horace Liveright. "I am sick of doing business with Jew publishers who will not carry out their part of the contract unless they are forced to," Eliot wrote. "I wish I could find a decent Christian publisher in New York who could be trusted not to slip and slide at every opportunity."[54] However, anti-Semitism was not the reason Knopf lost out on the chance to publish *The Waste Land.* That negotiation, for a reprint from Horace Liveright, broke down because Knopf was not willing to pay the asking price. With deep chagrin, he later admitted that in hindsight, the amount was not unreasonable, especially in light of Eliot's subsequent Nobel Prize.[55]

In later years, Knopf candidly acknowledged that budget constraints, in tandem with his innate tight-fistedness, caused him to start out as a publisher of debuts by authors who later sold their masterpieces to other houses.[56] During the 1950s, he also refused to participate in the growing trend of agents' auctions, forbidding his editors to review manuscripts that had been simultaneously submitted elsewhere. He considered it a waste of time if there was any risk that another house might beat Knopf to the contract.[57]

Notably, Knopf's written recollections rarely mention editors from the early days at his company, though they clearly played a role in developing his American works; for imported books, the editorial process has already been completed. Though more recent decades saw the rise of high-profile Knopf editors such as Judith Jones, Robert Gottlieb, and Gordon Lish (whose heavy edits are credited with shaping Raymond Carver's minimalist style), the young Knopfs seem to have prohibited such a visible role for their initial editorial staffs.

Junior editor Edith Stern, on staff at Knopf for just nine months beginning in 1922, disliked what she described as the "bleak orderliness" of the company's culture, "where efficiency methods were applied to the mélange of business, profession, and gambling that is publishing." She left to become a manuscript reader at Boni & Liveright, where she was paid more generously and felt exhilarated by an office where intellectual fervor flourished in step with "the extravagances, the orgies, the empty bottles that occasionally littered the stairs in the morning."[58] Early Knopf editor George Stevens also sought greener pastures, joining the newly formed W. W. Norton & Company in the late 1920s and making a name for himself as an exceptionally good fiction editor.

During this period, designers, not editors, were the celebrated members of Knopf's publishing process, reaping prestige through their dedication to artisanal craftsmanship.[59] While the 1920s saw Scribner's prestige closely linked to well-known editor Maxwell Perkins, the Knopfs gave the impression of executing a majority of the editorial work themselves during the company's initial years. In fact, they did not seem to believe that a manuscript should be acquired if it required substantial editing: uneven manuscripts were unworthy of becoming Borzoi Books.

Later in his career, as his editorial staff grew, Alfred Knopf continued to decry the notion of buying a weak manuscript, believing that the job of the writer is to write, and the job of the publisher is to publish: "I really think that the kind of work Perkins did, and the resulting legend that grew up around him, has persuaded too many authors to depend far too much on help from publishers' editors in getting their books written."[60] Such beliefs were tied to his attitude toward college English as well, tracing the problem to "absence of training—rhetoric and composition it used to be called when I was young—the consequent lack of an ear, and laziness, sheer laziness. Above all—and this I want to emphasize—the ever-present editor who makes it so easy to get a book accepted for publication."[61] While celebrity editors such as Perkins remained the exception during the 1920s, the profession of book copyediting emerged during this period in response to writers' complaints about excessive compositors' errors.[62]

An anecdote from Judith Jones indicates that, despite Alfred's proclamations to the contrary, his editorial staff may have done more editing than he admitted to, while he and Blanche may have believed that company's reputation and assets—built on their own arguably successful taste in acquiring books—should not be jeopardized by a staff member's questionable ability to make acquisitions decisions. (This principle did not seem to apply to acquisitions recommendations from authors serving as scouts.) Joining the company in 1957, Jones was soon immersed in the paradox of responsibility without authority:

> I heard via the grapevine that Blanche Knopf was looking for an editor. She had just fired a very capable young man and would have preferred, I'm sure, a

male replacement. But fortunately I seemed the right person to fill the spot, particularly when she learned that I was responsible for Doubleday's publishing of *Anne Frank: The Diary of a Young Girl.* It still rankled that her editors . . . had turned it down. When she interviewed me, she pulled out from a drawer a thick file of reports including that calamitous one as well as many others she had been hoarding. . . . Blanche had hired me primarily to work with translators of French authors she had signed up after the war, such as Jean-Paul Sartre and Albert Camus. . . . But the thrill—and the presumption—of editing as distinguished an author as Elizabeth Bowen was something I had not anticipated. Blanche and Elizabeth were good friends, and I understood without being told that when Blanche asked me to act as her editor any editorial suggestions I might have would be strictly anonymous—that is, they would be passed along to Elizabeth Bowen as Blanche's ideas.[63]

Within months, Jones was championing Julia Child's *Mastering the Art of French Cooking,* a mammoth book that Houghton Mifflin had rejected on the grounds that it "might well prove formidable to the housewife." Jones had not been with the firm long enough to be allowed to attend editorial meetings, but when her colleague Angus Cameron presented it on her behalf, "Alfred said, 'Well, let's give Mrs. Jones a chance.' Whereupon Blanche walked out of the meeting, no doubt miffed that her French editor was going to be wasting her time on culinary pursuits." Arriving at a suitable title for Child's cookbook proved to be its own challenge, but Child and Jones settled on the one that has now become classic, only to be denied Alfred's seal of approval: "When I triumphantly showed our title to Mr. Knopf, he scowled and said, 'Well, I'll eat my hat if that title sells.' I like to think of all the hats he had to eat."[64]

During the 1920s, establishing a cadre of celebrated editors such as Perkins might have been a prudent defense for retaining top authors. In addition, an editor's celebrity could enhance an author's. This would have been an easy feat for marketing masters such as the Knopfs. Yet Blanche and Alfred resisted letting their celebrity become overshadowed by a mere editor's.

American Investors

Despite the fiscal hemorrhage in the London office, sales from the New York operation flourished throughout the 1920s. Though financial records from this period are scant, a report to directors and stockholders produced in 1940 provides sales figures of $1,148,190 for 1927; $1,156,455 for 1928; and $1,223,550 for 1929.[65] Sales figures for an American publishing house during the 1920s are a rare find for a contemporary researcher. As Tebbel notes, within such privately held firms during this time period "the publishers were secretive about their financial data . . . and even if this had not been the case, it would have been difficult to resolve their varied bookkeeping methods, from the primitive to the relatively sophisticated."[66]

Published histories of Knopf's competitors during the 1920s do not list sales figures for these years, and such figures would have to be averaged across the total number of titles in print for each house (taking into account the profitability of a backlist) in order for them to be useful. However, the Census of Manufactures and *Publishers' Weekly* provide other measures of comparison. These indicate simply that Knopf's shareholders owned stock in a highly productive house whose sales figures echoed the nationally rising trend of value of products sold. A Census of Manufactures was not taken annually, but it reported for publishers (specifically, those that had no printing establishment) value of products totaling $115,002,643 for 1927 and $126,185,514 for 1929, an increase of 10 percent. Knopf's sales increased 7 percent during the same period. It is also impressive to see Knopf's sales figures increase for each of those three years despite the fact that the company produced fewer new titles in 1928 and 1929. Knopf released 154 frontlist titles in 1927, 136 in 1928, and 140 in 1929. Offering another barometer, the *Publishers' Weekly* established four levels of productivity in its early surveys: publishers issuing fewer than 5 books; from 5 to 49 books; 50 to 99 books; and 100 or more. In 1927, 1928, and 1928, just 19 publishers out of an average of 199 reporting were included in the top category. Knopf was therefore in the top 10 percent of America's most productive houses.[67]

Knopf's investors were a crucial component of the company's early network, but their motives may not have been purely financial ones; many of the investors were relatives of Blanche and Alfred. Before the house became incorporated in February 1918, Alfred periodically incurred bank debt, sometimes borrowing as much as $5,000 at a time. The decision to incorporate with capital stock of $100,000 was meant to reduce the company's debt. Debt made Alfred anxious, unlike many of his contemporaries in an era now remembered for margin loans and other forms of leveraged, risky investing. Though the company was never publicly traded on a stock exchange, Knopf advertised in an attempt to attract investors.[68] He issued a thousand shares at $100 each, half of which were common shares (all taken by Knopf himself). Of the preferred shares, half were retained by Knopf and half were sold. Despite the advertising, almost all of the initial investors were already affiliated with the company. They included Jacob "Jake" Fassett, Jr., son of an industrialist; Desmond Fitzgerald, one of Borzoi Books' commission sales representatives, who sold books for multiple houses; Blanche; Samuel; Blanche's mother, Bertha Wolf; Alfred's sister, Sophia Knopf Josephy; their stepmother, Lillie Knopf; and half-brother Edwin Knopf. By 1927, $30 Class C shares also had been created for purchase by other employees, and for use as dividend payments to those who held common and preferred shares.[69]

Samuel's influence on Borzoi Books' early years is well established, but whether non-employee shareholders exerted any direct influence on the day-to-day operations of the company is difficult to ascertain. Alvin Josephy recalls that when he was having trouble finding work after his graduation from Harvard, his mother, Sophia, asked her brother Alfred to intervene. Alvin, who "had had enough of nepotism" was relieved when Alfred told him that he and Blanche were reserving a place in the company for their son, Pat, and "the company was doing so badly in the Depression that they had had to let some loyal employees go and they couldn't afford to take on any new person, not even me."[70]

Limited investor involvement is also captured in a 1941 in-house report that expresses frustration toward the investor and former Board of Directors member Samuel Knox, a family friend who first bought shares in the company in 1925. Apparently, Knox was dissatisfied with the return on his investment. The anonymous author of the report decries Knox's failure to realize that he had invested for sentimental reasons, as did the other Knopf investors who paid more than $100 for a single, nonvoting share in a company that had essentially no promise of paying dividends.[71]

Further details of dividend payments and, to an even greater extent, salaries are elusive, but a report from Joseph Lesser reveals Samuel Knopf's return on investment. Written upon Samuel's death, the memo states that from 1921 through 1932, his stock investments totaled $182,150, and his dividends totaled $72,730. Between July 1922 and June 1932, his salaries amounted to $221,000.[72] For his son and daughter-in-law, the financial rewards were surely just as impressive, though they also reaped the intangible dividend of prestige.

Competing against such bastions as Harper & Brothers, Charles Scribner's Sons, and Houghton Mifflin Company, Alfred A. Knopf, Inc., took less than a decade to be recognized by numerous authors and literary critics as a premier American publishing house. Like legacy publishing firms run by scions, Alfred's "house" was a symbolic extension of his father's "home" in numerous ways that extended well beyond Samuel's role as investor; he was surely also part of the audience for whom Alfred wish to perform the role of successful literary powerbroker.

Much to Blanche's frustration, Alfred would remain enmeshed with his father until Samuel's death in 1932. Unlike a number of Knopf authors who developed literary lives in Manhattan (Willa Cather, Carl Van Vechten, and Floyd Dell among them) as an alternative to their less cosmopolitan family origins in other states, Knopf's launching a publishing house became a way of "staying home" with his father and relishing the traits they shared. These traits included an affinity for salesmanship, a desire to be connected to affluent circles, and a taste for expensive travel, housing, dining, and tailoring. The most crucial component of this symbiosis was lacking, however: knowledge of literature. For this, Alfred had to adopt surrogate parents, whom he found in Joel Spingarn and John Galsworthy, and in the many communities of writers to which they led him.

CHAPTER FIVE

Distinctive by Design

Her reaction to color and texture has always been subtle and sensitive: the shock
of a cloth manufacturer when he was given a lovely crêpe de chine handkerchief
and asked to match it for color is something I still remember.

Knopf Production Manager SIDNEY JACOBS, describing Blanche Knopf

EARLY KNOPF ADVERTISEMENTS and jacket copy often touted the beauty of
Borzoi Books, assuring consumers that Blanche and Alfred Knopf were at the
forefront of setting superior trends in American book design. The Knopfs' use
of visual rhetoric shaped the company's identity as well as the cachet of their
authors. In later years, the Knopfs were frequently celebrated for developing
a new aesthetic standard as vigorously as they developed new literary talent,
confirmed in Blanche and Alfred's recollection of the Borzoi's early days as a
period of originality and spontaneity. Yet it's difficult to categorize the appearance of early Borzoi Books. Did early Borzoi Books look modern? Or did they
inspire an image of a traditional gentleman publisher who would have resisted
the femininity implied in production manager Sidney Jacobs's recollection of
Blanche? Ultimately, was the Knopf marketing promise of superlative "beauty
in the binding" mere hyperbole?

Longtime Knopf designer George Salter insisted that "there *is* a Borzoi
style," but he emphasized the variety of traits within that style: "A mode rather
than a fixed graphic form, it lacks the stringency of a set formula."[1] Sidney
Jacobs observed that "it is . . . the catholicity of Alfred's taste and his toler-
ant receptivity to many design attitudes that make up the complex mosaic of
Knopf design." Jacobs paid equal homage to Blanche: "Frequently she selected
the designers and jacket artists to be used for her books and, like Alfred, usually
gave them free rein to interpret the author's work."[2] Yet Knopf came of age in
an era when many publishers were revitalizing aesthetic technique. What made
the Borzoi approach truly exceptional is that it married book production with
book promotion.

A Brand of Beauty

The Knopfs transformed a book's title page into a subtle form of advertising space by keeping the Borzoi mark visible, even integrating it into flourished borders, and thereby reinforcing the appearance of the wolfhound on the spines and back covers of the books. In one of the era's most striking Borzoi designs, Thomas Maitland Cleland created a vine pattern formed from a line of Borzois leaping end-to-end. Making its first appearance in 1925, this border was a striking feature of numerous Knopf ads, title pages, and other promotional materials,

Borzoi vine designed by Thomas Maitland Cleland

including British ads for Knopf Ltd. The AK monogram, and sometimes the full name Alfred A. Knopf, were also used to form border patterns.[3] In each of these approaches, Cleland's designs for Knopf combined a spirit of whimsy and novelty with the precision of fine-printing houses such as Stone & Kimball or Copeland and Day. Not coincidentally, other Knopf designers included the Stone & Kimball veteran Bruce Rogers, whom the Knopfs met through master printer Elmer Adler.[4]

The designs produced during Knopf's launch are a far cry from the elegance that would shape the brand in subsequent years. The first book published by Knopf, Émile Augier's *Four Plays,* is evidence of Alfred's attempts to make all design choices himself, taking suggestions from Blanche under advisement. His only employees at that time were an "office boy" and an assistant.[5] *Four Plays* features unusual proportions of 203 mm. in height by 132 mm. in width, making for a book that stands slightly taller than the typical octavos one might have found on a store shelf during this period. The book was bound in orange paper, with a top edge stained in a teal. Teal ink was also used for the stamped lettering on the cover. On the back, Alfred's initials tower in 108-point Art Deco typography. In the future, this monogram would shrink considerably and was sometimes combined with an image of a Borzoi leaping over it. The earliest years at Knopf also saw the use of an Art Nouveau monogram, applied to numerous bindings, jackets, and sheets of letterhead through the early 1920s. The existence of both the Deco and Nouveau styles captures the modern and traditional characteristics that flourished within the company's identity.

Predicting his penchant for limited editions, Alfred ordered two specially bound copies of *Four Plays* in morocco leather (goatskin) for presentation to

Early Knopf emblems

Samuel ("Pater") and Blanche ("V.V.").[6] Alfred chose Cheltenham for the book's interior, but for some reason he regretted this decision. Later calling Cheltenham "a face I have never dared use for a book again," he rejected a type-face created in part by the venerable Hannibal Ingalls Kimball, a book designer revered and imitated by the Borzoi's artisans.[7] The other design features of *Four Plays* are decidedly unremarkable. Except for the leaping wolfhound emblem, making its première appearance in a book, the title page is devoid of ornamentation; the plain, double-line frame is possibly hand-drawn. Over the years, dozens of incarnations of the dog emblem would emerge, ranging from Kahlil Gibran's lamb-like interpretation to Peter Andersen's minimalist line drawing. An extensive kennel is documented in Jack W. C. Hagstrom's "Alfred A. Knopf's Borzoi Devices."[8]

The paper used in Augier's collection—for endpapers as well as interior pages—is plain, and the edges are trimmed. Future Borzoi Books would make use of the "rough front," a machine-made process for developing shaggy edges, which creates the illusion that a book has been printed on handmade paper. Among the nine hundred pre-1930 Knopf volumes I examined in the Beinecke Library's Tanselle Collection (approximately 70 percent of all Knopf titles issued during the time period covered in this history, with even representation for each year), 75 percent have rough-front edges, reflecting an appreciation for European *fin de siècle* aesthetic qualities. Almost all of the volumes have stained tops, regardless of the trim style. Although Knopf's clear preference for deckle edges may have been tied to his belief that they conveyed a prestigious antiquarian aura, not everyone in the book trade saw them in a complimentary light. The renowned book historian John Carter described deckle edges as "an affectation . . . they collect dust and, being technically obsolete for a century and a half, hardly avoid a self-conscious air. In books of reference they are intolerable."[9]

Though the overall design of Knopf's first book is rudimentary, it is an example of the modern strand of his branding effort, demonstrating an attempt to differentiate his company from older houses; at other times, the design of his early editions contradicts this effort, reflecting the Knopfs' initially old-world persona. Regardless of those classifications, Alfred Knopf was known for bindings that were unusual, and he was often credited with the use of colorful bindings. Of course, any survey of used-book sellers turns up colorful bindings produced decades before the launch of Borzoi Books, and G. Thomas Tanselle's "A System of Color Identification for Bibliographical Description" was written in response to the profusion of descriptive approaches that arose after the nineteenth-century introduction of publishers' cloth and its kaleidoscopic variants.[10] Knopf clearly did not introduce such bindings, but his designs were often colorful. Nonetheless, 61 percent of Tanselle's Knopf specimens produced during the company's first five years were bound in unremarkable dark or neutral cloth (black, navy blue, dark green, maroon, tan, or gray). Knopf's use of bright-colored cloth and paper (including teal, yellow, orange, pink, violet, red, vibrant greens and blues, and multicolored patterns) did not rise sharply until 1923, accounting for 71 percent of the books he published that year. The trend continued in subsequent years, reaching 81 percent in 1928 and 85 percent in 1929. The initial increase coincides with the Knopfs' first trip abroad, where, Alfred recalled, they "were constantly on the lookout for new and more attractive binding materials. In Germany we discovered unfinished cloths that we imported until American mills caught the idea . . . as well as those remarkable batik papers. . . . In England we had met Lovat Fraser and were able to buy from the Curwen Press many of the charming binding papers he designed. Manufacturing costs in those days made it possible to indulge in such eccentricities."[11]

Jackets also afforded a way to distinguish the Borzoi brand in the market-place. A 1926 profile of the Knopfs published in the *New Yorker* asserted that "it was Alfred's idea—and Blanche has backed him in everything—to give the public something different in the format of books. He introduced into the trade brilliantly colored jackets which attracted the eye."[12] The article's author, Lurton Blassingame, appears to have relied on the Knopfs themselves as his primary source. In fact, the use of color in jackets had emerged at least eighty years before the rise of Knopf; G. Thomas Tanselle's landmark study of jackets states that the earliest known detachable English paper book-covering (an advertising wrapper that enclosed an 1833 edition of the literary annual *The Keepsake*, published in London) featured red printing on yellow paper, a color scheme continued by the publisher, Longmans, for subsequent works.[13] By the time of the launch of Borzoi Books, a book's price was customarily printed on the spine of the jacket, making it appropriate for display in a bookstore, but it would have been gauche to display a price in a home library. Possibly for this reason, many jackets were discarded. Nonetheless, the Tanselle Collection preserves some three hundred specimens of early Knopf jackets, almost all of which were printed on color stock. Of these, approximately 25 percent feature illustrations, sometimes showcasing art that was not featured in the book. The jacket on Tanselle's copy of the 1923 novel *Weeds*, by Pio Baroja, is a good example of this, featuring a vivid, modernist landscape painting by John Dos Passos, with the borzoi logo printed on the back in fuchsia. Blassingame was correct to state that Knopf jackets were eye-catching, but it is hyperbolic to credit Knopf with *introducing* the concept of colorful jackets.

It's reasonable to assume that all Knopf books published before 1930 were sold in jackets. Very few production records exist for early editions of Knopf books; many files were destroyed during an office move in the twenties. Yet a surviving photograph taken of the young Alfred Knopf in his office shows that his bookshelves were lined with jacketed Knopf editions, and jacketing was common practice by the time his firm was founded.[14] The Borzoi was usually featured on multiple surfaces of the jacket, including varying combinations of the spine, the front cover, the back cover, and one or both flaps. Often printed on uncoated stock that spanned a spectrum of blue, yellow, orange, and green, the jackets were sometimes paired with a vibrant batik binding underneath whose hues surprisingly clashed with those of the jacket. In other cases (including a majority of the examples in the Borzoi Plays series) the jacket stock and decoration are identical to the book's paper binding. The layout of Knopf's early typographical jackets is not elaborate, echoing minimalistic formulas used widely at the time by publishers such Boni & Liveright, particularly for their Modern Library series, launched in 1917. Not surprisingly, the tone of the Borzoi jacket copy is always sensational.

Today, innovative jacket designs by Knopf's celebrated associate art director, Chip Kidd, have received considerable attention. The company's first illustrated jackets do not predict such an illustrious outcome. The early layouts reflect an awkward, conflicted attempt to create commercial appeal while appearing highbrow. Illustrated Knopf jackets appeared as early as 1916, when Alfred Ollivant's *The Brown Mare* featured a facile two-color image of a horse and rider drawn by an artist identified simply by his last name, Schutte. The front-cover copy is much bolder than the art, promising readers that in this collection of fictional vignettes "the thunder and lightning are far away: but the reverberations of the storm echo across the sea in the crowded streets and quiet lanes of England under the cloud. A distinctive little book—unlike anything the war has yet produced."

A number of Knopf's jackets were designed by William Addison Dwiggins, a master typographer and calligrapher associated with the rise of the field of graphic design. His career had begun in advertising, including designing labels for canned goods, a skill that easily translated into the creation of paper labels for book covers and spines. Dwiggins was introduced to Knopf in 1923 when *Publishers' Weekly* co-editor Fred Melcher brought him to the Borzoi offices.[15] Though he created attractive jackets for Knopf and other publishers, he had tremendous disdain for the advertising role the sheath had assumed. Pining for the days when a jacket was simply a protective sleeve, he observed that "a walk down the aisle between the tables of best-sellers gives you something of the kick of a cocktail. . . . The jackets are very jolly things. There is only one count against them: they have taken the joy out of book covers."[16]

The architect and stagecraft designer Claude Bragdon was another well-known designer who produced jackets for Knopf.[17] The two met while Knopf was serving as an apprentice in Mitchell Kennerley's publishing firm.[18] Bragdon's interest in geometric ornaments was his artistic signature, leading to an approach for Floyd Dell's novel *Moon-Calf* that looks surprisingly simplistic. He sketched a large, black, moon-like orb, which spans most of the upper half of the jacket, and used it to reverse the book's title and author in white typography. It's worth noting that the novel's title has nothing to do with celestial topics; "mooncalf" is a slang term meaning "fool." In this case, the highly personal tone of the copy is far more intriguing than the jacket art. Though the book was published in 1920, when Blanche and Alfred's company was merely five years old, Alfred presents himself as a veteran, perhaps even elderly publisher: "MOON-CALF is by far the most distinguished and most significant first novel by an American that has ever been offered me." No mention is made of Floyd Dell's radicalism. Instead, Knopf anticipates that the novel will easily gain mainstream acceptance and "command wide attention and universal respect."[19] Copyright pages confirm that the book reached its eighth printing within its first six months on sale.

The Knopfs entrusted Bragdon with the high-pressure task of designing jackets, bindings, and interiors for Willa Cather's first two Knopf books, *Youth and the Bright Medusa* and *One of Ours*. Designing an all-typographical jacket for *One of Ours*, he succeeded in pleasing the author. For the book's other design elements, he emphasized interpretation rather than realism; he believed she would reject any design direction that reminded her too much of poster art.[20] The jackets were issued in variant colors and were updated to reflect how often Knopf had gone back to press; the printing number appears prominently on the spine.

Almost a decade later, after Bragdon's involvement with the Borzoi was eclipsed by better-known designers, Elmer Adler told Alfred that he thought the jacket for *One of Ours* was weak.[21] Nonetheless, Bragdon left his mark on hundreds of the first Borzoi Books. His geometrical ornaments appear on at least one hundred half-title pages and numerous cloth bindings of early

Borzoi endpapers in *The Borzoi 1925*

publications, and he created kaleidoscopic endpapers that were printed in a wide spectrum of colors, adding beauty to at least fifty Borzoi Books between 1922 and 1927.[22]

Despite Bragdon's contributions, the vast majority—82 percent—of the endpapers I examined in the Tanselle Knopf collection are plain. Only 16 percent use colored paper or decorations, and very few of them were printed with an illustration. One of these rarities is the sylvan scene printed in yellow ochre for Englishman Walter de la Mare's 1919 novel *The Three Mulla-Mulgars* (later republished as *The Three Royal Monkeys*), a book that features many line drawings and full-color artwork by the prolific, award-winning American illustrator Dorothy Lathrop.[23] This is the earliest evidence of decorated Knopf endpapers I have found. Another rare Knopf endpaper uses the wolfhound device, printing it repeatedly in a series of colored grids. Unlike the Modern Library, which used Rockwell Kent's notable endpaper design to brand "ML" on dozens of titles, Knopf uncharacteristically refrained from using the Borzoi endpaper with any significant frequency.

For select books, the Borzoi logo also appeared as a watermark on the sheets used for printing, and it was used for special stationery. Referred to as "Borzoi rag," the paper features a framed Borzoi mark ranging from 31 mm. tall x 37 mm. wide to 35 mm. tall x 52 mm. wide. The paper and trimming were coordinated so that the watermark could be positioned on the lower right corner right-hand pages, where a reader's eye falls when a page is about to be turned. As the page is lifted, light can illuminate the watermark, which also bears the words BORZOI BOOKS. Though watermarks are usually intended to brand the paper manufacturer, Knopf was hardly the first publisher to feature his name and emblem on specially made paper; Stone & Kimball's paper featured a torch shedding light on an open book.

An early occurrence of Borzoi rag paper appears in a 1923 limited edition of *From an American Legation,* written by America's minister to Sweden, Ira Nelson Morris, who was also an investor in Alfred A. Knopf Ltd. Again in 1923, the Borzoi watermark could be found in the limited edition of Carl Stern-heim's satirical novel *Fairfax.* Perhaps it was an equally satirical choice to use "upper-class paper" for a book that, translated from the German, pokes fun at the American bourgeoisie. Borzoi rag paper sometimes appeared in both a limited edition and its accompanying standard issue. Carl Van Vechten's 1928 novel of Hollywood decadence, *Spider Boy: A Scenario for a Moving Picture,* is an example of this dual application.

In lauding the design of early Borzoi Books, it is important to remember that the designers who lent their names to the Knopf identity were generally in business for themselves and did not serve the Borzoi exclusively. William Dwiggins was heavily involved with the designs for some of Knopf's most popular authors, but he served other houses as well. Of particular note were his fine slipcased editions for the new firm Random House and his service as a key member of the design team for the Limited Editions Club. On behalf of the Mergenthaler Linotype Company (not Knopf), Dwiggins created eleven typefaces, including Electra and Caledonia, widely used throughout trade publishing. George Salter had perhaps the broadest network, creating designs for a total of more than eighty American publishers other than Knopf.[24] In addition, though Alfred drew attention to his use of the Japan Paper Company, he was not the shop's only customer; their highly decorative papers could be found on the covers of many other American publishers' books, ranging from small houses such as Bostonian Bruce Humphries and upstart Coward-McCann to stalwarts such as Charles Scribner's Sons and Dodd, Mead & Co.

Neither was Knopf the only publisher who associated his name with the quality design, typesetting, and manufacturing provided by Elmer Adler and his colleagues at Pynson Printers, the name of whose firm harked back to the sixteenth-century kings' printer Richard Pynson. The manifesto for Adler's company was "we will do no work in which quality must be sacrificed to exigencies of time and cost," which ultimately cost him a sizable portion of his family's garment-business fortune. Adler eventually created the Graphic Arts Collection at Princeton, where he taught book and print collecting, fostering a greater integration between academia and the rare-book trade.[25] Knopf rarely used the printing and bindery services of Pynson Printers, complaining about the firm's steep prices. The numerous colophons in the Tanselle Collection attribute only eight books to Pynson, primarily limited editions, but numerous interior and title-page designs are attributed to Adler, whose productions would be sent to press at the large commercial firms of Vail-Ballou or Plimpton. Thus, the Borzoi could be associated with Adler's handicraft while the actual manufacturing took place at more affordable, industrial establishments. It was an arrangement that often frustrated Adler, who called it "irritating" to work piecemeal.[26]

Limited Editions and Series

The Knopfs' enthusiasm for limited editions is often held up as evidence of the Borzoi's setting a new standard for book publishing, but it is important to note that collectors' editions had existed long before the arrival of Borzoi Books. Knopf's company came of age in tandem with the emergence of the field of graphic arts (the American Institute of Graphic Arts was founded in 1914) along with a profusion of limited editions. While Knopf's advertising may have enhanced an awareness of the physical traits of a book, he was not responsible for the inception of that awareness. Neither did the Knopfs set the standards of an ideal book's physical traits. American collectors had previously relied on British private presses such as Kelmscott, but by the 1920s, in part because of the emigration of English publishers such as Kennerley, America was home to a number of highly skilled artisans. Organizations such as The Grolier Club flourished.[27]

Although Knopf was not the instigator of the trend, he was without doubt an inspiration to Bennett Cerf, who credited him with establishing protocols for gaining prestige as a publisher. In March 1928, the newly formed Random House announced a limited editions imprint, managed by the Broadway producer, book collector, and printer Crosby Gaige. Bruce Rogers designed many of those initial titles, which John Tebbel describes as "some of the most strikingly beautiful volumes of their time." Two of the titles, *Reminiscences of Andreyev* by Maxim Gorky (translated by Katherine Mansfield) and *Letters of Joseph Conrad to Richard Curle,* would have been at home on Knopf's inaugural list.[28] Modern Library historian Jay Satterfield writes, "In his own words, Bennett Cerf 'worshipped' Knopf, and, using his highest accolade, he testified,

'Alfred Knopf had the one thing Liveright lacked: he had class.' His assertion located Knopf and Liveright on a social hierarchy based on a concept of good taste. . . . By the 1920s, the term had been transformed to mean a superiority of personal style. That Knopf 'had class' denoted that he possessed a certain elegance of sensibility."[29]

In many ways, Bruce Rogers had the greatest influence on the look of Knopf's limited editions. After serving as a freelance designer at Stone & Kimball, Rogers joined Houghton Mifflin's Riverside Press, which created a limited editions division in 1900. For the next decade he produced extraordinary title pages, typefaces, and interior designs for more than one hundred Riverside editions. By the time Knopf launched his firm in 1915, Rogers was renowned on both sides of the Atlantic and had become the first living typographer to be showcased in a paper presented in London before the Bibliographical Society. His title-page frames often featured intricate line drawings and miniscule flourishes, proliferating into borders that are sometimes as much as an inch wide. His signature aesthetic was developed during the late nineteenth century but translated easily into modernist sensibilities: It conveys clarity, precision, and beauty with a spirit that is infused with whimsy.

His designs for Knopf were often in collaboration with fine printer William Edwin Rudge, whose operations were housed in a Tudor mansion in Mount Vernon, New York. Rudge employed Rogers between 1920 and 1928, producing books and promotional pieces that were destined to become collector's items.[30] Rudge-Rogers collaborations for Knopf include a slipcased edition of W. H. Hudson's *Ralph Herne,* featuring elegant running heads and chapter openers and bound in a combination of black cloth and red paper over boards; and Joseph Hergesheimer's autobiography *The Presbyterian Child,* bound in paper over boards decorated with a pink floral motif. Displaying the humor that permeates his letters to Alfred Knopf, Rogers wondered if his approach to the title page would have been different for a novel with a Methodist or Baptist storyline.[31] A review in the *New York Times* assessed the design as much as the writing, declaring the book to be "a consecrated chalice. First, there is a black board box, chastely labeled in old rose. Inside the box is something wrapped in oiled paper. Inside the paper is a binding of riotous design . . . and inside the covers is a book . . . with its title page ornamented by a round arch in which typography maintains the ecclesiastical atmosphere. . . . Such a vessel could hardly contain anything less than a splinter of the True Cross."[32]

For a 1923 imported edition of Stanley Morison and Holbrook Jackson's *A Brief Survey of Printing: History and Practice,* Knopf's jacket copy invokes the name of "our own Bruce Rogers" to place himself in transatlantic communities of prestige:

The constantly widening circle of book collectors interested in the art of the book welcomes this contribution made by real lovers of good printing. The simple narrative of the ten chapters develops the printed book from its manuscript model through the superb craftsmanship of our own Bruce Rogers. So highly do these English authorities think of our share of contemporary work that of the eight full page illustrations, three show work done on this side of the Atlantic. And the book was not designed especially for American consumption. Also, there are shown thirty-six examples of type faces entertainingly arranged for comparison. THIRD LARGE PRINTING.

Nonetheless, when in 1953 Rogers compiled a handsome commemorative monograph humbly called *Pi: A Hodge-Podge of the Letters, Papers, and Addresses Written During the Last Sixty Years,* he did not include any Knopf samples when selecting more than thirty illustrations for the book. This choice underscores the fact that although Rogers produced beautiful books for Borzoi Books, Knopf was not his sole client, and Rogers perhaps felt that his designs for the Riverside Press, The Grolier Club, university presses, and others would better exemplify his best work. Regardless, the omission indicates that he did not feel the need to place himself in Knopf's company.

In any case, limited editions permitted the Knopfs to place their works in the hands of affluent bibliophiles, melding packaging and promotion. More than three dozen titles published by Knopf between 1915 and 1931 were issued in limited editions, often with variations that reflected the recipient's rank within the Knopf circle. A limited edition created for *Tampico,* Joseph Hergesheimer's 1926 novel, bears the following message: "Of the first edition of *Tampico,* two hundred and fifty five copies have been signed by the author, as follows: fifty five on Shidzuoka Japan Vellum (of which five are not for sale) numbered from 1 to 55, and two hundred copies on Borzoi rag paper (of which eight are not for sale) numbered 56 to 255." The design elements for this limited edition evoke royalty: white paper over boards, a white ribbon bookmark, gilt ornamentation and a gilt top edge, uncut signatures of heavyweight stock, and a wolfhound gold-stamped on the back cover. The Borzoi's distinctive design was often enhanced by references to the Japan Paper Company, whose wares bore exotic names: Kinkami, Patria, Japanese Shadow Paper, Italian Wood Block Paper. Despite the firm's name, many of the papers were manufactured not in Asia but in Europe, often in France, Holland, and Italy.[33]

Knopf's limited editions were competitively priced; when the Limited Editions Club was launched in 1929, the subscribers' price was ten dollars per book. Carl Sternheim's *Fairfax* was issued only in a limited print run of 950 numbered copies, priced at $7.50, typical for limited editions featured in *The Borzoi 1925,* which simply describes *Fairfax* as having a "cloth back, hand colored board sides." In fact, the edition features gold-stamped vellum-and-batik sides issued in varying colors ranging from dark crimson to bright pink.[34] *Fairfax* is particularly noteworthy for being the only Knopf book designed by Frederic Goudy, who implemented heavily flourished ornaments throughout the text.[35]

Sometimes Knopf copyright pages let readers know that their copies were not particularly limited. Such was the case with a 1923 novel by Willa Cather: "This first edition of *A Lost Lady* consists of twenty thousand two hundred and twenty copies as follows: twenty on Borzoi all rag paper signed by the author and numbered A to T; two hundred copies on Borzoi all rag paper signed by the author and numbered 1 to 200; and twenty thousand copies on English featherweight paper." Cather bibliographer Joan Crane noted no physical difference between the lettered and numbered copies and proposed that the chronology of textual changes "indicates that the limited issue was not put into press until the first and second printings had been printed."[36] The 220 readers who possessed limited editions may not have possessed first-printing copies. Conversely, the possibility of corrected plates did not mean that Knopf's limited editions were immune to editorial gaffes. At least one copy of a morocco-bound 1919 edition of the Abbé Prévost's *Manon Lescaut* featured a title page and spine that misattributed the novel to Gustave Flaubert.[37]

Dwiggins was one of the few Knopf designers who disliked producing limited editions. Expressing relief that a limited edition for a series on the secretaries of state might not be commissioned, he told Alfred that it was frustrating to balance cost constraints with a mandate for elegance. He much preferred to design less expensive "garden-variety" books.[38] Cather shared his dislike for limited editions, expressing disdain for the boxed, batik-bound version of *One of Ours*, which she claimed was produced without her knowledge. In a letter to Dorothy Canfield Fisher, she equated this high-priced edition with the death of a book; this special edition was sold with its page edges folded, gathered, and bound but uncut, making them unreadable unless the collector chose to slice them open, which would diminish the value. Cather also mourned the fact that the lavish packaging did not match the careful editorial approach she had taken to tell the story of a soldier, stating that she had even reduced her use of adjectives. In addition, she believed that the type of collector who would purchase such an expensive book was too far removed from the protagonist's rural world.[39]

On Dwiggins's advice, Knopf launched a series called Pocket Books in 1923, attempting to produce smaller-format, lower-priced, "garden-variety" volumes. In the end, they were sometimes more ornately packaged than many standard Borzoi Books. Pocket Books featured Borzoi end papers in variant colors and elegant title pages designed by Elmer Adler. Other Knopf series

Title-page frame for Pocket Books designed by Elmer Adler

developed during the 1920s included Borzoi Classics and the Blue Jade Library, but Pocket Books was perhaps the company's most elaborately designed line during that decade. Other features included green cloth binding with lavish stamping depicting a leaf pattern and the Borzoi device. The jacket design echoed these motifs. Priced at approximately one dollar, Pocket Books were marketed as affordable editions that would nonetheless deliver a superior reading experience, including a few health benefits derived from good typography. Ophthalmology is the focus of the flap copy for Nobel Prize winner Sigrid Undset's *Jenny*, a novel reprinted in the series in 1929:

> PERIL IN THINE EYE. It hurts to read poorly printed books. Headaches or permanently injured eyesight may result. Just how the damage is done is not exactly known, but the countless little twists, wrenches, and strains which the eye undergoes in reading a poorly designed and printed type may be likened to the 20,000 jolts a day suffered by those who do not wear rubber heels.... There are many factors in the making of a transparently readable book: good size type, proper type design, even inking, even impression, good paper surface. Great skill is needed to combine all these requirements successfully. The fine results achieved in the Borzoi Pocket Books are due to the long experience of their publisher, who, for more than a decade, has led the way in the making of more beautiful books.[40]

Knopf advertising exalted the books' aesthetic appeal and quality manufacturing as much as the quality of the writing. One *New York Times* advertisement went so far as to reproduce a facsimile of a page from Willa Cather's *My Mortal Enemy*, showcasing not only the author's exceptional prose but also the designer's lavish folio ornamentation and elegant typography. William Dwiggins and the Pynson Printers are credited in the ad for producing what Knopf proclaims to be "a beautiful edition."[41] The process of working with Cather to produce such an edition was always arduous; Adler complained to Knopf that he lost money on the Cather projects because she requested many time-consuming changes.[42] Dwiggins, on the other hand, seemed to have a better tolerance for her heavy involvement in design decisions. After he created a jacket, title page, and folios for *My Mortal Enemy*, he didn't hesitate to accept other Cather assignments, and his aesthetic sensibility appears to have quashed excessive revision requests from her.[43] She wisely wanted new designs tailored for the theme of each of her books. For *Lucy Gayheart*, she rejected the re-use of the rustic approach that was initially taken with the layout for *Death Comes for the Archbishop*—a design approach that she compared both to a country press and a children's book. Not wanting to leave the production staff baffled, she suggested that they refer to the type treatment of *A Lost Lady* for inspiration in coming up with a new approach.[44] While it may be more efficient to produce books for an author whose taste is consistent, Cather's painstaking, customizing method mirrored the artisanal quality for which Knopf is still admired.

A Note on the Type

Among bibliophiles, the house of Knopf is especially known for printing an informative colophon at the back of all its books, using the space as a form of advertising that blends book promotion with book production. Knopf's "note on the type" distinguished Borzoi Books in a unique way. The lengthy, often narrative version of the Knopf colophon as we know it today did not appear until the 1920s; earlier versions simply listed the name of the printer on the copyright page and was therefore not a true colophon, which etymologically refers to a finishing touch (i.e., found at the conclusion of a book). During Knopf's initial years, the copyright-page information grew to include the name of the paper supplier, bindery, and typesetting firm as well. The earliest of these listings that I have found appears in a 1918 edition of Joseph Hergesheimer's *Wild Oranges*. Going beyond the words "MANUFACTURED IN THE UNITED STATES OF AMERICA," required to secure domestic copyright, the Knopfs inform us that *Wild Oranges* was printed by Binghamton's Vail-Ballou Company on paper furnished by the Japan Paper Company, and bound by H. Wolff Estate. The word "estate" belies Wolff's decidedly industrial home in a newly constructed concrete building that grew to eventually occupy 376,000 square feet on Manhattan's West 26th Street.[45]

While Borzoi Books promised durability, the practical process of attaching the binding to the sheets was perhaps the most important component in delivering on that promise. Paradoxically, this service is virtually impossible to brand because, if done correctly, its results are invisible. The H. Wolff Book Manufacturing Company is the bindery most commonly listed in Knopf colophons during the 1920s, and the firm, founded by Harris Wolff in 1893, would likely have used a state-of-the-art process. The problem of sewing the text block to its case, partly solved by Smyth's book-sewing machine but still time consuming, was further lessened by the invention of spiral hook needles and side-sewing machines that increased the speed of binding, as well as the book's durability. Nonetheless, Dwiggins believed it was a waste of resources to focus on the durability of bindings: "They don't need to last so long. Their cost is all out of proportion to the work they do."[46] He was surely exasperated, then, by the few collectible editions that Knopf produced at William Rudge's bucolic printing house. These would have shown the influence of Edith Diehl, a Wellesley graduate who devoted more than a decade, in America and abroad, to mastering the craft of bookbinding by hand and by machine. She bound all of Rogers's books for Rudge between 1918 and 1920, organizing Rudge's edition bindery before establishing her own hand bindery in Manhattan.⁴⁷

Exemplifying this rising interest in the craft of book-making, a *Publishers' Weekly* essay reported on Knopf's "very interesting innovation" in 1922, stating that "on the back of its title pages [Knopf] gives complete information as to who is responsible for the manufacture of its books."⁴⁸ Paying homage to book manufacturers in a colophon was by no means innovative in the early twentieth century. For bibliophiles, it was a quaint reminder of a practice renewed by William Morris and his followers, dating back nearly five hundred years to a time when printers were publishers.⁴⁹ The *Publishers' Weekly* article goes on to praise other publishers that were enhancing the physical quality of books, including good typesetting in Macmillan's *Maria Chapdelaine,* a two-color title page for Doubleday's *The Ragged Edge,* and an attractive binding with yellow stained tops for the Atlantic Monthly Press's *The Atlantic Book of Modern Plays.*

Though Knopf's early colophon is often thought to have been motivated by the desire to create a fine-printing aura, it should be noted that 1919 was the year of crippling strikes on the part of New York pressmen and compositors. Typographical Union No. 6 asked for a 50 percent increase in wages, from 75 cents an hour to $1.13, shutting down on October 1. "Outlaw" pressmen and feeders (members of unions that had been outlawed among New York's printing trades for refusing to abide by the international body's regulations) followed suit, leading 200 periodicals to suspend publication, which slowed book publication. Tebbel reports that "the strike came to an abrupt end in what *PW* described as a 'nebulous way' with no discernible advantage to either side in the new agreements that were signed," though compositor and printing prices escalated afterward.⁵⁰ Labor shortages and demanding workloads led to further strikes in New York as well as in Boston, Philadelphia, and Chicago, joined by mill workers. As these well-publicized tensions emphasized the industrial nature of book production, Knopf's colophon may have served as an antidote, rewarding manufacturers with free advertising on the pages of a Borzoi book. The Knopf colophon also reshaped the identity of a book manufacturer as someone who was devoted to the art of craftsmanship, as opposed to an overworked factory employee whose main concern was the promise of a living wage.

The two presses most commonly mentioned in Knopf's early colophons— the Plimpton Press in Norwood, Massachusetts (not far from Dwiggins's home, which facilitated his work with Plimpton), and Vail-Ballou, in Binghamton, New York—employed a combination of unionized and non-union labor. The history of the latter is not well documented, but considerable information exists on the years when Plimpton Press and Knopf forged their relationship. Despite the sylvan image conjured by the colophon's reference to rural Massachusetts, the Plimpton Press was very much an industrial facility, employing approximately 500 workers in 1917 (200 of whom, including the employment manager, were women) and relying heavily on textbook publishing for revenue. Plimpton undertook a variety of measures, including spacious work rooms, bonuses, and a savings bureau, to reduce workforce turnover. Yet the labor shortage, combined with higher wages paid by urban presses, made it a challenge to retain a stable workforce. The Press's agreement with union representatives gave unions first rights to provide skilled workers, but for unions headquartered in cities (as the Typographical and Pressmen's unions were), a small-town press such as Plimpton was less desirable and therefore faced greater turnover.[51] The effects of union leverage were still felt by Knopf as late as 1923, when *The American Mercury* ran an article that was unflattering to union workers; Rumford Press refused to print the job, and Knopf took the contract to the Haddon Craftsmen (an industrial plant, despite the name) in rural Pennsylvania.

Overcoming these realities, the colophon served to evoke a quaint image of customized artistry that endures in the Knopf brand to this day. It was Dwiggins who urged Knopf to adopt the elaborate back-of-the-book colophon as a way to more powerfully spark readers' interest in the physical traits of Borzoi Books.[52] The earliest occurrence of it that I have found appears in Katherine Anthony's 1925 biography of Catherine the Great, though Knopf historian Paul Bennett listed the inaugural year as 1926.[53] The narrative begins with the now-widely recognized words A NOTE ON THE TYPE IN WHICH THIS BOOK IS SET and informs the reader that the volume was composed on the Linotype in Scotch, and that "there is a divergence of opinion regarding the exact origin of this face, some authorities holding that it was first cut by Alexander Wilson & Son, of Glasgow, in 1827; others trace it back to a modernized Caslon old style. . . . The essential characteristics of the Scotch face are its sturdy capitals, its full rounded lower case, the graceful fillet of its serifs and the general effect of crispness."[54] By telling us that the book was printed on Scottish esparto, the Knopfs remind us that the paper was imported, though few readers would be able to define "esparto" or explain why its fibers make for a high-quality paper.[55]

In the early years of Knopf, the colophon served as a bridge between tradition and innovation. American literary modernists had renewed an interest in fine printing, which had flourished in late Victorian and Edwardian England. A response to the increasingly industrialized nature of book production—which Alfred claimed to scorn—England's fine printing movement was a prelude to modernism. Alfred's apprenticeship with Kennerley linked him to Britain's Bodley Head, where Kennerley had served with the house's co-founder John Lane in both the London and New York offices. Matthew Bruccoli described Lane as a man who was "regarded as the principal publisher of the new aesthetic movement" and whose books "physically and textually proclaimed the message of art for art's sake."[56] These sensibilities were passed through Kennerley to Alfred, although he set his sights on far greater profitability than Lane's firm, which, Megan Benton reminds us in *Beauty and the Book*, "explicitly catered to a small, vaguely avant-garde fringe of British book buyers."[57]

Publisher of Oscar Wilde and the experimental quarterly *The Yellow Book*, John Lane embraced "the 'decadent' world of Naturalist fiction, feminist polemics, and Beardsleyan eroticism," which resonated with late-Victorian artists who rebelled against the Industrial Revolution.[58] Although Alfred did not seek a following of radicals, he was well versed in how to produce industrially manufactured books that evoked images of a handpress or handmade paper. Yet his greatest talent was salesmanship. Lack of business acumen and marketing were his chief complaints against Kennerley, which underscores the distinction between the Knopfs and Arts and Crafts maestros such as the socialist William Morris, who saw no place for commercialism in a publishing house. Addressing Britain's Bibliographical Society in 1893, Morris said, "By the ideal book, I suppose we are to understand a book not limited by commercial exigencies of price: we can do what we like with it, according to what its nature, as a book, demands of Art."[59]

The practical and aesthetic challenges faced by early Borzoi designers are easy to dismiss when we examine the pristine result of their efforts, but Knopf's records reveal the many design hurdles encountered and overcome when industry, author, and publisher were at odds. In a letter to William Aspenwall Bradley, Alfred Knopf refused to pay for additional changes requested by author René Lalou to his forthcoming *Contemporary French Literature*, which was being printed by Vail-Ballou. Knopf gives advance warning that he will not pay for excessive corrections on another Bradley project, Wanda Landowska's *Music of the Past*, scheduled to be printed at Plimpton. He states that he will not pay for corrections that exceed 10 percent of the composing expense, and his letter reveals that Plimpton, which billed for corrections at an hourly rate, therefore charged more than Vail-Ballou because Plimpton used Monotype, which made it more time-consuming to set corrections.[60] Such details underscore the effect of print technologies on the economic relationship between manufacturing and editorial choices.

Though Borzoi Books were meant to look rarefied, the Knopfs maintained high aspirations for sales, pitching to book clubs and department stores. They achieved healthy sales in America despite the fact that their price points were between 10 and 20 percent higher than the industry standard; charging more than the norm, which ranged from a dollar-fifty to approximately three dollars by 1929, may have enhanced the perception that Borzoi Books were valuable.

Knopf made his prestige-pricing decision in a climate of public outcry against the high price of books, voiced in numerous editorials that attacked publishers and bookstores for pricing books so high that the general public might be forced into "abandonment of the reading habit."[61] (Steady increases in book sales proved that this fear was unfounded.) In 1920, publishers faced a steep postwar rise in production costs, which had increased 67 percent since 1918, primarily because of increased demand for paper and binding cloth combined with higher wages for printers and electrotype compositors as the result of the union pressure previously described.[62]

Far from hiding their above-average pricing, the Knopfs drew attention to it and used it to enhance their firm's cachet. In his postscript to *The Borzoi 1920*, Knopf assures us that his pricing has nothing to do with greed: "By the way, I should like readers to realize this: that I try to make Borzoi Books as well as I know how. Then I base the price on what they cost to make. I do not fix the price first and then try to trim the quality so as to come within that price."[63] However, letters between Knopf and authors, designers, and printers show the young publisher adjusting prices and production budgets in an attempt to respond to projected or actual sales figures. In 1927, he told Kahlil Gibran that he would regretfully have to raise the price of *The Prophet* to at least $2.50 because bookseller discounts and production costs were eating into the profits.[64]

In 1927, four years after Pocket Books was launched, Dwiggins proposed that Knopf could increase sales by selling even lower-priced yet still attractive books, spurring competitors to lower their prices and altogether reducing production costs within the trade. He recommended that the firm "give up the game of faking a standard of book-making that we can't even approximate under present cost conditions, and restudy book-manufacturing on another basis entirely."[65] Dwiggins's suggestion was not heeded until after the onset of the Great Depression.

Whether it's true that a cloth manufacturer was truly shocked to see Blanche present a handkerchief for precise color matching, the presence of such tales is evidence of a more important element: a lasting reputation for obsession with design, regardless of whether that reputation was an exaggeration. There are numerous examples of Borzoi Books that reflect a high level of artistic achievement, but it was Blanche and Alfred's ability to commercialize this achievement that caused the young firm to differentiate itself from other houses that were also implementing high production standards. The Knopfs cleverly united an aura of discipleship to the fine-printing movement with a branding strategy that defied everything for which the fine-printing movement stood.

Perhaps no aspect of the publishing process is more steeped in symbolism than the design of a book. Courting notables such as Adler, Rogers, Cleland, and Dwiggins, the Knopfs were able to build on more than the notoriety of their authors, touting the designers' names in colophons and in other forms of publicity. The heraldic wolfhound presided with an air of refinement, whimsy, beauty, quality, and innovation, transforming the covers and interior pages into a sort of theatrical stage, where the publisher could hold forth alongside the author. Soon after the company's launch, as the Borzoi image became sufficiently well respected to attract other "agents" (both literary agents and authors) as well as booksellers and consumers, the performance of prestige began a run that shows no signs of waning.

It's worth noting that the illustrated wrappers, customized endpapers, decorated title pages, and vibrant bindings of Borzoi Books reflected the sartorial choices of both publishers. Through Alfred's loud but expensive wardrobe, often procured on Savile Row, and Blanche's tasteful but equally expensive clothes, the young publishers packaged themselves as carefully as they chose designs for their books. "She dressed very fashionably in Christian Dior creations," asserted the anonymous author of Blanche's *New York Times* obituary. "At the office she sometimes wore a carmine scarf over the shoulders of a smart frock. Mr. Knopf is a large man, addicted to purple shirts and loud neckwear."[66]

The results of this image-building are echoed in Kenneth Burke's rendering of a reader who purchases self-help books. "*The reading of a book on the attaining of success is in itself the symbolic attaining of that success,*" he observes. "It is *while they read* that these readers are 'succeeding.' I'll wager that, in by far the great majority of cases, such readers make no serious attempt to apply the book's recipes. The lure of the book resides in the fact that the reader, while reading it, is then living the aura of success. . . . He gets it in symbolic form by the mere reading itself."[67] Whether displayed on a shelf or carefully read in solitude (with an audience of only the self), early Knopf books bore heavily branded packaging that surely delivered an experience of custom-crafted luxury, bestowed by a pair of young, highly fashionable literary connoisseurs.

CHAPTER SIX

Bookselling and the Borzoi

It takes talent to write books, but it takes genius to sell them.
Bookseller ADOLPH KROCH, paying tribute to Alfred Knopf

BLANCHE AND ALFRED KNOPF produced catalogs, made sales calls, sent special keepsakes to booksellers, and ran trade advertisements—standard practices that didn't need genius to execute. What was special about the Knopfs' approach to bookselling was the Borzoi brand itself, a memorable, enticing identity that easily became ubiquitous among booksellers and their customers. In the company's early years, Borzoi Books were also available through mail-order directly from the house of Knopf, for customers who were willing to pay a surcharge. This led Blanche and Alfred to play the role of booksellers themselves, corresponding directly with their readers and sometimes even packing the parcels themselves. In each of these interactions, the marketing message was almost always a reflection of Alfred's image: youthful exuberance woven with the gravitas of an old-world literary arbiter.

Blanche's authority in the company grew throughout the twenties, but her voice remained in the margins of Borzoi marketing during these years. As Mrs. Alfred A. Knopf, she cultivated a public identity that was an extension of her husband's. A rare example of her attempt to create a persona distinct from his appears in an unusual *New York Times* advertisement from 1922. The simple typographical announcement could be mistaken for a classified ad, but the copy is striking in an era dominated by male publishers: "MY FIRST CATALOG OF FIRST EDITIONS of (for the most part) younger English and American writers is now ready. . . . *A few desirable French titles are also listed.* BLANCHE W. KNOPF/The Borzoi."[1] During the 1950s, a series of Knopf advertisements carried signed messages from Blanche promoting French translations she had acquired, but in the company's early years, Borzoi advertising messages were signed (literally, in ads that reproduced an autograph) by her flamboyant husband. The fact that Blanche produced her own catalog in 1922 is also a significant anomaly.

Although Alfred appears to have heartily supported Blanche's involvement in the firm, in 1927 he created a unique lunch club called The Book Table and deemed it to be an all-male enterprise. Members included publishers, retailers, librarians, authors, designers, and others in the book trade.[2] Excluding women made little business sense; although few women were achieving positions of power in publishing houses, a 1928 *Publishers' Weekly* study reported that 36

MY FIRST CATALOG
OF
FIRST EDITIONS

of (for the most part) younger English and American writers is now ready for distribution and will be sent on request post free. Almost all my stock is in condition as new.

A few desirable French titles are also listed

BLANCHE W. KNOPF
The Borzoi
220 West 42nd St., New York

New York Times advertisement promoting Blanche Knopf's catalog, 1922

percent of the new book shops launched between 1919 and early 1928 (almost 400 out of 1,100) were owned by women. Nevertheless, it was Alfred's personality that distinguished the company from its competitors. Booksellers remembered his flashy wardrobe, particularly his crimson silk shirts, as a reflection of his dynamic salesmanship. When he was accompanied by Blanche, who quietly cultivated a reputation for dressing in couture, she surely made the pitch seem tasteful.

Introducing the Borzoi

Knopf's inaugural trade advertisement in the *Publishers' Weekly* was decidedly unrestrained. Published in the 25 September 1915 issue, the ad bears the headline "BOOKS YOU MUST HAVE" while the loquacious publisher bubbles away for more than two dozen lines, delivering a pitch that reinforces Kroch's descriptions of the young Knopf. "In the first place these books of mine are good books," Knopf asserts, "and though I have been thinking about it for a long time I cannot recall a single good book out of which both bookseller and publisher have failed to make money." His conclusion reflects a clear understanding of his audience: "Well, the first of the books are ready," the copy continues. "You will sell a lot of them right now and you will go right on selling them as long as you remain in the book business. Not one of these books will ever become a 'plug'; they have already made their way to a lasting fortune. It is up to you now to have them on hand when some of your very best customers ask for them."[3] Only the Russian authors from his debut season are featured in this ad.

Though the *Publishers' Weekly* announcement features the Borzoi logo, the phrase "Borzoi Books" is absent.[4] The illustration of the wolfhound marks one of the few clearly documented instances of former advertising executive Samuel Knopf's involvement in the marketing of his son's company. Though a "kennel of Borzois" (as W. A. Dwiggins called it) would be drawn by various artists over the years, Knopf recalled that the first one was created "by an artist in Barron Collier's organization whose name I have long since forgotten, if indeed I ever knew it. My father had this drawn—he was, at the time we started the business, associated with Collier."[5] The initial Borzoi features a clumsy rule beneath the dog's feet, presumably to ensure correct alignment in the layout. By 1916, a more elegant Borzoi was introduced, leaping freely. With very few exceptions, the borzoi faces "west," to the left, perhaps because of a comment William Addison Dwiggins made when he encountered proofs showing the dogs running "east." He jotted a note of displeasure to Knopf: "These hounds are in retreat, heraldically. What scared them?"[6]

The emblem appears on Knopf's text-heavy early catalogs and copious brochures, but otherwise they reflect a tactic he learned from his competitors; after all, his first lessons in producing promotional materials were learned at Doubleday. Yet his vibrant, self-assured tone established him as a new standard-bearer: "I love books physically," he proclaimed in his 1917 fall catalog, "and I want to make them beautifully. I do no one a serious injustice when I say that American books are *not* beautiful."[7]

Discovering an inventive way to convert books themselves into a catalog, the Knopfs released two unique publications that showed the world who the members of the Borzoi circle were and collected their voices under the imprimatur of Alfred, who clearly loved serving as a master of ceremonies. Produced as commemorative volumes, *The Borzoi 1920* and *The Borzoi 1925* contain essays (sixteen and forty-eight, respectively) commissioned from Knopf authors. Sold today as collectors' items, they are generally thought of as anthologies, but Geoffrey Hellman got it right when he called the 1920 edition an "elaborate catalogue" in his 1948 profile of Alfred.[8]

Blanche and Alfred solicited the essays for each volume, asking Knopf authors to write about one another or provide commentary on broader topics. In *The Borzoi 1920*, Willa Cather's musings, "On the Art of Fiction," are succeeded by an essay on Willa Cather written by H. L. Mencken, which is succeeded by an essay on H. L. Mencken by George Jean Nathan, and so on. Both books feature numerous photographs of the authors, though the frontispiece for *The Borzoi 1920* consists of a hand-written, ink-stained page from the manuscript of Max Beerbohm's *Seven Men,* a lighthearted survey of lesser-known authors who were immersed in *fin de siècle* literary decadence. Both volumes contain A Brief Who's Who of Writers Particularly Identified with the Borzoi as well as bibliographies of all Borzoi Books published to date. *The Borzoi 1925* includes D. H. Lawrence's pithy replies to letters from readers who found his work to be scandalous. Other noteworthy essays include Edwin Björkman's confession that books by Thomas Mann are difficult to read, and a tribute to Kahlil Gibran by Witter Bynner, who used the opportunity to produce a stirring call to end xenophobia. Both books create an alluring image of Borzoi authors as a close-knit, highbrow literary family with Alfred Knopf as their wise old patriarch.

The design features of these hardcover "catalogs" are handsome. *The Borzoi 1920,* produced before the emergence of Knopf's narrative colophon, is bound in lavender paper that is decorated with a black and yellow arboreal motif and was likely procured from the Japan Paper Company. The book is printed on laid paper with modern, smooth-cut edges and a blue stained top. On the spine, the title looks hand-lettered in a clean sans serif script. *The Borzoi 1925* reflects the Knopfs' progression to the use of highly skilled artisans of design. It is bound in varying forms of Japan Paper Company batik with rough-front edges, a gold-stamped spine, and Borzoi endpapers. Thomas Cleland's Borzoi frame appears on the title page and surrounds the initial capital letter of each chapter opener. The volume features an extensive colophon, which states that the print run was 5,000 copies.

Clearly meant to serve a promotional purpose, these anthologies were given as gifts to booksellers, agents, critics, and authors, though they were also sold to the public. Knopf attempted to drum up pre-publication sales of *The Borzoi 1920* with an announcement in the *New York Times* that described "an unusual and unusually interesting little book. . . . *The Borzoi 1920* will be ready in a few days. Your bookseller will take your order now. The price is only one dollar."[9] However, his effort to attract consumers appears to have been unsuccessful. *The Publishers' Trade List Annual* indicates that it took eight years for *The Borzoi 1920* to sell out and seven years to deplete the inventory of *The Borzoi 1925.*

Despite the modern look of *The Borzoi 1920,* in the foreword Knopf places himself in the company of old-world European publishers, saying that the book was inspired by "the catalogs issued now and again by European publishers—no bare lists of authors and titles, but such wholly charming productions as, for example, the annual almanacks [*sic*] of the Insel-Verlag of Leipzig," and hoping that the book would serve "the individual reader, the bookseller, and the librarian."[10] It is not the *concept* of a "yearbook" but the voice—capturing Knopf's savvy role—that makes these anthologies unique marketing devices.

Batik binding, *The Borzoi 1920*

It is also worth noting that *The Borzoi 1920* contains traces of Knopf's early days as a procurer of reprints. The book's introduction by Maxim Gorky, for example, was reprinted from a translation that had appeared in the *Athenaeum* (London) in June of that year.

Consumers did not buy *The Borzoi 1920* and *The Borzoi 1925* in bestselling quantities, but Knopf received copious thank-you letters from those in the trade, often far removed from the publishing nexus of New York City. What's more, he saved these letters as if they were fan mail. Brimming with praise, though written out of obligation to acknowledge the Knopfs' promotional gift, the letters were composed by a range of literary critics at newspapers (such as C. Lester Barnard of the *Tampa Morning Tribune* and George Sargent of the *Boston Evening Transcript*), booksellers (including U. P. James of Cincinnati), agents (Curtis Brown of London), and other publishers, Arthur H. Scribner among them.[11] Retailers found it easy to match these handsomely packaged

Borzoi with the vibrant Alfred, who gave memorable sales presentations and somehow managed to sound wise beyond his years.

This image was perhaps best captured by Adolph Kroch, whose recollections of the young Knopf were echoed in later years by many other booksellers. "A tall, sparse figure, a pink shirt-front, a black tie, and a black mustache," Kroch wrote, describing the first time Knopf called on him as a representative for Mitchell Kennerley. "What did I hear? Garshin, Andreyev, Gogol, Maupassant, Barbey d'Aurevilly, Artzibashev, Kropotkin, and more Russians. Names cherished by me a few years before, revived with a gusto, a slow-burning seriousness, and a fanatic enthusiasm. . . . I felt instinctively that here was a personality who would make his mark in literature or, still better, in American publishing. . . . His letters implied grandeur. They were not sales talks, but literary dissertations and elucidations."[12] Kroch's use of the word "personality" (rather than "person") captures the continuum between the Borzoi's image and Knopf himself, which extended from the acquisition of seemingly prestigious authors to a passion for prestigious book design, forming a cohesive marketing message. Kroch claimed that the binding of *Four Plays* made as much of an impression as Knopf's wardrobe: "The physical appearance [of *Four Plays*] was a departure. No sombre [*sic*] cloth, but gay batik for the binding, with the top harmoniously stained." Kroch continues by perpetuating the myth that 100 percent of Borzoi Books featured colorful bindings: "Booksellers stocked the colorful books that stood out on shelves and tables of their shops. . . . Just what Knopf wanted! Food for thought and a stimulant to the eye. You could see the colorful volumes on boudoir tables of attractive women and carried, unwrapped, by young moderns."[13]

As head of Chicago's largest bookstore, Kroch also reflects Knopf's national sales efforts. Though Borzoi Books were associated with New York, Alfred often proudly credited Midwest booksellers—rather than shops frequented by East Coast intelligentsia—as being his best initial retail outlets.[14] His first order did not come from a bookshop popular with Manhattan bohemians; in fact it did not come from a bookstore at all, but from the department store Marshall Field and Company.[15] By 1925, Alfred was touting the availability of Borzoi Books in Honolulu, where his books had begun receiving praise in the media.[16]

Postcards provided an efficient way for Borzoi Books to build seemingly personal relationships with a wide network of booksellers. One card received by the legendary San Francisco bookseller John Howell is a particularly compelling artifact of this. The Knopfs promoted the publication of Joseph Hergesheimer's *Berlin* with *postkartes* mailed from that city, featuring a photograph of Hergesheimer "in native Bavarian dress," with Alfred's message on the reverse side: "Mr. Hergesheimer has recorded his impressions of Central Europe, and especially of the great cities, Berlin, Munich, Egern, Vienna and

Budapest, in a book entitled BERLIN, which will be published on July 22, at $2.50, by Alfred A. Knopf, Inc."[17] The book was published in 1932, during a decade when publishers saw seismic cultural and financial shifts, departing from Jazz Age prosperity. With a jacket photo that invites tourism, *Berlin* went on sale one week before Nazi candidates won more than 200 seats in Germany's national elections. Hitler was appointed Chancellor the following year, fracturing the transatlantic connections that had heavily influenced Knopf's formative years.

While young Knopf's early publishing activities in Europe consistently generated publicity, he was equally passionate about the less glamorous duty of establishing a Borzoi network within the American bookselling community. Alfred used the contacts he had made as a traveler for Mitchell Kennerley and set about planning ambitious sales trips as far west as St. Louis, Omaha, and Minneapolis–St. Paul. He also hired national sales representatives who worked on a straight commission basis, making an agreement with Louis Greene (later chairman of R. R. Bowker Company) to handle sales in smaller towns on the east coast and in the Midwest. Industry veteran James Crowder was soon retained to represent Knopf in the Chicago territory. Knopf found it a challenge to find representation on the west coast but eventually enlisted Desmond Fitzgerald, who became an initial shareholder in Alfred A. Knopf, Inc. In 1918, Alfred's brother, Edwin, began covering an unusually broad territory that included New England, the mid-Atlantic region, and the South—including Texas. A recent graduate of the Mackenzie School, his brother's alma mater, Edwin was described by *Publishers' Weekly* as "the youngest traveler of any in this year's portrait gallery."[18] Five years later, Edwin left Borzoi Books for the west coast, building a successful career in Hollywood.

Though his sales force grew throughout the twenties, reps such as Greene, Crowder, and Fitzgerald represented multiple publishers. Knopf did not believe anyone could sell Borzoi Books better than he could, so he often felt compelled to call on New York and Midwest accounts personally.[19] In doing so, he was also following a custom of the trade; it was not unusual for the head of a publishing house to make sales trips. He would not make his first trip to the west coast until 1930.

Knopf publicly praised booksellers, but he privately expressed exasperation with them. If he had been able to make time for personally selling his books to customers in stores, he surely would have relished the opportunity. When describing publishers' dummies (blank mock-ups that demonstrate the binding, bulking, and title page of an upcoming book), Knopf claimed that such devices were necessary because some booksellers were not smart enough to buy books based on the contents. Despite his enthusiasm for the physical beauty of his books, Alfred looked down on retailers who couldn't decide whether to order (and in what quantity) without seeing sample bindings and jackets.[20]

Samuel Knopf involved himself in retail matters as well, scoring a victory in a censorship incident—a rare example of the house of Knopf refusing to comply with censors, though the battle was spearheaded by H. L. Mencken, not by Alfred. In 1926, Mencken published a work of nonfiction titled "Hatrack" by the journalist Herbert Asbury in *The American Mercury*. The essay recounted the story of a woman from Farmington, Missouri, who worked as a maid by day and a prostitute by night. Called "Hatrack" because of her angular physique, she was shunned by her church when her secret became public. The essay highlights small-town religious hypocrisy (which is surely why Mencken liked it) but sparked the ire of the Reverend J. Frank Chase, secretary of the New England Watch and Ward Society. The April 1926 issue of the *Mercury* became the subject of litigation when Mencken arranged to have himself arrested in Boston for selling a copy of the banned magazine. Though the *Mercury* prevailed in court, the case cost Knopf $20,000 in legal fees.[21] Nonetheless, he proceeded with plans to publish the essay in a collection of Asbury's works titled *Up from Methodism*. Though he was a descendant of the first Methodist bishop in America, Asbury had turned his back on religion. The book was not banned in Boston, but the bookseller Richard Fuller refused to carry it in his Old Corner Book Store, described by Alfred as a key account. The shop stood in venerable literary real estate; the building had been occupied by Ticknor & Fields from 1833 to 1864. Knopf sales representative and shareholder John Mullen reported the refusal, and Samuel angrily spearheaded a campaign to intimidate Fuller, traveling to Boston to successfully coerce the bookseller into stocking *Up from Methodism*. In the end, the book sold barely 4,000 copies despite the enticing publicity.[22]

This was not Knopf's first tangle with the Old Corner Book Store. In 1922, he reported to Joseph Hergesheimer that he had closed the shop's account because Hergesheimer's *Cytherea*, a novel featuring adultery, was sold from the counter rather than being displayed on shelves.[23] In an odd reversal of roles, the situation was resolved when Fuller invited Knopf to lunch and persuaded the young publisher to allow the old-guard bookseller to remain a customer.[24]

Knopf cultivated relationships with bookstores and department stores in equal measure, participating in an important aspect of early twentieth-century American book pricing. On 1 December 1913, the Supreme Court ruled unanimously in favor of department stores in a case that resolved more than a decade of litigation between R. H. Macy and Company and the American Publishers' Association. Macy's often charged less than the publishers' retail price, creating the potential for price wars with bookstores. Books proved to be lucrative "loss leaders" for Macy's, attracting a clientele that purchased high-margin merchandise in other areas of the store. The APA contended that its members had the right to dictate the retail price of their books. The association also asserted a publisher's right to refuse to sell to Macy's (or any retailer) that would not comply. In the end, the APA was required to pay more than $100,000 in damages to Macy's, an expense that forced the association to dissolve.[25] In a 13 December 1913 *New York Times* interview, a Macy's book buyer referred to as Miss E. L. Kinnear dismissed the concept of loss leaders, asserting that Macy's never technically sold books at a loss because books attracted profitable customers to the store. She also described the channels she used to acquire books while APA members refused to sell to her:

> I found booksellers [relatives and friends] as far South as Texas and as far West as Denver who were in sympathy with me. They would buy books and ship them to Macy's. . . . When the trust [APA] succeeded in locating a dealer who was selling me books, he would be notified to stop that sort of thing or be driven out of business. They were obliged to pay the highest price charged by the trust to dealers. . . . We even went to the extreme of opening book stores in other cities in order to get books. . . . When the commission and the freight charges were paid the price was never far from the price at which we sold the books. But it is not true that we ever sold books at a loss. We sold them, of course, at a loss of profit, but never at less than they cost us in order to attract people to the store.[26]

Her anecdotes capture noteworthy aspects of the market conditions faced by the Knopfs when they launched the company. Books possessed such broad appeal that they were considered necessary department-store merchandise; some leading department stores even had rare-book departments. Much like today, these powerful retailers posed a threat to independent booksellers who could not afford to offer steep discounts to price-conscious consumers. Knopf's decision to set his prices slightly higher than the norm (Tebbel even refers to him as "the pioneer in the $2.50 novel") was an extension of his image as a purveyor of literature whose intrinsic value kept it immune from price wars.[27]

The bookselling marketplace was also characterized by cheap editions distributed by jobbers who sold to drugstores and other non-bookstores. The Knopfs clearly sought to differentiate themselves from this level of drab mass production—and their prices clearly signaled the elite aspect of their identity. The Borzoi identity implied a preference for well-read intellectuals, yet Blanche and Alfred of course welcomed consumers from all walks of life (even department-store shoppers), scorning only retail outlets that purchased through periodical wholesalers.

The Knopfs were publishing in a period that saw cheaply produced hardcovers proliferate as dime novels waned, while ubiquitous paperback lines such as

Simon & Schuster's Pocket Books or the Englishman Allen Lane's Penguin imports would not emerge until the 1930s. Nonetheless, a specter had been cast by newsstand wholesalers of the nineteenth century in incidents such as the 1883 overproduction of paperbacks that "caused such a glut that the American News Company . . . returned to Seaside Library 1,200,000 copies it could not sell."[28]

Perhaps surprisingly, Knopf actively pursued the Book-of-the-Month Club when it was launched in 1926 by former advertising copywriter Harry Scherman. Described by Janice Radway as "a modern selling machine for books . . . that, like Ford's assembly line, installed speed at the heart of its operation in the interest of facilitating ever-faster circulation of goods, messages, and ultimately capital itself," the club represented everything Knopf publicly eschewed.[29] Yet he never hesitated in suggesting Borzoi Books for BOMC, carefully following the club's instructions to submit six bound page proofs of any appropriate books for which he planned a print run of 25,000 or more.[30] Almost immediately, a Borzoi Book was chosen by the club: *The Orphan Angel*, a novel by the American poet Elinor Wylie. In the novel, Percy Bysshe Shelley's doomed sailing excursion takes him across the Atlantic. In Wylie's reimagining, the poet is rescued by an American ship, which brings him to the States for a literary sojourn.

Knopf was even able to persuade Willa Cather, who routinely turned down sizable offers for film or reprint rights for her works, to allow her 1931 novel *Shadows on the Rock* to become part of the BOMC program. Dismayed that Cather refused to allow Knopf to submit any of her works to his program, Harry Scherman tried to remedy the situation through BOMC judge Dorothy Canfield, Cather's close friend since their days as undergraduates at the University of Nebraska. Canfield's efforts failed. Cather "felt most strongly that only people who really *wanted* to read her books should be asked to buy them," Knopf recalled. "At the time the retail book trade was conducting a vehement, though ineffective, campaign against book clubs. I decided to telegraph each of our salesmen to ask the most important bookseller he visited that day whether or not we should let the Book-of-the-Month Club have *Shadows on the Rock*." He assumed that the retailers would agree with Cather's stance, yet all but one buyer very much wanted the book to become a BOMC selection in order to *increase* retail sales. "It was this refusal to sacrifice immediate sales for a longer objective that made the victory of the book clubs inevitable in this battle," Knopf said in his 1964 Bowker Memorial Lecture, adding that while visiting a Midwest shop whose owner scorned book clubs he found "right in the middle of his store—indeed in front of his own desk—a big display of the latest Literary Guild selection."[31]

The Knopfs did not restrict their efforts to retailers and book clubs. Alfred operated an extensive direct-mail business that maintained an air of friendly connections between publisher and reader. Providing illuminating samples of reader-response, the letters he received from loyal customers represent many perspectives on the Borzoi message. The variety of the correspondents is evidence that Knopf believed in giving personalized attention to all of his customers, whether they were members of the Greenwich Village intelligentsia or not. His replies cast Borzoi Books as inviting—never condescending. As a practical matter, Knopf's jacket copy encouraged consumers to write to him and ask for a catalog, permitting the company to develop extensive mailing lists that fostered these "personal" interactions with a fan base. It's a tactic that is most successful in the hands of a marketer like Knopf, who made recipients feel as if they had a pen pal in this publisher. In the early years, such consumers *did* have a personal correspondent in Knopf. His files are rife with carbon copies of replies to inquiries ranging from whether certain titles were out of print to whether a Borzoi translation was underway for various European works.

In some cases, the writers praise the catalogs as much as the books. W. A. Lyle of Atlanta professed to admire the illustrations and wished to obtain back issues of Knopf's other "exquisite catalogues." The reply delivers the unfortunate news that the old catalogs have been discarded, but Knopf says that he may begin to save copies in the future because he receives so many requests for the previous editions, as if the catalogs are becoming collector's items. In response to Lyle's additional inquiry about an out-of-print title, Coulson Cade's *Dandelions,* Knopf agrees to find out if the book can be tracked down, as if he will personally scour the stock room, but he recommends that Lyle place a classified ad in the *Times* or *PW* as a last resort. The Knopfs may have enlisted assistants to compose these many replies, but the effect is nonetheless of a communication from a close friend who caters to all literary desires.[32]

In several speeches decades later, Knopf proudly referred to a Prohibition-era letter he received from William Caven, an attorney in the northeast Texas town of Marshall, who relished being able to procure "intoxicating" Borzoi Books in his desolate locale. He attributes the books' power to their production quality. Caven hopes that the Borzoi will become a better-known oasis in a place that, he says, Mencken would call a desert of intelligence.[33]

Walter Kingsley, the press agent for a vaudeville troupe managed by Edward Albee II (whose son, Reed Albee, became the adoptive father of the contemporary playwright Edward Albee III), wrote to thank Alfred for the catalog and to express his appreciation for the superiority of Borzoi Books. He says he has placed a large order with his bookseller by telephone, inspired by the combination of innovation and intellect presented on the Knopf list.[34]

The perception of quality book-craft as a sign of quality literature is a theme of these missives, but some correspondents indicate that they can't afford Knopf's slightly higher prices. Carl Culpepper of Los Angeles clipped a Borzoi order form he had seen in an advertisement in *The Literary Digest*. Enclosing stamps to cover the postage, he says the books' high price point is a challenge for him, but he feels it is worth it to own as many of Knopf's "elegant volumes" as his budget would allow. The limited editions, however, seem very much out of reach to him. Like Caven, he invokes Mencken, saying that he has a strong following in Los Angeles even though he probably has a negative opinion of the west coast.[35]

Other correspondents include an assistant librarian for the US Army, Carl W. Hull, who relishes Knopf's blend of international and domestic luminaries, enclosing a check for Hamsun's *Growth of the Soil*. Hull declares *Hunger, Moon Calf,* and *Cytherea* to be artifacts of superior craft in book production.[36]

R. W. Pence, in the Department of Rhetoric at DePauw University, used satire to decry the books' high prices, wishing that Knopf would stop sending the Borzoi Books catalog because its wares compete with the cost of food, shoes for his child, and a new grate for his furnace. He praises the rhetorical power of Knopf's personal notes, which always make Pence give in, and he concludes by observing that a catalog stamped with the Borzoi seal delivers the same thrill as a catalog from an English purveyor of rare antiquarian literature.[37]

Book reviewers were of course included in catalog mailings, receiving free review copies as requested. Many reviewers took the time to write letters of admiration to Knopf—an unusual act in a relationship that is typically leveraged in the other direction, with the publisher reaching out to flatter the reviewer. Harry Esty Dounce at the *New York Sun* wrote Knopf to hail the variety and production quality of Borzoi Books and claimed that his reviewers would vie for copies like a pack of hungry animals. Dounce kept *Manon Lescaut* and *Madame Bovary* for himself, promising to comment on these two old-world reissues in his editorial columns. In contemporary publishing, such levels of publicity for reprints would be highly difficult to achieve.[38]

Although the catalogs encouraged consumers to place orders through their booksellers, the Knopfs greatly benefited each time a consumer ordered directly from them, allowing the company to pocket the discount that would have been granted to a retailer. During this period, the Knopfs were free from the contemporary publishers' burden of retailers who return unsold books for credit (a burden that is alleviated by e-books). Except in the college textbook market, this practice of returns did not become widespread until the 1930s, when Simon & Schuster began consignment relationships with bookstores, agreeing to accept unsold copies for credit to be used on future orders. According to Jason Epstein, Knopf described such agreements as "Gone today. Here tomorrow." Such agreements can indeed have a devastating financial impact on certain publishing projects. Designed to ease the financial burdens of the Great Depression, the practice had a negative effect on consumers as publishers tried to cover their losses by raising cover prices.[39]

Cash-receipt figures and other daily income totals from the early years at Borzoi Books are sporadically recorded in Alfred's diaries. Sales totaling $100 per day were not unusual in 1918, though it is not possible to confirm whether these figures include retailers' receipts or are limited to sales to private individuals.[40]

To introduce themselves and their books, the Knopfs were also prolific producers of promotional leaflets for consumer and trade audiences alike. One leaflet, addressed simply "To the Readers of This Catalog," captures rare data on sales figures, revealing that by the end of 1921, sales were up by 88 percent over the previous year, with a majority of those sales coming from books that were priced 25 percent above the industry standard.[41] Leaflets designed for consumers were promoted in Knopf's print advertising with the promise that he would personally send the requestor an informative publication on specified authors, in the spirit of Knopf's Conrad brochure for Doubleday. He often proudly proclaimed that there was no charge for this "service."

In the absence of the company's early mailing lists or geographical sales records, it is difficult to create a portrait of the typical consumer of Borzoi Books. Unlike the trove of data available for early BOMC subscribers, Knopf records tell us more about the type of consumer Blanche and Alfred *hoped* to reach through their extensive sales network. Even if demographic data were available, Lawrence Levine admits the possibility that lowbrow, middlebrow, and highbrow are merely "historically evolved systems of classification" within populations that sometimes defy categorization.[42] What is certain, however, is that whether Knopf's customers lived in Marshall, Texas, or Los Angeles, they could imagine that reading a Borzoi book—or even simply adding the wolfhound to their bookshelves—placed them in elite company.

The College Market

Alfred Knopf clearly believed that nurturing affiliations with universities was a key to prestige, and to prosperity. Ellen Garvey suggests that this belief was not far-fetched. Every time a publishing house's traveling textbook sales representative called on a professor, the reputation of the trade line was enhanced as well: "The cultivation of reputations did not create a brand name, except for those readers who occupied significant gate-keeping roles as critics, academics, and librarians. A strong reputation among academics, however, did benefit other, often more profitable parts of the firm's business."[43]

Knopf's Text-book Department, soon renamed the Educational Department, was launched in 1922 and directed by Columbia alumnus and Carnegie Foundation translator Paul Bernard Thomas. During the 1920s, it was not customary for trade books (i.e., those intended for sale through standard retail trade outlets) to be adopted for classroom use, motivating Alfred to create the new division, for which he paid Thomas only a modest salary.[44] The Educational Department is one of the few Borzoi endeavors for which there seems to be no evidence of Blanche's involvement, perhaps due to her lack of a college degree as much as to her gender.

During the next six years, Paul Thomas and his Education Department created many new series, including Political Science Classics, the Borzoi Historical Series, the Contemporary Thought Series, the History of Civilization Series, Tudor Translations, Borzoi Handbooks of Journalism (which included a guide to writing book reviews), and Students' Library of Contemporary Fiction, which housed a limited number of novels also sold in regular trade editions, including Hudson's *Green Mansions*. Knopf recruited professors to serve as scouts, paying them $100 if one of their suggested manuscripts was published. Among those who served as scouts as well as authors was Columbia alumnus Harry Elmer Barnes, a historian and sociologist at Smith College.

Despite their mutual goal of pursuing prestige, Barnes and Knopf were privately embroiled in ignoble squabbles over money and marketing. Dubbed "radical and aggressive" for being a champion of "revisionist history" (a reputation that only grew in later years, when he became a Holocaust denier), Barnes may have seemed an unlikely candidate to spearhead the Borzoi Historical Series and History of Civilization Series.[45] Nonetheless, his book *The Genesis of the World War* earned public praise from former Harvard President Charles Eliot, and he attracted a substantial number of authors to the series.[46] He also recruited high-profile scholars to write introductions, which served as a form of testimonial to enhance the Borzoi's growing academic circle.

Barnes's abundant correspondence with Paul Thomas and with Alfred Knopf reflects a professional relationship fraught with haggling and conflicting predictions about what constituted a promising manuscript. Barnes frequently complained that his compensation was too low, and he was annoyed by the fact that he received no compensation when he recommended a book that was published by Knopf's trade division. Thomas invoked the evidence of low sales figures for those trade titles, stating outright that Barnes should not be paid for books that were apparently never going to pay for themselves. Like many authors, Barnes was indignant when Knopf billed him for making excessive late-stage corrections to his own works, and Barnes complained that his books were not advertised sufficiently. He envied the campaigns launched by the upstart Simon & Schuster touting the widely read works of Will Durant. Alfred Knopf asserted that no amount of advertising would make Barnes as popular as Durant. Confident in the merits of *Genesis of the World War,* Barnes sent Knopf a check for $2,000, using his supposedly limited earnings to fund a Borzoi advertising campaign.[47]

There is evidence that in addition to the acquisitions fee, Barnes also received royalties on books for which he had served as impresario—a precursor to the model now used by contemporary literary agents. In composing his memoir decades later, Alfred Knopf asked his treasurer Joseph Lesser to clarify what the financial arrangements had been between Barnes and the firm. Lesser's research revealed that Barnes had received 2 percent retail royalty on four history texts released in the 1920s, none of which were written by him: A. C. Flick's *Modern World History,* J. E. Gillespie's *History of Europe,* Harold M. Vinacke's *History of the Far East,* and C. Wittke's *A History of Canada.* There is evidence that other Knopf textbook authors were expected to share royalties with the editor.[48] For example, Alfred Knopf encouraged Walter de la Mare to accept revised terms for the textbook edition of his prize-winning novel *Memoirs of a Midget.* His 10 percent royalty was to be reduced to 7.5 percent while the editor received 2.5 percent.[49]

Knopf was just as precise in crafting his terms of sale for college bookstores. Publishers generally grant a lower discount to bookstores on titles that are required for classroom use, reasoning that the instructor spurred this automatic sale, so the store is entitled to less compensation. The rise of Knopf coincided with the formation in 1923 of the College Bookstore Association, now the National Association of College Stores, an organization that aspired to gain greater bargaining power with publishers. The inaugural issue of the association's bulletin, published in 1928, offers a wry description of the textbook publishing environment at the time. A note from the CBA newsletter's editor, Marion Dodd of the Hampshire Bookshop in Northampton, Massachusetts, acknowledges that some college bookstores "find money in doughnuts or athletic goods or neckties to cover the loss in a text book department." Dodd assures readers that the CBA is "quietly demonstrating to the publishers that the sooner they give us a square deal on the discount proposition and stop discriminating against the College Bookstore as a legitimate outlet for general books, the better for all concerned." Dodd appears to have solicited houses in advance for publishable statements on their discount schedules, and on their interest in stocking college stores with trade books as well as textbooks. While

Macmillan and the John C. Winston Company offered broad good wishes without spelling out their terms, Knopf's notice was markedly detailed:

> The Educational Department of Alfred A. Knopf, Inc., takes this opportunity to wish you a prosperous New Year and to announce that from January 1, 1928, the discount on text-books will be 25%. . . . With this increased rate of discount we will maintain our policy of allowing a 20% return within ninety days from the invoice date, and we must ask that you strictly adhere to these terms. . . . Our trade discounts are decidedly generous. They are as follows: Before publication (all orders) 42%. After publication: All orders containing five books of one title, for the entire order (40%). All other orders (1/3). These discounts apply without distinction to all stores. There is no return privilege with these trade discounts.[50]

The ad also announces that Knopf is adopting a new policy prohibiting a Borzoi book from being classified as both a trade and a text book; all future productions are to be released as one or the other, but the textbooks will continue to have distinct pricing, "so as fully to protect the college bookstores." Knopf's candor regarding discounts may seem as striking as his discussion of a return policy. Some historians of the book have proposed that the "sale or return" plan, which allowed retailers to return unsold copies, had only gradually begun to emerge in the United States in 1907, after being standard in continental Europe.[51] However, ample evidence exists of nineteenth-century trial periods and consignment agreements in the American book trade (the Seaside Library incident among them). Some return periods were as generous as six months.[52] As mentioned previously, the practice did not become widespread in America until the 1930s.

Demonstrating Alfred's commitment to college sales, the new head of Knopf's Educational Department, Wilbur Pearce, gave a presentation at the CBA's first annual convention in 1928. His lecture, "Selling General Books," directly responds to the desire among college stores to be seen as more than textbook vendors. Replacing Thomas, Pearce was repeatedly praised in the CBA newsletter because he had come to Knopf from the Syracuse University Bookstore and, as a former member of the association, possessed considerable credibility.[53]

Despite Knopf's attempts to explain the difference between his trade and text books, a 1928 memo from Thomas to Knopf Treasurer Joseph Lesser indicates that internal tracking of this distinction was sometimes fraught with confusion. The memo spells out complex categories of books that were in Thomas's domain: textbooks "pure and simple"; books originally published by the trade division but later issued in textbook editions; textbooks published in both trade and academic editions; books published in trade editions due to the recommendations of the textbook department; and educational books, such as those comprising the History of Civilization Series, that had been transferred from the trade department.[54] A promotional leaflet blends novels such as *One of Ours* with Harry Barnes's *Sociological and Political Theory,* informing professors that the name Borzoi Books "applies to text-books as well as to books for the general reader. Borzoi Texts represent the most recent progress of scholarship in almost every field of intellectual inquiry." The next line might have had little appeal for an academic audience; it sounds as though it were written by someone who finds school to be dull: "They are not dry compendiums of facts and figures; they are entertaining as well as informative."[55]

The textbook division was launched at an auspicious time, a year after Borzoi Books sales soared by 88 percent.[56] High school attendance in America rose from less than 5 percent to more than 50 percent between 1880 and 1940, in tandem with rising college enrollments and the founding of numerous research universities.[57] Nonetheless, by 1930 the division experienced the same fate as the London office, failing to produce substantial profits. Alfred Knopf sold it to F. S. Crofts & Co., which was owned by his longtime friend Fred Crofts. At least one title in the inventory had no commercial value: Harry Barnes's *The Making of a Nation.* Perhaps hyperbolically, Knopf claimed that he had not been able to sell a single copy.[58]

In today's academic marketplace, hundreds of Knopf titles are adopted for courses each year, primarily through the company's Vintage trade paperback line. Vintage was launched in 1954 at the urging of Pat Knopf, despite Alfred's strong misgivings about the "disposable" traits of the paperback form and the distribution channels associated with paperbacks. The timing for Vintage was ideal: college enrollments had surged as a result of the Servicemen's Readjustment Act of 1944 (G.I. Bill of Rights). Pat Knopf was himself a veteran of World War II, rising to the rank of captain before going to work for his father. Pat subsequently broke away from his parents, co-founding Atheneum Publishers in 1959, but in many ways his greatest contribution to his parents' company was creating a viable entry into the college textbook market.

It is curious that the Borzoi's message of excellence was not as well received among academics, at least not enough to make the venture of a textbook division profitable. In *A Rhetoric of Motives,* Burke reminds us that an essential function of language is as "a symbolic means of inducing cooperation in beings that by nature respond to symbols," a concept that, he notes, has remained fundamentally unchanged since it was implemented by Aristotle and Cicero.[59] For the targeted audience of college professors selecting books for adoption, the Borzoi's uniquely identifying trait—the aura of superior beauty in design and binding—was perhaps a symbol with less relevance. In fact, the reputation of

Borzoi Books as ornamental may have interfered with the Knopfs' attempts to compete with the utilitarianism and conformity favored by competing text-book publishers of that era. The voice of Knopf, embodying verve and elegance simultaneously, induced lackluster cooperation beyond the circles of America's standard book trade.

Although Knopf's first American textbook division did not succeed finan-cially, it lent an enduring trait that enhanced the prestige of the Borzoi identity: Alfred Knopf's stature as a publisher of critically acclaimed historians, includ-ing Henry May and public intellectuals such as Richard Hofstadter. Knopf's decades-long membership in the American Historical Association is further evidence of the significance the field eventually held for him. Affiliations with professors, historians in particular, shaped the image of a publisher who kept company with great minds.

CHAPTER SEVEN

A Majestic Brand

AN EMBLEM OF EXCELLENCE. The merit and success of BORZOI BOOKS is due to the fact that we never publish inferior work. . . . BORZOI is not alone a trademark, it is also an emblem of excellence in all departments of literature, and a guidepost to the best examples. It'll pay you to start reading BORZOI BOOKS today.

1923 *New York Times* advertisement

LIKE MOST SUCCESSFUL STARTUPS, the Borzoi venture owed much of its popularity to well-honed consumer advertising and publicity. While Knopf's publicity and advertising worked in sync with each other, it is the advertising that is continually exalted for taking a novel approach. *New Yorker* writer Geoffrey Hellman noted the unusual voice of the ad copy: "Knopf advertising has long had a peculiar stateliness—half-professorial, half impresario-like." Describing the Borzoi Broadside ads that appeared in *The American Mercury*, Hellman observed that "the publisher's majestic, dogmatic side came through strong and clear."[1] Yet Knopf wasn't the only publisher attempting to develop a distinctive voice. In the period after the war, many publishers sought to personalize their advertising, a practice that met with both praise and dismay. The addition of a publisher's signature was not distinctly Knopf's, either; Doubleday, Page advertising featured Frank Doubleday's signature at the bottom of what John Tebbel termed "take-the-public-into-your-confidence" ads, making it hard to determine whether Knopf or Doubleday was the innovator of this practice.[2] In fact, the use of hyperbolic advertising to sell books pre-dates the Knopfs by centuries.

The first known printed advertisement in English was, appropriately, for a book. Caxton's 1477 Salisburi pye, a collection of prayers and orders for religious services, was promoted through printed handbills addressed to "any man spiritual or temporal," promising "good, chepe" editions that were "well and truly correct," and "imprinted after the form of this preset letter."[3] This rhetorical approach—an earnest tone, despite a message that conveys pride—would flourish on American shores, where in the nineteenth century we find a profusion of approaches that are not so different from Knopf's.

Examples include the publisher John P. Jewett, whose advertising hawked the 1852 novel *Uncle Tom's Cabin* as "THE GREATEST BOOK OF ITS KIND" and contained multiple exclamation points.[4] The 1854 bestseller *Ruth Hall*, whose protagonist is saved from destitution by becoming a novelist, became popular as the result of a three-phase advertising campaign with exaggerated sellout claims, followed by headlines such as "A SUPPLY AT LAST—THREE THOUSAND COPIES PER DAY!" Mason Brothers Publishers also proclaimed the novel to be "THE MOST SUCCESSFUL AMERICAN BOOK."[5] Their promotion extended well beyond newspaper ads; a railway car was named in honor of the author, Fanny Fern (Sara Eldredge's pseudonym).[6] In the wake of campaigns like these, the *American Publishers' Circular* published an article titled "Where, When, and How to Advertise," which emphasized the utter necessity of advertising all new books.[7]

Nonetheless, a perception of innovation permeated the tone of Knopfs' branding efforts, shaping the forward-leaping identity of the Borzoi as well. It was the grandfatherly yet exuberant persona created in the voice of Knopf's ads, not the media placement or the personal tone, that made his strategies innovative. The unusual word "borzoi" was itself a reflection of the intriguing aspects of that persona. In the early 1960s, Alfred told the documentary filmmaker Jules Schwerin that the most appealing aspect of the phrase "Borzoi Books" was its ability to puzzle consumers, thereby making the company the subject of conversation. Anyone who asked what it meant, Knopf reasoned, was providing free advertising for his publishing company.[8] Not surprisingly, H. L. Mencken routinely mocked advertising copy and the gullible American "booboisie" who were seduced by it.

Publishing and the Dawn of the Advertising Age

When the Knopfs launched their company in 1915, the American marketing climate was shifting in ways that reverberated throughout the field of bookselling. Between 1900 and 1930, advertising in America matured into a high-revenue industry bolstered by attempts at market research, usually in the form of direct-mail surveys sent to subscribers. New production technologies such as the rotogravure process made it efficient for newspapers to run photographs in testimonial ads, and fields such as copywriting became professionalized. Granted, market research lacked the higher levels of empiricism of today's campaigns, but the creation of graduate programs such as the Harvard Business

School in 1908, which offered courses in marketing and advertising and housed a Bureau of Business Research, is evidence of an effort to introduce scholarly approaches to the field. In 1930, the trade journal *Advertising Age* was launched.

These signs of progress may have caused publishers to find greater respect for the potential of advertising, or at least greater curiosity about it, but it is important to remember that publishers' marketing budgets were not on par with those of mass-merchandise manufacturers who spurred these advances in advertising. Because much has been inferred about the psyche of the reading public that received publishers' marketing messages during these years, it is equally important to note that psychographic research, which drives highly successful contemporary campaigns by tracking consumers' values, fears, and other emotional traits, was primarily used in the 1920s to simply classify populations according to attitudes. Emanuel Demby, a pioneer in consumer research, notes that "no attempt was made to . . . suggest the existence of segments. . . . All seemed to lack what is now known as a good dependent variable for measurement—how close or how far each psychographic group was to a particular behavior or attitude."[9]

However, the data collected from door-to-door surveys of consumer purchasing habits (exemplified very well in a project undertaken in 1916 by the *Chicago Tribune*) or postcard questionnaires to determine magazine readership (such as the Kellogg Company's extensive 1911 survey) lent an aura of scientific precision to the field of advertising. Such surveys tracked income, home ownership rates, profession, gender, and other demographic data. Furthermore, the Audit Bureau of Circulation, founded in 1914, made it possible for periodical publishers to voluntarily undergo an audit of their newsstand and subscription sales as well as analyses that would aggregate statistics, such as the number of subscribers in rural areas versus in cities or small towns. As advertising rates are closely tied to circulation claims, ABC reports were seen as quelling deceptive industry attempts to exaggerate readership numbers.[10]

Despite a lack of sophisticated psychographic research, many scholars of book marketing during the 1920s describe a cultural crisis fed by the insecurities of a newly urbanized middle class. It's wise to acknowledge that the use of advertising messages as evidence for this "crisis of insecurity" is fraught with imprecision. The advertisements merely reflect the mindset of the almost entirely upper-middle-class advertising executives who sometimes used stereotyping in their attempts to speculate about the target market's mindset. Brewster and Palmer's widely adopted 1924 advertising textbook tried to encourage empiricism, but nonetheless it contains unfounded claims about how receptive an audience might be. One of these claims addresses perceptions of prestige:

We must consider not only the count and character of circulation of media, but also their prestige—that is, the regard in which they are held by their readers. There is a certain prestige in anything that is printed and people tend to place some confidence in a printed message because of the very fact that someone has gone to the expense and trouble of putting it into type. For this reason, even a dodger thrown around on doorsteps by the neighborhood will carry a little weight.[11]

In a similar vein, Helen and Robert Lynd's oft-cited Middletown study was a watershed for the field of sociology. However, it used a limited geographical scope and applied a cultural anthropological approach. In contrast, book-consumer *behavior* is documented in the form of bestseller lists and company sales data on select titles, providing a more accurate measure of purchasing trends than can be extrapolated from ethnographies or from the advertising messages to which an audience was exposed.

Stuart Ewen reminds us that, despite these vagaries, the 1920s was a foundational period for modern marketing: "The rise of advertising and consumerism in the twenties was part of a broader change in the character of capitalist society. Commercial propaganda didn't act as the determinant of change, but was in many ways both a reflection and agent of transformation. Advertising raised the banner of consumable social democracy. . . . As it became the voice of American mass-produced and consumed culture, it did so within a context of shrinking arenas for popularly defined culture," which brings to light a great irony in the use of advertising by publishing houses such as Knopf. Book advertising was occasionally used to pitch the alternative to mass-produced culture, promising readers a level of prestige that would help them rise above the masses and join the literate elite.[12]

The expansion of mass media, including not only national radio broadcasting companies but also nationally linked periodicals such as William Randolph Hearst's newspaper chains, gave manufacturers new venues for touting their wares to these somewhat un-knowable mass markets, creating new streams of revenue for the media moguls themselves. National magazines proliferated, their circulations soaring when subscription prices dropped as a result of increased ad revenue. Despite relatively low budgets that prohibited publishers from making extensive media buys (except for those book publishers who produced their own national magazines), book advertising rose in tandem with the available venues, directly leading to an expansion of book reviews.[13] At the same time, a profusion of "little magazines," such as the *Dial* and the *Little Review*, was seen.[14] Though their circulations often hovered below 3,000, such publications provided a useful means for shaping Manhattan's small but powerful publishing community. Not all small literary magazines went unnoticed by readers of high-circulation magazines such as the *Saturday Review of*

Literature. In "Popular Modernism: Little Magazines and the American Daily Press," Karen Leick notes that publications such as the *Little Review* received frequent attention in mass-market magazines.[15] One key to the Knopfs' success was their ability to attract authors and readers from both segments. In addition to mainstream media, the *Little Review* was part of Knopf's media mix, including a space inside the front cover of the March 1917 issue with copy that reads, "If Quality matters to you, even in a book, ask anywhere for Borzoi Books. Published in New York by Alfred A. Knopf."

Most established book publishers, as well as the many upstart houses founded during this period, experimented with new ways to promote their products. Even so, publishers' budgets were far more limited than those of major national advertisers. When the cultural historian Catherine Turner writes, "Knopf revered literature, but he never hesitated to advertise literary commodities in the same way Campbell's Soup or Listerine advertised their products," she refers primarily to the Borzoi logo's continual appearance in advertising alongside messages that conveyed a consistent corporate image.[16] This approach may have mimicked the branding strategies used to sell household goods, but the budgetary limitations of publishers' campaigns present significant distinctions between Campbell's or Listerine's approach to branding and the relatively small-scale budgets associated with modern American publishing. Emerging national advertising agencies such as N. W. Ayer & Son promoted brands through extraordinarily expensive multi-media blitzes, featuring large-scale sponsorship of radio shows, full-page magazine space (sometimes full color), and nearly daily newspaper advertising. Spanning dozens of cities, billboards were also essential to the mix. Grouping book publishers with leading national advertisers during this period, or in present-day America for that matter, does not make for apt comparisons. Knopf copywriter Frank Irving Fletcher underscored this fact: "A book cannot be 'put over' by advertising in the sense that a breakfast food or a talking machine can be 'put over' . . . books have one of the most limited markets of any commodity in the world."[17]

In setting his limited budget for ads, Knopf followed the norm for publishers: he adjusted his plans according to the sales of the books, assigning minimal dollars in advance of publication and tracking his advertising schedules alongside the tracking of sales and reviews. Unlike manufacturers of motorcars or tooth powder, publishers rarely designated a sizable advertising budget for launching each new "product." For several authors, including Warwick Deeping, Knopf created contracts in which advertising expenses were guaranteed only if the author agreed to take a cut in royalties.[18]

Despite the financial disparities between publishers and wealthier advertisers, the transformation of the advertising industry reflects a transition that enhanced the publishing field: increased literacy, urbanization, and consumerism changed the significance of books in America in the early twentieth century. Whether consumers actually read the books they purchased cannot be ascertained, but Knopf greatly benefited from the rising emphasis on books as status symbols. In *Fables of Abundance,* the historian Jackson Lears draws on two opposing images—the rural cornucopia and the sanitized modern home— to capture this well-documented social shift. As the emphasis in advertising messages turned from sprawling fields to the efficient factory, Lears writes, advertising reflected America's population shifts. Images of semi-corpulent women surrounded by nature were prevalent in magazine advertising in the late-nineteenth century.[19] In the wake of an increasingly urbanized society, the ideal woman depicted on advertising pages began to sport a slender, perhaps even boyish figure. A wise administrator of home economics and germ prevention, she had access to knowledge (standardized "book learning"). A survey conducted by the publishers of the *Literary Digest,* one of Knopf's ad vehicles, included questions about modernization, including whether a reader's home was wired for electricity, and whether the reader owned an automobile.[20]

The visual transition described by Lears was reflected in the voice of book-advertising copy that rejected the rural carnival barker and embraced the essence of an educated, sophisticated leader. Unprecedented levels of consumerism, bolstered by increased consumer credit, implied an audience of shoppers who were deliciously vulnerable to well-honed sales tactics. In a company speech, J. Walter Thompson executive William Esty declared, "We have got universal literacy without very much accompanying judgment; people are eager and anxious to be told what to do and how to do it and when to do it."[21]

Roland Marchand echoes Esty's assumptions, identifying several categories of "parables" that encompass most advertising messages from the Progressive Era, including "the first impression," in which merchandise saves an unwitting novice from social shame. Consumer goods, particularly books, could be advertised as admission tickets for an acceptable social realm—a way of leaving behind the agrarian poverty of the nineteenth century and entering a world where enlightenment would vanquish naïveté. Educating audiences about literature with the tone of a patient professor (or perhaps even a patient parent as described by Marchand), Knopf adopted advertising strategies that cast himself as a reassuring sage. However, as the advertising historian William O'Barr reminds us, "Despite the attractiveness of the inferences Marchand draws about the role of advertising in twentieth-century America, there is no real evidence in this otherwise carefully documented book about what members of the audience for these advertisements actually thought about them."[22]

Frank Irving Fletcher's advertising series for the Borzoi brand exemplifies this mystery of audience attitudes. Fletcher's is the only publishing campaign of its kind, running over a four-month period during the spring of 1923 without ever mentioning a single author or title. Each rendition featured new, amusing copy. Adding to the novelty of the campaign, the ads appeared in the *New York Times* alongside news stories rather than in the weekly book review section. Using books as an advertising medium, Knopf ultimately published the complete Fletcher project as a monograph titled *The Meaning of Borzoi: A Series of Advertisements and a Preface.*

The Borzoi campaign offers a corporate identity that promises to lend a hand to the befuddled, prestige-seeking reader. The use of plural pronouns implies the presence of Blanche: "We do the picking and choosing for you," one ad promises, emphasizing exclusivity. "To achieve the imprint of BORZOI. . . . It must attain a certain altitude above sea level, so to speak, before we will publish it at all." Another assures that "even if you don't know the author, the BORZOI imprint is a guarantee that his work is good." With equal verve, one ad warns the reader to "Never Lend Your Borzoi to a Friend! . . . It is beautifully bound, to begin with—a piece of real bookmaking—artistic in its covers and typography—and just a little too good to share the fate of an umbrella."

A particularly compelling headline in the series capitalized on the oppression of Prohibition, crying, "OH! FOR THE PROHIBITION OF LITERATURE AND AN ERA OF BOOKLEGGING!!" The subsequent copy describes the imagined impact if Knopf's wares were to become contraband, suggesting it would cause "the millions in New York, who never think of a BORZOI" to develop a craving for them. The ad positions Knopf as daring: "We wish that a BORZOI BOOK on the person were more perilous than a flask on the hip," the copy reads, equating the company's "productions of genius" with the "respect now lavished on a cellar of gin." For such a reader, inhabiting a thirsty city rife with ways to circumvent the Eighteenth Amendment, the ad's closing line conveys clever perceptiveness: "We know that if we can sell you a BORZOI volume now, we can come pretty close to keeping you interested forever in the immortal subject of books." Printed in minuscule type, the word "immortal" is easily misread as "immoral."

The effectiveness of the campaign would have been difficult to measure, as a spike in sales could be attributable to factors other than advertising. While national corporations with sizable ad budgets were paying for Starch tests (created in 1922 by psychologist Daniel Starch to measure recall and readership of print advertisements), book publishing budgets forced the literary industry to fend for itself. Tebbel describes a full-page ad run by Little, Brown in 1924 in the *Times Book Review* for Larry Barretto's *A Conqueror Passes* bearing the line, "Does display advertising of a book with quotations from highly commendatory reviews influence you to buy? . . . If you use the *New York Times Book Review* as a guide in your selection of books and are not led to purchase 'A Conqueror Passes,' we should welcome your statement as to why the advertisement has failed to accomplish its purpose." The copy also candidly states that the price of the ad could be recouped only if 3,000 copies of the book were sold. Responses would have resulted in merely anecdotal evidence, but it represents one publisher's attempt to measure the utility of display advertising.[23]

We cannot know how most readers reacted to Fletcher's messages, but the copy paints a vivid portrait of the Knopfs' attempt to define their circle. The Fletcher campaign underscores aspects of Max Weber's concept of status honor, which he describes as "normally expressed by the fact that above all else a specific style of life can be expected from all those who wish to belong to the circle. . . . As soon as there is not a mere individual and socially irrelevant imitation of another style of life, but an agreed-upon communal action of this closing character, the 'status' development is underway."[24]

Despite the dearth of extensive demographic and psychographic information about the readers of mass-market magazines, publications such as Henry Luce's *Time* carried mass-market advertising price tags to match their circulation numbers. Cost is surely the reason why Knopf emphasized free publicity efforts in these venues, saving his print-ad dollars for clearly literary magazines such as *The Saturday Review of Literature,* established by Book-of-the-Month Club editor Henry Seidel Canby, and newspapers in Chicago, Washington, D.C., Los Angeles, and New York. To some extent, Knopf engaged in targeted marketing as well. Ezra Pound's *Pavannes and Divisions,* for example, was not advertised in the *New York Times* but did appear under the headline "For the Intelligenzia [*sic*]" in *The Nation* during the summer of 1919.[25] Knopf's own *American Mercury* may not have possessed an empirically researched audience, but Mencken and Nathan clearly defined the audiences they hoped to offend, constantly satirizing the American middle class that Knopf appears to have wanted to educate.

The launch of the *New Yorker* in 1925 heralded the arrival of a publication that epitomized the irreverent "community insider" and helped authors and publishers broaden their reputations within seemingly prestigious circles. The *New Yorker*'s earliest issues include profiles of upstart book publishers, including Blassingame's piece on the Knopf "trinity" (Samuel, Blanche, and Alfred), and the magazine's first advertisers included Boni & Liveright; Haldeman-Julius; Doubleday, Page; and G. P. Putnam's Sons, all of which bought full-page space during the *New Yorker*'s first year alongside purveyors of tires, perfume, pianos, and fine clothing. Other periodicals came aboard as *New Yorker* advertisers, viewing the magazine not as a threat but as a good investment: The *New York*

Herald Tribune's weekly book review bought a full-page ad reminding readers that a subscription provides access to interviews, poems, and other features "for less than the price of one novel."[26]

The audience for publishers' ads running in the *New Yorker* surely comprised the New York–centric publishing community itself. In a form letter to solicit advance copies for potential review, editor Harold Ross says that the book-review column will be written by Harry Esty Dounce (who had managed book review sections for New York's *Sun* and *Evening Post*), choosing a broad spectrum of quality fiction and nonfiction for reviews that will be entertaining to read.[27]

Surprisingly, Alfred Knopf was slow to add the magazine to his advertising media mix, though it is a staple of today's Borzoi advertising. The first Knopf advertisement to appear in the *New Yorker* promoted Carl Van Vechten's novel *Nigger Heaven*. Published in the 28 August 1926 issue, one week after the magazine ran a laudatory profile of the house of Knopf, the single-column layout awkwardly combined Cleland's ornate Borzoi border with extracts of Miguel Covarrubias's modern jacket illustration. The headline casts Van Vechten's novel as a nightclub tour: "Why go to Harlem cabarets when you can read *Nigger Heaven*?"[28] The ad was placed near a section of the magazine devoted to entertainment venues.

During the magazine's first five years, it soon grew from a whimsical, gossipy, thin publication to a robust showcase of literary talent including Knopf authors, such as the poet Elinor Wylie. The pages became packed with spot-color advertising that bore sophisticated headlines for luxury products aimed at precisely the sort of well-heeled readers the Knopfs aspired to attract. Nonetheless, no further Borzoi advertising appeared in the *New Yorker* until 24 November 1928, an issue that carried a full-page quasi-testimonial approach for Francis Brett Young's novel *My Brother Jonathan*. "Mrs. Jerome Napoleon Bonaparte, prominent in the society of New York, Newport, and Palm Beach, is an enthusiastic admirer of Borzoi Books," the copy proclaims, beneath a large illustration of the pearl-bedecked Mrs. Bonaparte holding her handsomely jacketed new hardcover.[29] The ad was soon ridiculed in the magazine's "Talk of the Town" section, which on 8 December ran a lampoon beneath an illustration of a book-toting woman astride a pony-size borzoi:

> Mrs. Jerome Napoleon Bonaparte . . . is an admirer of Borzoi Books. . . . Her endorsement, incomplete though it was, touched us deeply; somehow we couldn't dismiss the matter, and went around thinking about it, wondering which Borzoi Books she had read, why she liked them, and why the publisher thought we cared whether she did or didn't. Before long a curious, haunting refrain was running through our head: "Mrs. Bonaparte likes Borzoi Books,

Mrs. Bonaparte likes Borzoi Books." Finally, the refrain became confused, and gradually changed into another song—a lilting lay such as shepherds used to sing: "But does she like animal crackers, does she like animal crackers!"[30]

Soon after, the *New Yorker* ran two cartoons that appear to mock the Knopfs' attempts to characterize their readers as highbrow. The first, published on 15 December 1928, depicts a conversation between two workers in a manhole: "Do you do much reading, Bill?" "Sure. I'm an enthusiastic admirer of Borzoi Books."[31] The second, appearing on 2 March 1929, features a woman in a drug-store requesting "some Pond's Extract and a Borzoi book," an affront to the Knopfs, who abhorred the mass-market editions distributed in drugstores.[32] It was brazen of the *New Yorker* to snub its advertiser by implying that the Knopfs' branding efforts made their books lowbrow; by this time, Knopf had published two Nobel Prize winners (Knut Hamsun and Sigrid Undset) and Willa Cather's Pulitzer Prize winner, *One of Ours.*

Knopf was faced with the task of preparing an advertisement to publicize his first Nobel Prize winner in the fall of 1920. An event that required no hyper-bole, the occasion was marked by advertising copy in which the Knopf voice remained uncharacteristically quiet. The text was set in space that measured just one column wide and two inches tall: "Knut Hamsun has been awarded the Nobel Prize for Literature for 1920. 'HUNGER,' one of his greatest novels, has just been published in America. $2.50 at all booksellers. ALFRED A. KNOPF, Publisher. Candler Bldg., New York."[33] The copy is framed only by a plain double-rule box for a layout commonly referred to as a tombstone. The restraint belies the complexity of the novel, whose author who was characterized by Peter Gay in *Modernism: The Lure of Heresy* as "an eccentric among eccentrics, a grimly isolated figure in the history of the novel, the most subversive of mod-ernists. . . . He remained an outsider for all of his large readership, despite the Nobel Prize. . . . Until Joyce's later work, Hamsun's stream-of-consciousness technique was unsurpassed."[34]

Knopf's humble approach to advertising an obscure Nobel Laureate would not last long, however. The following year would see the arrival of elaborate layouts for Knut Hamsun's *Growth of the Soil,* in which the braggadocio would once again dominate the page, complete with the publisher's signature, which was indecipherable but entirely recognizable to those who viewed his subsequent advertising with regularity. Such ads would also extol the hand-some design and production features of Borzoi books with consistent vigor and frequency. It is as if the Nobel Prize served as the ultimate tipping point in the company's advertising, leading Knopf to leave behind a gentler tone on the march toward elaborate, heavily ornate layouts and classically unapologetic Knopf headlines such as "Books for the Civilized Minority," which topped a group ad (showcasing multiple titles in a single space) featuring luminaries such as Camus in the *New York Times* nearly forty years later.[35]

Books "for Just a Few Intelligent People"

In 1921, the Knopfs used the humorous advertising headline "For Just a Few Intelligent People" to promote the works of H. L. Mencken, poking fun at their own elitist image while echoing his intolerance for small-mindedness.[36] For advertisers like the Knopfs, the dilemma of wanting to achieve broad, mainstream sales while maintaining an image of exclusivity was solved by the high circulation and high editorial standards of the *New York Times*, where the voice of Knopf evolved and matured during the Borzoi's first fifteen years.

The book-publishing industry spends more advertising dollars on space in the *New York Times* than in any other newspaper, despite the fact that the efficacy of advertising books in the *Times* has not been measured in any reliable way.[37] Knopf, who had briefly served as a sales representative for the paper during the summer of 1911, was vocal about the dubious correlation between the amount his company spent on ad pages in the *Times* and the amount of revenue generated by the books featured in such ads. Nonetheless, he followed the lead of most other houses and made the *Times* a significant component in his advertising plans, beginning with his first season as a publisher.[38]

For publishers, the *New York Times* represents an exceptional audience due to the high concentration of editors, literary agents, and book critics residing in New York City. Knopf also appreciated the national reach of the newspaper. Traveling to Seattle in 1930, he observed that in towns that had no substantial daily newspaper the *New York Times Book Review* and the *Saturday Review* were eagerly read.[39] Nonetheless, his notoriously colorful voice evolved gradually on the *Times*'s ad pages. The earliest Knopf advertising in that venue demonstrates only a glimmer of his personality's future luster.

Homo Sapiens is the sole title featured in Knopf's first *New York Times* ad. It is a compelling artifact because the design and copy are devoid of Knopf's legendary flair. Published on 30 October 1915, the small-space ad ran in the general editorial pages, grouped with other book advertising alongside journalism unrelated to the world of books. The ad ran again on the following day, appearing in the *New York Times Review of Books*. At first, the ad was assigned to the bottom of the page, though it garnered top billing for the second run on October 31.[40] It is not unreasonable to speculate that Knopf or his father may have called to complain about the poor placement of the initial run. No artwork is featured, but all-type layouts were typical in book advertising during that decade. The Borzoi logo would not be shown in *New York Times* advertising until the following spring.

Despite the constraints of a limited budget and fierce competition for attention on a page crowded with titles, traces of Knopf's hallmark exuberance are evident. Editorial coverage of *Homo Sapiens* in the *Times* included a pronunciation guide beside the author's surname, but no such phonetic assistance appears in Knopf's ad, contributing to the word's intriguing prominence. Positioned above it on 30 October is B. W. Huebsch's ad, hawking translations of Russian novels by Artzibashef.

Elegant borders and elaborate ornamental flourishes did not appear in Knopf advertising consistently until the 1920s. By 1922, Knopf's *New York Times* advertising had begun to feature a typographical border bearing the words "Borzoi" and "Alfred A. Knopf" repeated continually in a small point size. Another distinctive advertising border used by Knopf, comprising wolfhounds and "AK" monograms, emerged during that period as well, the result of Knopf's introduction to designer Thomas Maitland Cleland, through Elmer Adler, in 1922.[41]

New York Times advertisement framed by the publisher's name, 1922

Adler designed Knopf's advertisements throughout the 1920s, often to the designer's tremendous frustration. In 1927, for example, after at last gaining Willa Cather's approval for a series of ads he had set for *Death Comes for the Archbishop*, Adler complained to Blanche that his repeated requests for instructions on production had gone unheeded by Knopf staff.[42] Nonetheless, he was able to execute his production services for the Borzoi's many *New York Times* advertisements with relative efficiency; Pynson Printers was located in an annex of the Times building. Adler's shop first operated on the second floor of a garage on East 32nd Street, but when the *Times's* future president and publisher Arthur Sulzberger joined the newspaper in 1918, he became interested in Adler's work. "I believe it was through Alfred A. Knopf," Sulzberger recalled. "It was I who invited Mr. Adler to come and occupy space in the Times building, where for many years he maintained his typographical shop." Sulzberger also arranged for a loan to cover the rent until Adler's firm was solvent. Moving to his new quarters in 1924, Adler dedicated part of the square footage to gallery space, hosting exhibitions of the work of his favorite artists, who included Bruce Rogers and Thomas Maitland Cleland.[43]

The leaping wolfhound arrived in Knopf advertising in April 1916, coinciding with Alfred's marriage to Blanche. The ad also represents Knopf's first use of group advertising, comprising the only mention of Knopf's first book, Émile Augier's *Four Plays*, in *Times* advertising.[44] There was nothing innovative about the practice of running group ads, and the layouts and descriptive copy used to promote Borzoi Books in 1916 are markedly similar to that of other publishers' advertisements. The Borzoi device, however, makes a dramatic difference in the visibility of Knopf's messages on a crowded page of text. It is therefore surprising that Alfred did not make more extensive use of it in his advertising that year. Throughout 1916, he continued occasionally to run text-only, small-space layouts.

One of these would promote his most frequently advertised book during the company's first five years: *Eat and Be Well* by Eugene Christian, "America's Foremost Food Expert," whose book promises to tell readers "what to eat to be well, how to eat to keep well, what to eat to get well." Despite Knopf's description of the author, Christian had faced criminal charges in 1905 for practicing medicine without a license. Christian mounted an appeal and was successful in reversing a judgment against him.[45]

The typical Knopf "campaign" in the *New York Times* consisted of running a layout once. Occasionally a layout ran twice, almost always on consecutive days, presumably because the *Times* offered discounts for such a schedule. The one-column square ad for *Eat and Be Well*, however, featured no logo or other artwork, and it ran no fewer than ten times in 1916. After a two-year hiatus, the ads reappeared multiple times in the fall of 1919 through January 1920 in an attempt to capitalize on Christmas gift giving and New Year's fitness resolutions. The book's health claims may have also made it of particular interest during the influenza epidemic, but the advertising waves do not coincide with the epidemic's surge in the fall and winter of 1918.[46] In fact, the book was not advertised in the *Times* at all during the surge, despite the fact that Knopf himself fell ill with the flu that year.[47]

The first distinctive design approach in Knopf's *New York Times* advertising is evident in 1916 with arrival of a checkerboard border, from which the Borzoi emblem protrudes. The voice is distinctive as well, persuading by gently balancing charm, pride, and authority. The tone of these small-space messages is the precursor to the more aggressively charismatic voice that would come to dominate Knopf's promotional identity, or as Catherine Turner describes it, advertising that "combines snobbery with accessibility."[48] On 10 December of that year, unashamed of hyperbole, Alfred proclaimed to readers of the *Times* that he had "just issued the most beautiful book of the season, THE RUSSIAN SCHOOL OF PAINTING." The promise that Knopf books were available everywhere was also occasionally replaced with a humbler phrase that nonetheless presents Alfred as a personality: "At your bookseller. If not, write Mr. Knopf, 220 West 42nd St., NY."[49]

The first approximation of a Knopf book jacket in *New York Times* advertising was published on 30 September 1917, with *The Three Black Pennys*. Three-dimensional mock-ups of books in *New York Times* advertising were not common until 1924, a trend spurred by the novels of Zane Grey. Though the jacket elements are extraordinarily rudimentary in Knopf's 1917 layout, with crudely drawn ornamental pennies and a seemingly hand-lettered title belying a sophisticated novel that would remain in print at Knopf for more than fifty years, the copy touts the wrapper: "Jacket in full colors."[50]

Samuel Knopf officially assumed the role of treasurer in his son's company in 1918, which may explain why that year bears evidence of two shifts in Borzoi advertising in the *Times:* an investment in larger space and the presence of longer, more elaborate, and frequently more dramatic descriptive copy, such as lines for Italian poet Annie Vivanti Chartres's *The Outrage* that read, "Before deciding the amount of your subscription to the next Liberty Loan—imagine members of your family in the position of Louise and Chérie—two Belgian women caught in the German invasion. Imagine yourself facing their dreadful problem. Read 'THE OUTRAGE.' It is a story that will make you realize what German brutality and lust means to the individual—what it would mean to you. . . . It is a Borzoi book. 'THE OUTRAGE' is not just a story of Belgium's suffering—not 'just another war book.' It is a production of literary merit and lasting worth. The fact that Mr. Knopf has included it in his list of Borzoi books assures you of that."[51]

That year's advertising concluded with what was at the time the company's most sizable *Times* ad, measuring approximately two columns wide by 10.5 inches tall and featuring eleven books under the unremarkable headline "BOR-ZOI BOOKS FOR CHRISTMAS," which was set beneath a much more noteworthy tagline: "The Russian Wolfhound Identifies Borzoi Books."[52] The titles serve as a useful snapshot of the diversity of Knopf's three-year-old list. They include Carl Van Vechten's *The Music of Spain*, Kahlil Gibran's *The Madman*, and Ralph Kirk's *Zanoza*, described in the ad as "an exciting tale of mystery and adventure with a Russian Wolfhound (Borzoi) for its hero. A rattling good dog story. Pictures by Harvey Dunn."[53] In his foreword to the book, Knopf expresses a wish that he could give every bookseller a copy of *Zanoza*. From that year through 1929, most of Knopf's advertising budget would be spent on such group ads, reminiscent of the sort of line listings that Ellen Garvey noted were being phased out in the 1920s, though Knopf's flamboyant voice once again distinguished his crowded group ads from those of his competitors.[54]

The copy in most Knopf group ads emphasizes blurbs from critics and other authors. The effect, particularly in Knopf's numerous tall group ads, is to showcase a roster of names—reviewers, biography subjects, and authors—including George M. Cohan, Molière, Maupassant, Conrad, Ibañez (whose name was typeset without the tilde but was accompanied by a phonetic guide for Castilian Spanish: "ee-bahn-yeth"). The message to the publishing community is that Knopf travels in good company, while novice consumers can join in without worrying about making pronunciation gaffes.

Throughout the 1920s, it was the distinctive Knopf persona that proved to be so successful in setting Borzoi Books apart. Even the simple detail of referring to Knopf with the honorific "Mr." added personality to the identity behind a company that, by its fourth year of existence, was receiving consistent review attention and enjoying financial solvency.[55] In his advertisements, he emerged as a master of ceremonies that year: "Mr. Knopf's List just published" (6 June), "Mr. Knopf recommends . . ." (4 July), "Mr. Knopf's Fall Announcement" (25 July).

In a persuasive sleight of hand that certainly distinguished Knopf from other publishers, he satirically referred to himself as a master of understatement. In long-winded promotional commentary that fills two back pages of Warwick Deeping's novel *Kitty*, Knopf wrote:

Shortly after the publication of *Sorrell and Son* the publishers received from an American author [subsequently identified as Alice Brown] noted for her own beautiful and careful craftsmanship a letter of criticism and protest. Her complaint was that the advertisements of the book—written, it should be explained, by a publisher who has convictions about the force of understatement—erred on the side of carefulness; she called for a greater enthusiasm, a little more lavishness of adjective. She said that, from the advertisements, one "didn't get an idea of the unusual character of the book—written as it is with such distinction, truth, and charm."[56]

In fact, Knopf's advertising copy for *Sorrell and Son* was not lacking in flamboyance. An early *New York Times* ad for the book even contained the word "adjective": "A Book for Every Father and Every Son. Delightful, moving, engrossing, fascinating are adjectives that may well apply."[57] His praise is underscored by exuberant praise from the British press, set in boldface above the equally exuberant Borzoi emblem.

On 7 November 1920, Knopf ran a group ad featuring not one but four Borzois, stacked in a striking row to signal announcements of the novel *Moon-Calf,* by Floyd Dell, and the short-story collection *Youth and the Bright Medusa,* Willa Cather's first book to carry the Borzoi mark.[58] Cather believed that Houghton's advertising copy was too impersonal, and she admired the fact that Knopf's ads showcased quotations from favorable reviews within just days of the reviews' publication. Houghton had attempted to promote her books using a personal epistolary tone in October 1915, two weeks before Knopf launched his company. However, the advertisement, which ran in the *New York Times,* contained an unfortunate typographical error in its opening lines, hailing the release of *The Song of the Lark* thus: "Messrs. Houghton Mifflin Company take pleasure in announcing a new and impotant novel."

When Cather approached Knopf and subsequently allowed him to publish *Youth and the Bright Medusa,* she had not yet agreed to publish her novels with him. During this trial period, Knopf advertised the story collection not only in the *Times Book Review* but also in the *New Republic,* a vehicle rarely used by Houghton to promote fiction. The copy for this 29 September 1920 advertisement included the lines, "There are not many living writers from whom a new book commands the attention with which each successive volume of Miss Cather's is now awaited. There seems to be no disputing the fact that she is our foremost living woman novelist."[59] Regardless of whether such copy would influence a consumer, the message does a marvelous job of flattering the author. Cather made Knopf her publisher soon afterward, and the timing was a boon for him when, in 1923, *One of Ours* became the first Pulitzer Prize–winning novel to bear the Borzoi logo. For books that sold as well as hers, Knopf prominently listed the number of printings in advertisements—a move that was surely aimed at authors more than at consumers.

Knopf celebrated his acquisition of Cather's work in a remarkable advertorial published in the *New York Times* in 1922. Under the headline "History of a Publishing Season," with typesetting, photo credits, and a layout that blended seamlessly with the editorial look of the *Times*, this advertisement ran adjacent to the day's news, not in the *Book Review*. The tone is anything but journalistic as Knopf chats about his authors as if they were a close-knit circle, announcing his new publishing agreement with Ernest Boyd in patriarchal prose: "I am glad to take this opportunity to announce publicly that Mr. Ernest Boyd, formerly of the editorial staff of *The Evening Post*, is now one of the Borzoi official family." He also notes the recent death of two Borzoi authors, W. H. Hudson and Wilfred Scawen Blunt, with the observation that although "the year has been saddened by the death of two friends and authors . . . each will live through his books." The ad closes with Alfred's signature and an invitation to correspond with him "about the above or any other of his publications."[60]

Though Knopf's consumer advertising plans throughout the 1920s mirrored the Cather program, featuring group ads in magazines and in the *New York Times*, he also occasionally purchased space in city newspapers other than the *Times*. Such buys were not innovative for publishers: Knopf bought 410 lines total in Chicago's *Daily News*, *Tribune*, and *Post* in January and February of 1919, for example, but that paled in comparison to the lines of Chicago ad space bought by E. P. Dutton & Co., Harper & Bros., or Charles Scribner's Sons, all of which numbered in the thousands.[61] Knopf advertising also appeared in the *Washington Post* in the 1920s, though evidently none of the layouts featured the works of Langston Hughes, who received copious publicity in the paper as the city's "Negro poet." Carl Van Vechten's *Nigger Heaven*, however, was included in a holiday group ad run in the *Washington Post* under the headline "LANDMARKS OF A MEMORABLE SEASON."[62]

Not surprisingly, Knopf advertising in the *Los Angeles Times* often featured books that were made into motion pictures, including Deeping's *Sorrell and Son* and Hergesheimer's *Cytherea*. One advertisement in the *Los Angeles Times* provides evidence that Knopf very likely offered cooperative advertising agreements with retailers in his company's early years. Such agreements allow a bookseller to receive accounting credit from a publisher for the cost of bookseller advertising that is dedicated to that publisher's books. Published on 10 February 1924, an ad placed by the west coast department store chain J. W. Robinson Co. touts "eight new Borzoi Books which might have been planned as Valentines," including Storm Jameson's *The Pitiful Wife*.[63]

New Media

While magazines and newspapers proliferated, non-print media also evolved during this time period. Radio, which many publishers feared would eliminate their industry, actually helped to sustain readership in America. Publishers emphasized radio publicity rather than sponsorship of individual shows, probably due to budget constraints. By 1926, at least ten regularly scheduled talk shows featuring books, hosted by locally well-known speakers, were broadcast in the United States. These ranged from Joseph Henry Jackson's Oakland program on Monday nights (Jackson was the literary editor of *Sunset* magazine) to Chicago's Harry Hansen of the *Daily News*, who broadcast on Tuesday nights. Doubleday used this medium more than other publishers, garnering an unprecedented sixteen million listeners in a historic book-radio tie-in with the release of Edna Ferber's *Show Boat*. "A front-cover advertisement in PW announced that the house was 'Broadcasting *Show Boat*!' and three days later, the Eveready Hour did just that, with Lionel Atwill announcing and Russell Doubleday introducing the performers and musicians. . . . It was the widest publicity ever given to a single book," John Tebbel asserts.[64]

On a smaller scale, the *New York Times* radio-program listings for the 1920s include frequent references to programs featuring books, such as the 9 p.m. literary hour from Newark's WJZ, but authors are not specified.[65] Though it is reasonable to assume that Knopf authors would have been among them, also appearing on shows listed in other newspapers coast to coast, I have found no evidence that the house used this medium before 1930, when Joseph Hergesheimer sent a telegram to Blanche extolling the dignified and charming promotion she delivered on air for his fiction.[66]

Joan Shelley Rubin explores the relationship between early radio programs and innovations in book promotion in her groundbreaking work *The Making of Middlebrow Culture*. Noting that the airwaves were often used for educational purposes in the days after the Great War, with the emergence of licensed stations, Rubin argues that the medium was heavily influenced by the involvement of scholars, which in turn led book publishers to want to be a part of it—a synergy that Knopf clearly valued, as demonstrated in his attempts to gain prestige through textbook publishing. "By 1923," Rubin writes, "seventy-two universities, colleges, and schools had obtained broadcasting licenses. Many educational institutions, regarding the medium as an arm of university extension divisions, gave listeners the opportunity to pay tuition and receive degree credit for courses they 'took' on the air. They often paraded a procession of faculty members before the microphone."[67]

Rubin also describes a climate in which radio's literary lectures further enhanced the perception of authors as learned authority figures, whose books could promote the reader's prestige and social mobility. Joy Elmer Morgan, who chaired the National Committee on Education by Radio, championed radio's power to improve "quality thinking among the masses."[68] But eventually the quest for bigger profits obliterated the surge in educational radio programming that marked Borzoi Books' early years. Competition for available channels, combined with the rise of privately owned stations financed by ad dollars and an increase in network broadcasting backed by national advertisers, forced many colleges and universities to either share their air time or withdraw altogether. A 1930 Supreme Court ruling sounded the death knell, declaring that educational stations were not entitled to special standing.

The refined aura of books and authors endured, however. The commercial book programs for radio retained a theme of empowering a supposedly insecure audience while delivering tasteful messages. Protestant minister Edgar White Burrill's "Literary Vespers," launched in 1922, also united the threads of practical living and Matthew Arnold's character-building. Burrill would read literary passages aloud, then link them to current events. But the most significant marriage between book promotion and radio emerged in the form of book reviews, sometimes delivered by managers of bookstores. One of the most successful radio book reviewers during the medium's dawn was Joseph Henry Jackson, a newspaper critic and travel writer whose "Reader's Guide" series began in San Francisco in 1924 but eventually aired nationwide on NBC. The key to his popularity may have lain in his concerted efforts to avoid sounding like a teacher, envisioning himself addressing people in a living room rather than a classroom, facing "easy chairs rather than rows of desks."[69] The conversational tone he adopted set a new standard for the form and, in a reality not lost on publishers, lent itself beautifully to sales pitches under the guise of criticism. It was not until the 1930s, however, that network book broadcasts became the norm, and nationally recognized authorities blended celebrity with book criticism. In their early years, radio book reviewers were generally obscure commentators who perfected the voice of the friendly "living-room conversation."

An additional turning point in the use of radio for book promotion occurred, surprisingly, in the wake of the stock market crash that signaled the Great Depression. Despite (or perhaps because of) looming economic peril, ten publishers, ranging from Knopf to Simon and Schuster, joined with the American Book Bindery to sponsor the first nationwide book-review program, "The Early Bookworm," which debuted in October 1929. Hosted by the legendary theater critic and Algonquin Round Table regular Alexander Woollcott, "The Early Bookworm" aired not early in the morning but during the lucrative 7:45

to 8:00 after-dinner time slot. It was broadcast on the CBS affiliate WABC, a station that could provide hook-ups to thirty-three affiliates. Though the audience was vast, Woollcott's tone was intimate, conveying the spirit of a gossipy, dynamic buddy who would speak candidly about the publishing world's latest products and his opinion of them. The advertisers required Woollcott to restrict his reviews to their books, though he could choose freely among them.

Promotional tie-ins for the show were diverse. One such tie-in contributed to the sense of intimacy and audience involvement that was Woollcott's hallmark: a thirty-two-page "Radio Book Chat" booklet was printed by the American Book Bindery and distributed to listeners as well to bookstore owners, featuring personal information about upcoming authors whose works were going to be reviewed on "The Early Bookworm." This lengthy brochure also promoted contests for the best review, written by a listener, for any of the titles featured on the show.

An additional way in which Knopf capitalized on emerging media was his decision to film his top-selling authors and submit the footage to Pathé News, a French motion-picture company and distributor of newsreels. The *Washington Post* film critic Felicia Pearson called the scheme "an advertising stunt that will acquaint us with the faces of our best-known names. Which is like looking t'other end of the telescope for us movie fans who are usually busy learning the names of our best known faces."[70]

Not all book-promotion strategies reflected technological innovations. One "new" practice involved a centuries-old medium: the human street hawker. In 1921, Knopf hired a group of men to wear sandwich boards promoting *Moon-Calf*, the autobiographical novel by the socialist Floyd Dell, who recently had been acquitted on charges of violating anti-espionage laws related to his work for *The Masses*. The sandwich-board crew was instructed to troll Times Square and Wall Street wearing artists' smocks and tam-o-shanters, presumably to position Dell as a bohemian. Samples of the book were displayed on the boards, which also showed the names of nearby retailers who had been enlisted to track the effectiveness of the campaign. *Moon-Calf* was indeed a top seller, though the direct impact of the street team is not known; the book was advertised in newspapers as well. The only evidence that Knopf was pleased with the results of the street team is the fact that he continued to use the technique for other works, including Henry Aikman's novel *Zell*.[71] While Knopf was hawking books by old-fashioned means at the street level, however, the small, new progressive house of Covici-Friede hired a skywriter to emblazon the skies over Manhattan, the Bronx, and Brooklyn with the word MURDER, followed by a question mark, to promote the title of a novel by Evelyn Johnson and Gretta Palmer.[72]

Mass transit provided another opportunity for publishers to experiment with advertising. In 1924, Brentano's (at the time both a publishing house and a book retailer) rented advertising space inside Fifth Avenue buses.[73] The book that Brentano's chose for this campaign was Ernest Pascal's *Dark Swan*, which was also made into a silent film that year, as were several of Pascal's other novels. Knopf also experimented with transit ads, but this was the result of convenience rather than innovation. Samuel Knopf was able to negotiate complimentary train-car advertising on the Long Island Rail Road for Borzoi Books, with the promise of adding an air of sophistication to the commuter rail in an era that equated books with prestige.[74] Samuel negotiated this with his employer, Barron Collier, who in addition to owning a large advertising firm was also a streetcar and real-estate magnate.[75]

Publishers' budgets do not appear to have permitted advertising on the spectacular electric signs that transformed Times Square into a colorful commercial showcase during this period. However, billboards formed a supplemental advertising medium for book publishers in an era that saw outdoor advertising proliferate alongside sales of the automobile. Knopf's major bestseller, Warwick Deeping's *Sorrell and Son,* was advertised on a large, upper-Broadway billboard in 1926. Knopf used the medium again the following year to promote the Borzoi brand itself, under the headline "Now you can buy books by the label."[76] Again, Knopf was not the innovator in the use of this medium to promote books. Boni & Liveright, for example, made use of billboard space at 42nd Street and Fifth Avenue, visible from the New York Public Library. Reflecting the budget disparities between the branding of toiletries and the branding of publishing houses, Boni & Liveright touted Emil Ludwig's *Napoleon,* one of the bestselling books of the decade, on a diminutive sign that was perched atop a far more noticeable four-story billboard promoting Colgate's Ribbon Dental Cream.

Once one of the most widely known book-advertising agencies, Spier New York (now WKP-Spier) was founded by a member of Knopf's marketing team whose duties extended well beyond the realm of advertising.[77] On staff as Knopf's publicist in the early 1920s, Franklin Spier played a key role in developing the voice of Knopf in the media, jockeying with dozens of other book publicists for media attention.[78] Curiously, Knopf rarely mentioned Spier in later interviews. Though he engaged in frequent name-dropping regarding book designers and literary agents when looking back on the success of Borzoi Books, Knopf seldom mentioned the names of marketing personnel who had fostered the growth of his company, almost giving the impression that editorial and promotional coups were solely the result of his and Blanche's efforts. Spier was one of many marketing mavens who participated in the professionalization of publicists in the early twentieth century. A landmark publication in the field was the 1928 release of *Propaganda,* published by Horace Liveright and written by Sigmund Freud's nephew, Edward Bernays, who is often hailed as the father of modern public relations. In candid chapters, Bernays boldly equates public relations with the free world: "The conscious and intelligent manipulation of the organized habits and opinions of the masses is an important element in democratic society."[79]

In addition to procuring media attention for Borzoi Books, Spier's duties also included coordinating an extensive network of touring authors, who were encouraged to accept invitations for book signings in towns far removed from the entertainment centers of New York and Los Angeles. Joseph Hergesheimer's bookseller visits ranged from an afternoon at Stokes and Stockell bookstore in Nashville to the Brick Row Book Shop on the Yale campus, for example.[80] Of course, not all authors felt comfortable with the carefully strategized, exhaustive book tours recommended by the Knopfs. Kahlil Gibran received a delicately persuasive letter from Blanche assuring him that giving readings at bookfairs across the country (particularly one hosted by department store Joseph Horne Company in Pittsburgh, which she cited as a good starting point for the fearful author) was not necessarily distasteful.[81] Touring was a Knopf imperative, and Spier often handled the logistics of this process.[82]

Dozens of Borzoi authors demanded that Spier execute their publicity ideas, ranging from the minutia-laden to the grandiose, and Carl Van Vechten was surely the most prolific of these authors. When Van Vechten informed Spier that a local fan had recently commissioned an elaborate bracelet reflecting the catalog of jewels described in *Peter Whiffle,* Spier patiently requested the woman's address so that a photographer could be dispatched, accompanied by a newspaper columnist to conduct an interview with the bracelet.[83]

Spier was equally tenacious in the publicity campaigns that truly set the Knopfs apart from their publishing peers, promoting the publishers themselves in equal measure with the promotion of their authors. From Blanche's affection for "riding the hounds" in Westchester County to Alfred's affinity for pink shirts, the Knopfs basked in the limelight to a degree that could have only been the result of tireless efforts on the part of a shrewd publicist. Their trips abroad were a routine theme of this continual campaign.[84] In addition, because the publishing industry is one of the few creative ventures in which the artists (writers) incestuously also serve as critics, Spier's efforts to expand the Borzoi's network of book reviewers was crucial to the development of the Borzoi's author roster as well. Each time his secretaries produced a mailing list for review copies, they did more than fulfill a clerical task on the Addressograph labeler. Reviewer mailing lists often contained the names of current and future

Knopf authors, preparing editorial inroads that Spier and other publicists were expected to exploit to the fullest possible extent. Clarence Day, for example, whose autobiographical collection *Life with Father* became one of the top-selling Borzoi Books, was brought to Knopf's attention by house author Max Eastman, who liked Day's book reviews in *Metropolitan* magazine.[85]

The Borzoi's marketing image was effective because the aura of prestige was seamlessly blended with brash promotional techniques. The unique flair of the Knopf voice was presented consistently to retailers, consumers, authors, critics, and agents alike. This formula proved to be enduring perhaps because it was as versatile as it was consistent, uniting an array of traits. The Borzoi managed to conform while rebelling, surprise while maintaining a sense of dependability, lend an air of sophistication to middlebrow titles while popularizing obscure literature, and merge with the establishment while reveling in the opportunities of being a newcomer.

Blanche and Alfred performed dual roles, arbitrating literary taste and creating an appetite for their brand of literary prestige. Conveyed through a sales representative's brochures, an announcement in the *Washington Post,* or a publicity blurb in the *New York Herald,* the Knopfs' marketing messages formed the script through which their company's identity could be performed, while their company's sales figures swelled. By enlisting designers who created both the books and the advertising, the firm could seamlessly communicate their ideals.

In such communication transactions, whose purpose is commerce, the rhetor (agent) is typically thought to be someone who has a commodity to sell, while consumers comprise the audience. For the Knopfs, however, the audience included not only consumers but also literary agents, booksellers, authors, and to some degree other publishers, who had the ability to accept Alfred Knopf into their circles, satisfying his appetite to be seen as a member of a band of elite powerbrokers at the helm of America's literary marketplace. During the company's early years, the scripts he chose gave Blanche a public voice that was only an extension of his, yet her presence, made known more frequently through publicity or sales calls than through traditional advertising, became a paradoxically unspoken aspect of his script, reminding the audience that he had not struck out alone in his publishing venture. Where Blanche appeared to loyally follow him, so might other bibliophiles.

The Knopfs came of age upon a new stage, in a scene populated by publishers such as Liveright and Kennerley—men whose reputations ranged from daring to foolish. As the Knopfs crafted their identity, their marketing messages alluded not only to who Blanche and Alfred were but also to who they *weren't.* To differentiate Borzoi Books, the Knopfs' marketing script by necessity carried claims that distinguished their house from competitors—those ignoble publishers who would sell formulaic, commercial plots, packaged in cheap bindings that would not endure (and did not need to endure, as the pages within them bore disposable works that had no chance of longevity).

Capitalizing on an era rife with new media strategies, Borzoi Books became both an enticement and a fulfillment for readers (including the publishers themselves) who craved being seen as cosmopolitan, enlightened, and more intelligent than mass-market throngs. This was the promise of the company's marketing messages, symbolized by an elegant, energetic, exotic dog and conveyed in entertaining copywriting that urged America to believe in the majesty of Mr. (and Mrs.) Knopf.

AFTERWORD

The Legacies

> When all scores are settled, it will be written that Alfred Knopf was the greatest publisher this country has ever had.
>
> JOHN HERSEY, eulogy for Alfred Knopf

WHEN THE HOUSE OF KNOPF turned fifty in 1965, *Newsweek* published a tribute written by Saul Maloff, who claimed that the house "harks back to a time when publishing was a profession for cultivated gentlemen instead of a more or less hot investment for bull-market speculators who wouldn't know a book from a portfolio."[1] Blanche, who clearly contributed to the "cultivated" image of her profession, died the following year at the age of seventy-one, six months after the firm's anniversary gala. Alfred survived her by eighteen years, marrying Knopf author Helen Hedrick in 1967.

Maloff's tribute was published in the wake of the sale of Alfred A. Knopf, Inc., to Random House. The sale was tied to a 1959 decision by Bennett Cerf and Donald Klopfer to offer 30 percent of Random House stock on the New York Stock Exchange. Within a year, the share price had rocketed from $11.25 to $45.00. Motivated to encourage investors further, Cerf and Klopfer expanded their business, purchasing Knopf in 1960 and Pantheon in 1961.[2] Cerf reportedly bought Knopf for a price tag of $3 million paid in Random House stock, placing Blanche and Alfred among the corporation's principal shareholders. Borzoi sales in 1959 topped $4 million, while Random House's sales for the same year topped $12 million. The merger made front-page news in the *New York Times,* and *Time* magazine announced the venture with the headline "Borzoi at Random," characterizing the players in colorful terms: "Former employees of Alfred A. Knopf, a publisher with the appearance and manner of a retired Cossack sergeant, recall that on frequent occasions when Knopf was displeased, he would rumble: 'If this keeps up, I'm going to sell to Bennett Cerf.' . . . Knopf and his wife Blanche, an aloof, astringent woman . . . will still run the publishing house as an independent fief under the Random suzerainty, and their books will retain the familiar Borzoi escutcheon. . . . Knopf wears a walrus mustache and alarming purple shirts with pink ties, while Cerf blends into the grey-flannel landscape."[3]

Blanche and Alfred had groomed their son, Pat, to inherit their firm, but to their bitter disappointment, he struck out on his own, co-founding Atheneum Publishers in 1959. Just six years after Cerf orchestrated the Knopf acquisition, he sold Random House to the Radio Corporation of America (RCA). The merger was commemorated on Knopf letterhead with the image of a borzoi cocking its ear toward RCA's gramophone logo.[4]

Although Alfred Knopf continued to oversee operations at his firm, his involvement was sporadic. He officially retired in 1972 and subsequently served as chairman emeritus until his death in 1984. After he sold his firm, the reality of Borzoi Books as valuable commodities was proven repeatedly during the additional corporate mergers that continue to mark America's book trade. If Pat had assumed the reins, his father's firm might have remained independent, but with the exception of W. W. Norton (which is employee-owned), all of America's major houses have eventually become part of a conglomerate. Knopf's award-winning, lucrative backlist enhanced the prestige of its parent company in 1988 when RCA sold Random House, Inc., to Si Newhouse's Advance Publications. Knopf was once again a key asset in 1998, when Newhouse sold "big Random" to the German media corporation Bertelsmann A.G., whose American publishing arm comprised Bantam, Doubleday, and Dell.

Following the Bertelsmann acquisition, which put Knopf in the hands of German owners, *New York Observer* reporter Elizabeth Manus contrasted the lavish Newhouse budgets with Bertelsmann's austerity plans: "Life under Mr. Newhouse was freewheeling: Lincoln Town Cars, long lunches, large author advances. . . . Expenses for hotels and airline trips have been trimmed. The mailroom has been outsourced. . . . And Knopf, always known for beautifully designed books, now finds itself with a new paper merchant." Manus quotes Andrew Hughes, then vice president of production and design for the Knopf Group, as saying, "It's a matter of opinion whether you think it's as good as the paper we used in the past. The mill said they'd make enhancements." It is obviously unusual for news coverage of a publishing merger to turn to speculations about whether the quality of a house's paper will be diminished, but this underscores Knopf's enduring blend of book production and promotion.

Manus reminds readers that the Random House Trade Group and Alfred A. Knopf, Inc., are "two of the nation's most prestigious houses," and "with flair, edge, and gravitas, Alfred A. Knopf has set a high-water mark in American publishing." Despite fears of budget cuts, Knopf fared well after the 1998 merger, retaining its prestige within its new corporate home in part because of the profitable Vintage editions of Knopf's backlist—a trade paperback line created in 1954 by Pat, who overcame fierce opposition from his paperback-abhorring parents. Pat was following in the shadow of Jason Epstein's new Anchor Books line at Doubleday, which created the revolution of quality paperbacks in 1953. Knopf publisher Ajai Singh "Sonny" Mehta redesigned and revitalized Vintage when he joined Knopf in 1987. A decade later, Vintage had become a $100 million imprint, with rewards that extended beyond a healthy balance sheet. Manus reports that Peter Olson, Bertelsmann's chief executive in the wake of the 1998 merger, told Knopf staff members that Vintage would have first right of refusal on the new corporation's best books.[5] Soon afterward, Olson oversaw a reorganization in which the profitable Anchor imprint was removed from Doubleday's oversight and merged with former protégé turned rival, Vintage. Yet Olson's management of Random House, Inc., failed to achieve expected levels of return on investment. In 2008, Bertelsmann replaced him with Markus Dohle, a native of Germany who had never before worked in book publishing but who had served as director of a printing operation. Educated in industrial engineering at the University of Karlsruhe, he represents the antithesis of the Knopfs' artisanal literary persona.

Under a mandate from Dohle, the firm where Alfred Knopf landed his first publishing job—Doubleday—was subsumed under the Knopf Publishing Group. Reflecting the new reality of an emphasis on the conglomerate's bottom line, rather than the success of individual imprints, the restructuring was announced during a period of exceptional commercial triumphs for the house of Effendi: in 2009, Doubleday published more bestsellers than Knopf, and the two top-selling novels in America were Doubleday's (Dan Brown's *The Lost Symbol* and John Grisham's *The Associate*—modern-day equivalents of the blockbuster Tarkingtons whom Blanche and Alfred eschewed).[6] Blanche and Alfred might not have approved of Dohle's industrial background, but they might have been quite pleased by Knopf's "acquisition" of Doubleday because it indicated European approval; it was a sign that Bertelsmann's leaders recognized the overall achievements of their most prestigious American *verlag*.

Despite its clout, Knopf is currently just one among more than fifty imprints (including the original "little Random" division) operating within Random House, Inc.—imprints that must compete against one another for media attention and sales. Yet Knopf's revenues from a prestigious backlist, combined with an enduring reputation for excellence, continue to give Borzoi Books a competitive edge. This will be especially crucial in the wake of the 2013 merger between Penguin and Random House. The new company, called Penguin Random House, is controlled 53 percent by Bertelsmann and 47 percent by Pearson, parent company of Penguin.[7]

Underscoring the dilution of individual imprints' ability to capture their earnings, in December 2012 Dohle announced that every employee of Random House, Inc., who had been with the firm for at least twelve months would receive a $5,000 bonus in celebration of the extraordinary profits realized that year. Among the top sellers were John Grisham's *The Racketeer,* Gillian Flynn's *Gone Girl,* and Cheryl Strayed's *Wild,* but it was obvious that the *Fifty Shades of Grey* erotica series—published by Vintage—was the true fiscal phenomenon. While this was happy news after years of layoffs and shrinking budgets, the bonus was a reminder that Dohle has the power to redistribute the fruit of an individual publishing group's labor.[8]

While Alfred Knopf would have been pleased by the continued economic power of the brand he created, for him the rewards of a publishing life were always equally tied to making a prestigious name for himself. Not only did he satisfy the business goals his father emphasized, he was able to achieve his own goal of acquiring personal prestige, eventually landing memberships at the Grolier Club, the Club of Odd Volumes (Boston), the Caxton Club (Chicago), the Century Country Club, the Publishers' Lunch Club, and other exclusive organizations.[9] The company's fame is evident in equally profuse ways, such as the inclusion of Knopf in the *Oxford English Dictionary* as an example of how the word "borzoi" was being used in 1969 (from the *Times Literary Supplement:* "One inevitably comes up with Gollancz's yellow jackets, Alfred A. Knopf's borzoi colophon, and so on").[10] Researchers have even tried to assign a numeric value to the prestige of Borzoi Books. In 1981, a team of sociologists surveyed American book editors in an attempt to determine which houses ranked as the most prestigious among their publishing peers. Knopf received high marks from scholarly, trade, and university press editors. "In fact," the researchers concluded, "no trade house rated more highly."[11]

As their company reached its fiftieth anniversary, Blanche and Alfred nonetheless downplayed their initial vision for the company. Alfred Knopf depicted his early prospects as dodgy at best. Narrating a montage of his home movies, he insisted that "our ambitions and hopes for the future were very modest indeed. It was clear to me that there was room on the American scene for a publisher, a small one, who would choose books with discrimination, produce them in a better style than was customary at that time, and above all pay his bills promptly."[12] In a fiftieth-anniversary interview with *Publishers' Weekly,* Blanche was unable to define their target consumers with clarity, and her definition never invokes Nobel Prize winners: "'Quality middle-brow' is the way Mrs. Knopf characterizes the firm's editorial program," the unidentified reporter wrote, quoting Blanche as saying, "We're not *avant-garde,* but we're not pure middle-brow either; we don't aim especially at the book clubs or the *Reader's*

Digest." While making these statements, she puffed away on a cigarette in the study of her apartment on West Fifty-Fifth Street, relaying the reporter's drink request to her maid in "rapid colloquial French."[13] The profile respectfully omitted the fact that Blanche's eyesight was failing, as was her overall health. By this time, the Knopf receptionists had been trained to rush to Blanche's assistance when she came through the office door, guiding her so that her near-blindness would not be apparent to the rest of the staff.[14]

According to Harding Lemay, Knopf's publicity manager from 1958 to 1961, Blanche had become Alfred's fierce competitor, and employees as well as their heir apparent, Pat, frequently found themselves embroiled in their manipulative attempts to undermine each other.[15] The novelist and poet Robert Nathan was one of many Borzoi authors who asserted that it was not possible to be edited by both Blanche and Alfred: an author "belonged" to one or the other.[16] Willa Cather perhaps represents one of the few exceptions to this rule, requesting Alfred as her editor from the beginning but nonetheless corresponding with Blanche profusely. Far from weakening Borzoi Books, the notorious feuds between Blanche and Alfred, seen by some as childish and by others as evidence of the couple's passion for publishing, only stoked the fame of their company. Despite the discord, Alfred's interviews and reminiscences, as well his tribute to Blanche upon her death in 1966, describe his life with her as a complete partnership, professionally and otherwise, as if his public image (or his private self-image) required the myth that she was a supportive wife with whom he never engaged in tempestuous bickering. United under his single moniker, their separate publishing endeavors fulfilled a common purpose.

Whether working together, as Blanche and Alfred did in the company's initial years, or memorably at odds, the media-hungry Knopfs left a legacy of marketing savvy that equaled the critical acclaim received by their many prize-winning acquisitions. It would of course be grossly inaccurate to say that the company's prestige was wholly manufactured from the colorful personalities of its publishers. The Knopfs' editorial choices often proved to be as wise as their marketing and packaging choices, further enhancing a prestigious identity for the Knopfs themselves and for those who were professionally involved with them.

They launched their company in an era when old-guard publishers were dubious about such an overt marriage of marketing and books. Henry Holt warned readers of this in a 1905 screed published in the *Atlantic Monthly:*

During all this time of upheaval and chaos, the experiments that make up the miscellaneous publishing business, even in the calmest times, have grown much more expensive. Drumming has been introduced, and advertising has been quadrupled,—both in cost and volume,—dummies are sent out with the drummers, posters have become works of art, and each novel must have a fifty-dollar cover design, where a couple of dollars' worth of lettering used to fill the bill. Yet not as many books pay for themselves as did before. . . . Hence the mad quest of the golden seller, the mad payment to the man who has once produced it, and the mad advertising of doubtful books in the hope of creating the seller. . . . Even temperately conducted, the miscellaneous publishing business—the kind that advertises and, to a large extent, the kind that drums—is an extremely hazardous business.[17]

Alfred Knopf excelled in this "hazardous business" because he avoided overspending in acquisitions and made scrupulous use of every potential advertising space in which he invested—including the space provided on the jackets and title pages of his own books. The salesmanship decried by Holt was executed by the Knopfs in such a way that they were never classified as mere "drummers," and Alfred very likely would have preferred the fiscal constraints imposed by Bertelsmann over Si Newhouse's permissive expense accounts.

Today, with Sonny Mehta in command (under the watchful eye of Dohle) the company is led by a soft-spoken, elusive native of India, a diplomat's son whose Oxbridge lilt was developed during his nearly two decades in England as a student and, eventually, as a prominent member of the British publishing scene. His predecessor, Robert Gottlieb, served as director of Knopf from 1968 to 1987, perpetuating both the Knopfs' business approach and their corporate identity in a seamless transition. Mehta, who received the London Book Fair's Lifetime Achievement Award in International Publishing in 2011, embodies much of what the Anglophile Knopf wished to have been (Mehta appreciates Savile Row tailoring, on the rare occasions when he wears a suit). While he is also said to perpetuate Blanche's tradition of elusiveness, Knopf's prestigious reputation has only occasionally become the subject of public debate. In a 1991 profile of Random House published in *New York* magazine, David Streitfeld wrote, "Even if they're not [the best books in the world], they seem that way. 'Gilt by association,' one observer termed the phenomenon nearly 40 years ago. If Anne Rice were only known by the paperback editions of her novels, for instance, she would be generally dismissed as a writer of florid, overdone, spooky stuff. But in their handsome Knopf editions, her books seem as literary as *The Turn of the Screw*."[18]

E-books raise the question of whether it is possible for a publisher to create a "handsome" electronic edition, but the elimination of paper, cover art, and binding has not negated an interest in typography and other interior-design features that perhaps matter even more if a book is being read on an iPad. The economic boon of e-books was realized at Random House in the first half of

2011 (before the *Fifty Shades of Grey* phenomenon), when operating profits rose 73 percent over the same period in 2010, in part due to reduced costs associated with manufacturing, shipping, and returns.[19] For a scene in which profit generates power, the profit margin for e-books may create new channels of status for Knopf without negating the firm's artisanal aura.

Knopf advertisements are now devoid of a sensational publisher's voice, relying instead on sensational quotes from copious laudatory reviews. In orderly layouts, well-honed headlines retain the cachet of Knopf's voice by emphasizing cleverness more than braggadocio. This refinement was the work of the legendary advertising director Nina Bourne, who joined Knopf in 1968 as Alfred neared retirement. She, along with Robert Gottlieb and Tony Schulte, had forged a renowned team at Simon and Schuster and were perceived as bringing new creativity, bordering on commercialism, when they were lured to the house of Knopf. One month before they joined the company, Bennett Cerf called the trio "a publishing business in themselves." Cerf continued, "Bob Gottlieb is a very strong, attractive publisher and knows his business, and Tony Schulte is a fine administrator. Nina, of course—there's nobody like her in the advertising business. So to get even one of them would have been a coup, I think. To get the three of them is a miracle. I'm very happy because this assures the Knopf succession."[20] Cerf's concern over the "succession" refers not only to a personnel plan but to the company's aura of prestige and success. Bourne remained with the company until 2009, a year before her death at the age of ninety-three.

When I had the privilege of meeting Nina Bourne in 2008, she recalled her lasting image of Alfred, formed in March 1968 during her first days on the job. Because Cerf had done the recruiting, she was not required to have an interview with Knopf, meeting him for the first time after she was hired. During their first interaction, he was wearing a long coat and an expensive fur hat, conveying an affluent, towering presence despite his 5' 9" height. Alfred no longer came to the office on a daily basis when Bourne joined the company, but she quickly learned that he would continue to express strong opinions regarding her work. In 1969, he sent her a particularly scathing memo, typed on the unmistakable raspberry-colored stationery he used for internal correspondence, to express disapproval over a "sassy" (her word) ad she had run for Joseph Heller's play *We Bombed in New Haven*. Bourne was credited with fostering the success of Heller's now-classic novel *Catch-22* while she was at Simon & Schuster. She had begged for a higher initial print run and, as the book climbed British bestseller lists, chided American readers in ad headlines that said, "Come on, Yanks! Don't let the English beat us!"[21] Nonetheless, her achievements in her thirty-year career prior to joining Knopf did not make her immune to Alfred's wrath.

The Knopf ad for *We Bombed in New Haven* featured the book's cover art, comprising the title and author name typeset in the shape of a bomb. The copy is far from risky and echoes Alfred's early ads: "WE BOMBED IN NEW HAVEN is just published. It will speak directly to the great number of readers for whom CATCH-22 is the most urgent book of our time. $4.50. Alfred A. Knopf." The layout, however, is not traditional: the bomb appears to soar down a full column of white space.[22] What might have been especially upsetting to Alfred was the absence of his wolfhound logo. In any case, despite her gentle, cheerful temperament, Bourne responded to "Mr. Knopf" with an equally scathing memo, telling him that she had never before been addressed in such harsh tones. Conceding that the promotional "voice of Knopf" had always been his (she speculated that Franklin Spier and Frank Fletcher had little influence over the tone of Borzoi copy), she succeeded in gradually modernizing Knopf advertising without diminishing the company's prestigious persona.[23]

The term "Borzoi Books" no longer makes a regular appearance in ads, but the wolfhound continues to sprint across the copy, and the line "THIS IS A BORZOI BOOK" appears on the copyright page of every Knopf book. Though the ubiquitous colophon also continues to appear in every Knopf book, bindings and interior book design are not the focus of marketing messages anymore. Instead, trendsetting jackets created by associate art director Chip Kidd are more often the subject of publicity.

One of the company's most enduring features has proven to be the transatlantic legacy. Julia Child's *Mastering the Art of French Cooking*, originally published in 1961, experienced resurgence in 2009, quickly ranking no. 1 on the *New York Times* list after the release of the film *Julie and Julia*, and the Knopfs' affection for Scandinavian fiction is reflected in Swedish detective novels by Stieg Larsson, whose books held fast to bestsellers lists after the release of *The Girl with the Dragon Tattoo* in 2008. Unlike the works of Knut Hamsun, the Larsson novels reflect a strand of edgy, often violent yet erotically charged literature that some credit Mehta with daring to bring to Knopf, beginning with his acquisition of Bret Easton Ellis's *American Psycho* in 1990 and recently evidenced in Haruki Murakami's bestseller *1Q84* in 2011.

Whether they were negotiating for the rights to Eunice Tietjens's poetry or a collection of satire by Mencken, the Knopfs' formative years created widely varied scenes in which they could act as publishers. The traits of these disparate "circumferences" (as Burke would call them) encircled one unified message: perceived superiority. In a 1965 tribute to the Knopfs, the writer and translator Harriet de Onís summarized the theatricality of the Borzoi's invention by claiming that "if Blanche and Alfred had chosen the stage as their profession they would have given the Lunts a run for their money. They play their parts as publishers up to the hilt." Onís recalls that when she was first interviewed by Blanche, she thought, "Here is Rosalind Russell in a role she might have dreamed of. Everything was perfect: setting, voice, attire." Yet Onís concludes her observations with a reversal: "On second thought perhaps what I have just said falls short of the truth. What seems a role is really their life, and they are only doing what comes naturally."[24]

They crafted a definition of prestigious publishing that was closely linked to their personal identities, but it has been easily perpetuated by their descendants in the industry—the authors, agents, editors, designers, marketers, booksellers, critics, and prize committee members who continue to associate the Borzoi emblem with superior standards set by "the greatest publisher this country has ever had."[25] Whether we attribute this success to Henry Holt's much feared "drumming" or to Blanche and Alfred's genuine love of literature, the Knopfs achieved their goal of becoming prestigious producers, setting a stage and refining a script that has remained in performance well past their lifetimes.

 NOTES

Abbreviations Used in Notes

AAKI: Alfred A. Knopf, Inc., Records
CUA: Columbia University Archives
HRC: Harry Ransom Humanities Research Center, Austin, Texas
NYPL: New York Public Library

Introduction

1. Alfred Knopf gave conflicting dates for the launch of his firm. For the article "50 Years of the Borzoi," appearing in *Publishers' Weekly* on 1 February 1965, he supplied 29 October 1915 as the anniversary date, taken from the publication date of the first book. In earlier advertising and interviews, he gave the date as 25 September 1915, perhaps because this was the date of his first *Publishers' Weekly* ad, in which he announced to booksellers, "Well, the first of the books are ready." The copy continues, "You will sell a lot of them right now and you will go right on selling them as long as you remain in the book business."

2. John Tebbel, *A History of Book Publishing in the United States,* vol. 2: *The Expansion of an Industry, 1865–1919* (New York: R. R. Bowker, 1975), ix–x.

3. James F. English, *The Economy of Prestige: Prizes, Awards, and the Circulation of Cultural Value* (Cambridge: Harvard University Press, 2005), 9.

4. Max Weber, *Economy and Society,* vol. 1 (Berkeley: University of California Press, 1978), 346–47.

5. Evan Brier, *A Novel Marketplace: Mass Culture, the Book Trade, and Postwar American Fiction* (Philadelphia: University of Pennsylvania Press, 2010), 121.

6. John Tebbel, *A History of Book Publishing in the United States,* vol. 3: *The Golden Age between Two Wars 1920–1940* (New York: R. R. Bowker, 1978), 128.

7. Jay Satterfield, *The World's Best Books: Taste, Culture, and the Modern Library* (Amherst: University of Massachusetts Press, 2002), 32. See also Catherine Turner, *Marketing Modernism between the Two World Wars* (Amherst: University of Massachusetts Press, 2003), 77.

8. "50 Years of the Borzoi," *Publishers' Weekly,* 1 February 1965, 49 and 54.

9. Ibid., 54.

10. "Mrs. Blanche Wolf Knopf of Publishing Firm Dies," *New York Times,* 5 June 1966.

11. Satterfield, *The World's Best Books,* 96.

12. "New and splendid . . . books for the civilized minority . . ." advertisement, *New York Times,* 21 September 1958.

13. Diane Davis, "Burke and Freud on Who You Are," *Rhetoric Society Quarterly* 38, no. 2 (April 2008): 125.

14. Bobst Awards program, AAKI, 675:1, HRC.

15. John Guillory, "The Ideology of Canon Formation: T. S. Eliot and Cleanth Brooks," *Critical Inquiry* 10, no.1 (September 1983): 174.

16. Pierre Bourdieu, *The Rules of Art: Genesis and Structure of the Literary Field* (Stanford: Stanford University Press, 1992), 232–34.

17. Cathy Henderson and Richard Oram, *Dictionary of Literary Biography*, vol. 355: *The House of Knopf, 1915–1960* (Farmington Hills, MI: Gale Cengage, 2010). Authors featured are Elizabeth Bowen, James M. Cain, Albert Camus, Willa Cather, Raymond Chandler, Roald Dahl, Kahlil Gibran, Dashiell Hammett, John Hersey, Langston Hughes, Thomas Mann, H. L. Mencken, Kenneth Millar (whose pseudonym was Ross MacDonald), Yukio Mishima, and Carl Van Vechten.

18. Correspondence between Alfred Knopf and Susan Sheehan, ca. 1970, AAKI, 656:3, HRC.

19. "Scholar Discusses Work in Knopf Publishing Collection," Cultural Compass Page, HRC, 12 July 2011, www.utexas.edu/opa/blogs/culturalcompass/2011/07/12/scholar-discusses-work-in-knopf-publishing-collection/.

20. Promotional brochure, AAKI, 595:6, HRC.

21. Sheryl Englund, "Publicity to Overawe the Public: Marketing 'The Second Sex,'" *The Library Chronicle of the University of Texas at Austin* 22, no. 4 (1992): 103.

22. Michel Foucault, "What Is an Author?" in *Textual Strategies*, ed. Josué V. Harari (Ithaca: Cornell University Press, 1979), 141–60.

23. Jonathan Galassi, "There's More to Publishing Than Meets the Screen," *New York Times*, 3 January 2010, www.nytimes.com/2010/01/03/opinion/03galassi.html?_r=0.

1. Educating a Future Publisher

1. Michael Korda, *Making the List: A Cultural History of the American Bestseller, 1900–1999* (New York: Barnes and Noble, 2001), 26.

2. *Publishers' Trade List Annual* (New York: Offices of the *Publishers' Weekly*, 1915), 52.

3. Alfred Knopf's unpublished memoir, page 12, AAKI, 610:2, HRC.

4. John Tebbel, *A History of Book Publishing in the United States*, vol. 2: *The Expansion of an Industry, 1865–1919* (New York: R. R. Bowker, 1975), 26.

5. Peter Prescott, unpublished biography of Alfred Knopf, chapter one and interview notes. Private collection of Dr. Anne Lake Prescott, viewed at her home in 2008. Prescott's primary source for Knopf family histories was a series of extensive personal interviews conducted with Alfred Knopf and his relatives, now deceased, during the 1980s and '90s. In addition, in his memoir Alfred Knopf recalls receiving a letter from one of his mother's former students, confirming her former job as a teacher.

6. Alfred Knopf's notes for biographer Susan Sheehan, AAKI, 656:3, HRC.

7. Samuel Knopf's citizenship certificate, 10 October 1892, AAKI, 656:3, HRC.

8. Advertisement, *Cincinnati Enquirer*, 20 December 1894; "Horseless," *Cincinnati Enquirer*, 2 February 1896; "Samuel Knopf," *Cincinnati Enquirer*, 5 October 1896; "Men and Matters," *Cincinnati Enquirer*, 3 September 1896.

9. "Confirmed: Mrs. Knopf's Awful Death," *Cincinnati Enquirer*, 18 February 1897; "Infidelity Is Charged by Mr. Knopf," *Cincinnati Enquirer*, 9 February 1897; "Withdrawn: The Knopf Divorce Suit," *Cincinnati Enquirer*, 20 February 1897.

10. Prescott unpublished manuscript, chapter one, page 26.

11. Alvin Josephy, *A Walk toward Oregon* (New York: Knopf, 2000), 8.

12. Jeffrey Gurock, *When Harlem Was Jewish* (New York: Columbia University Press, 1979), 6 and 40.

13. Josephy, *A Walk toward Oregon*, 5.

14. Cathy Henderson and Richard Oram, *Dictionary of Literary Biography*, vol. 355: *The House of Knopf, 1915–1960* (Farmington Hills, MI: Gale Cengage, 2010), 38.

15. Alfred Knopf's unpublished memoir, page 12, 610:2.

16. Ibid., pages 13–14.

17. Josephy, *A Walk toward Oregon*, 8.

18. Eugene Exman, *The House of Harper* (New York: Harper & Row, 1967), 182.

19. "Gifts to Columbia . . . $34,609,091 under Dr. Butler," *New York Times,* 28 January 1922.

20. *Columbia University in the City of New York, Catalogue and General Announcements, 1909–1910,* map on unnumbered page between 170 and 171, CUA. For statistics, see Frederick Paul Keppel, *Columbia* (New York: Oxford University Press, 1914), 275.

21. Joyce Ross, *Joel Spingarn and the Rise of the NAACP, 1911–1939* (New York: Atheneum, 1972), 7.

22. William Ward, "A Short History of the NCTE," *College English* 22, no. 2 (1960): 71–77.

23. Quoted in Donald C. Stewart, "Harvard's Influence on English Studies: Perceptions from Three Universities in the Early Twentieth Century," *College Composition and Communication* 43, no. 4 (1992): 462.

24. Keppel, *Columbia,* 179–80.

25. Jerome Karabel, *The Chosen: The Hidden History of Admission and Exclusion at Harvard, Yale, and Princeton* (New York: Houghton Mifflin, 2005), 1–2.

26. *Columbia University in the City of New York, Catalogue and General Announcements, 1909–1910,* CUA.

27. Joel Elias Spingarn, *A Question of Academic Freedom: Being the Official Correspondence between Nicholas Murray Butler and J. E. Spingarn* (New York: privately published). University Archives and Columbiana, 295:13, CUA.

28. Korda, *Making the List: A Cultural History of the American Bestseller, 1900–1999,* xvii.

29. Spingarn, *A Question of Academic Freedom.*

30. Van Wyck Brooks, *Days of the Phoenix: The Nineteen-Twenties I Remember* (New York: E. P. Dutton, 1957), 141–58.

31. James Berlin, *Rhetoric and Reality: Writing Instruction in American Colleges, 1900–1985* (Carbondale: Southern Illinois University Press, 1987), 80–81.

32. Arnold Goldsmith, *American Literary Criticism: 1905–1965* (Boston: Twayne, 1979), 26.

33. Joel Elias Spingarn, *Creative Criticism and Other Essays* (New York: Henry Holt, 1917), 217.

34. Joyce Ross, *Joel Spingarn and the Rise of the NAACP, 1911–1939* (New York: Atheneum, 1972).

35. Alfred Knopf's unpublished memoir, page 32, AAKI, 610:2, HRC.

36. Alfred Knopf to Joel Spingarn, n.d., Joel E. Spingarn Papers, 6:3, NYPL.

37. Joel Spingarn to Alfred Knopf, 7 June 1911, AAKI, 595:4, HRC.

38. Alfred Knopf to Joel Spingarn, n.d., Joel E. Spingarn Papers, 6:3, NYPL.

39. Alfred Knopf to Joel Spingarn, 6 December 1911, Joel E. Spingarn Papers, 6:3, NYPL.

40. *Columbia University Bulletin of Information,* 1909–1910 and 1911–1912, CUA.

41. Alfred Knopf's unpublished memoir, page 31, 610:2.

42. Ibid., page 29.

43. Alfred Knopf, "Some Random Recollections: An Informal Talk Made at the Grolier Club, New York, 21 October 1948," in *Portrait of a Publisher 1915–1965,* vol. 1: *Reminiscences and Reflections* (New York: The Typophiles, 1965), 5–6.

44. "Sees Artists' Hope in Anarchic Ideas," *New York Times,* 18 March 1912.

45. Alfred Knopf's unpublished memoir, page 22, 610:2.

46. The Reminiscences of Bennett Cerf (1967–1968), page 245, session 6, in the Columbia Center for Oral History Collection.

47. Alfred Knopf's unpublished memoir, page 24, AAKI, 610:2, HRC.

48. Alfred Knopf, "John Millington Synge," in *Portrait of a Publisher 1915–1965,* vol. 1, 215–19. Originally published in the *Columbia Monthly,* June 1911. *Playboy of the Western World* was first published in the US that year, by J. W. Luce, with a subtitle that referred to the play as a comedy.

49. "The Core Curriculum," Columbia University, www.college.columbia.edu/core/oasis/history2.php.

50. *University Catalogue and General Announcement,* 1912–1913, CUA.

51. Travel certificate. AAKI, 595:4, HRC.

52. Alfred Knopf's unpublished memoir, page 61, AAKI, 610:2, HRC.

53. Alfred Knopf's notes for the memoir, AAKI, 595:4, HRC.

54. Alfred Knopf to Joel Spingarn, 26 May 1912, Joel E. Spingarn Papers, 6:3, NYPL.

55. Alfred Knopf's notes for the memoir, AAKI, 595:4, HRC.

56. Ibid.

57. Assorted correspondence between Alfred Knopf and Alfred Ollivant circa 1911–1912, AAKI, 723.10, HRC.

58. Alfred Knopf's notes for the memoir, AAKI, 595:4, HRC.

59. Matthew Bruccoli, *The Fortunes of Mitchell Kennerley, Bookman* (San Diego: Harcourt Brace Jovanovich, 1986), 75.

60. Haldane Macfall, "Claud Lovat Fraser: English Art's Untimely Loss," reprinted in *The Living Age,* vol. 313, no. 4061, 6 May 1922, page 358. Originally published in the UK in *Form,* January 1922.

61. Alfred Knopf's unpublished memoir, page 58, AAKI, 610:2, HRC.

62. Alfred Knopf's notes, AAKI, 595:4, HRC. Though he is identified in Knopf's notes as a son-in-law of Morris named Spaulding, the correct surname is Sparling. His marriage to May Morris had ended in divorce in 1898.

63. Kenneth Burke, *A Grammar of Motives* (Berkeley: University of California Press, 1969), 103. First published in New York: Prentice-Hall, 1949.

2. Apprenticeships and Partnerships

1. Alfred Knopf, "My First Job," in *Portrait of a Publisher 1915–1965,* vol. 1: *Reminiscences and Reflections* (New York: The Typophiles, 1965), 166–68. Originally published in the *Atlantic Monthly,* August 1958.

2. Alfred Knopf, "The Old Days at Garden City," in *Portrait of a Publisher 1915–1965,* vol. 1, 161–64. Originally published in *Double-Life* (New York: Doubleday, 1947). See also Knopf memoir, pages 65–66, AAKI, 610:2, HRC.

3. *The Country Life Press* (New York: Doubleday, Page & Company, 1919), 20.

4. Ibid., frontispiece and pages 22 through 78.

5. Clifton Knight to Federal Trade Commission, 21 July 2009, Federal Trade Commission, www.ftc.gov/os/comments/prenotnegativeoprule/541909-00014.pdf.

6. Knopf memoir, page 69, AAKI, 610:2, HRC.

7. Ibid., 67.

8. Harley Granville-Barker to Alfred Knopf, 18 October 1913, AAKI, 501:2, HRC.

9. Knopf, "The Old Days at Garden City," 163.

10. Joseph Conrad to Alfred Knopf, 20 July 1913, AAKI, 501:2, HRC.

11. Alfred Knopf to Joseph Conrad, 10 September 1913, AAKI, 501:2, HRC.

12. Alfred Knopf's unpublished memoir, page 84, AAKI, 610:2, HRC.

13. Assorted correspondence in response to Knopf's Conrad solicitation. AAKI, 501:2, HRC.

14. Knopf, "The Old Days at Garden City," 164.

15. Matthew Bruccoli, *The Fortunes of Mitchell Kennerley, Bookman* (San Diego: Harcourt Brace Jovanovich, 1986), 75.

16. Sinclair's *The Jungle* was not among the books published by Kennerley. It was issued instead by Doubleday, Page & Company in 1906.

17. Blanche Knopf, speech delivered at a Hotel Astor banquet celebrating the house's fiftieth anniversary, 29 October 1965. AAKI, 675:2, HRC.

18. Advertisement for *The Three Black Pennys, New York Times,* 30 September 1917.

19. Ibid.

20. Bruccoli, *The Fortunes of Mitchell Kennerley, Bookman,* 66.

21. Ibid., 76.

22. Ibid., 85.

23. Alfred Knopf to Joseph Hergesheimer, May 1915, AAKI, 595.4, HRC. Written in pencil and ending abruptly in midsentence (subsequent sheets are not on file), this is perhaps a page from a draft of a letter.

24. Alfred Knopf to Howard Vincent O'Brien, n.d., AAKI, 595.4, HRC. Because it is preserved in the sender's archive, this is perhaps a draft.

25. Alfred Knopf's unpublished memoir, page 65, AAKI, 610:2, HRC.

26. Meaghan Dwyer-Ryan, et al., *Becoming American Jews: Temple Israel of Boston* (Lebanon, NH: University Press of New England, 2009), 5–6.

27. Charles Dellheim, "A Fragment of a Heart in the Knopf Archives," *Chronicle of Higher Education* 45, no. 45 (16 July 1999): B4.

28. Alvin Josephy, *A Walk toward Oregon* (New York: Knopf, 2000), 11.

29. "New York Incorporations," *New York Times,* 8 February 1907.

30. Dwyer-Ryan, et al., *Becoming American Jews,* 3.

31. Peter Prescott, unpublished biography of Alfred Knopf, chapter three, manuscript pages 56–63. Private collection of Dr. Anne Lake Prescott.

32. Ibid.

33. Richard Perren, "The North American Beef and Cattle Trade with Great Britain, 1870–1914," *Economic History Review* 24, no. 3 (August 1971): 433.

34. "New Incorporations," *The Horseless Age* 21, no. 12 (18 March 1908): 331.

35. "Mission & History," Ethical Culture Fieldston School website, www.ecfs.org/about/missionhistory/history.aspx.

36. Blanche Wolf to Alfred Knopf, ca. 1912–1915, AAKI, 561:2, 561:3, and 561.4, HRC.

37. Transcript, Edwin Knopf's speech delivered at a banquet commemorating the 50th

anniversary of his brother's publishing firm, 29 October 1965, AAKI, 675:2, HRC. The protagonist of *V. V.'s Eyes,* a male physician named V. Vivian, has nothing in common with Blanche Knopf. Alfred simply adopted V. V. from the book's title because he thought Blanche's eyes were beautiful.

38. *Borzoi Quarterly* 15, no. 2 (1966), AAKI, 681:4, HRC.

39. Alfred Knopf's unpublished memoir, page 122, AAKI, 610:2, HRC.

40. Ibid., 123. See also Cathy Henderson and Richard Oram, *Dictionary of Literary Biography,* vol. 355: *The House of Knopf, 1915–1960* (Farmington Hills, MI: Gale Cengage, 2010), 41.

41. "Women Cast Votes as Readily as Men," *New York Times,* 6 November 1918.

42. Alfred Knopf's unpublished memoir, page 105, AAKI, 610:2. HRC. See also Knopf's War Department card, AAKI, 682:3, HRC.

43. Alfred Knopf's unpublished memoir, pages 105–9, AAKI, 610:2, HRC.

44. Geoffrey Hellman, "Publisher: Flair Is the Word," *New Yorker,* 27 November 1948, 46–48.

45. Josephy, *A Walk toward Oregon,* 11–12.

46. Geoffrey Hellman, "Publisher: A Very Dignified Pavane," *New Yorker,* 20 November 1948, 52.

47. Marjorie Keyishian, "A Soviet Visitor and a Quest: Preserving the Borzoi," *New York Times,* New Jersey weekly edition, 14 July 1991.

48. Alfred Knopf, "Russian Literature," *New York Times Review of Books,* 16 April 1916.

49. Henry W. Lanier, ed., "ABC of Copyright" in *The Author's Annual 1929* (n.p.: Payson & Clarke, 1929), 205.

50. "New Publisher to Specialize in Russian Literature," *Publishers' Weekly,* 3 July 1915: 10.

51. "Makers of Books in Vacation Time," *New York Times Review of Books,* 25 July 1915.

52. Alfred Knopf's unpublished memoir, pages 109–10, AAKI, 610:2, HRC.

53. Paul Avrich, *Anarchist Portraits* (Princeton: Princeton University Press, 1988), 96.

54. Alfred Knopf's unpublished memoir, page 110, AAKI, 610:2, HRC.

55. John Tebbel, *A History of Book Publishing in the United States,* vol. 3: *The Golden Age between Two Wars, 1920–1940* (New York: R. R. Bowker, 1978), 120.

56. Blanche Knopf to D. H. Lawrence, 3 April 1928, AAKI, 693:1, HRC.

57. Blanche Knopf to Radclyffe Hall, 20 September 1928, AAKI, 691.8, HRC.

58. Malcolm Gladwell, *Outliers* (New York: Little, Brown, 2008), 125.

59. George Bornstein, "The Colors of Modernism: Publishing Black, Irish, and Jewish Books in the 1920s" (Lecture: Race, Ethnicity, and the History of Books symposium, The University of Texas at Austin, 7 February 2009).

60. The Reminiscences of Bennett Cerf (1967–1968), page 117, session 3, in the Columbia Center for Oral History Collection.

61. George Hutchinson, *The Harlem Renaissance in Black and White* (Cambridge: Belknap Press, 1995), 344–45.

62. Tom Dardis, *Firebrand: The Life of Horace Liveright* (New York: Random House, 1995), 165–70.

63. Alfred Knopf, "On Censorship: A Statement," in *Portrait of a Publisher 1915–1965,* vol. 1, 26–27. The statement is dated 7 May 1951, though its audience and exigency remain unidentified.

64. Eugène Brieux, preface to *Four Plays* by Émile Augier (New York: Knopf, 1915), ix.

65. Alfred Knopf's unpublished memoir, page 109, AAKI, 610:2, HRC.

66. Adolph Kroch, "To Alfred Knopf, from a Bookseller," in *Portrait of a Publisher, 1915–1965*, vol. 2, 41. The tribute was originally written in 1940, for the Borzoi's twenty-fifth anniversary.

3. The Borzoi Abroad

1. Kermit Vanderbilt, *American Literature and the Academy* (Philadelphia: University of Pennsylvania Press, 1986), 3.

2. Mary Ann Gillies, *The Professional Literary Agent in Britain, 1880–1920* (Toronto: University of Toronto Press, 2007), 22.

3. "50 Years of the Borzoi," *Publishers' Weekly*, 1 February 1965, 49.

4. Alfred Knopf's unpublished memoir, page 128, AAKI, 610:2, HRC.

5. In later years, Knopf would remind his publishing colleagues that his son shared a birthday with Carl Van Vechten, James Weldon Johnson. G. B. Stern, and John Hersey. Van Vechten hosted June 17 parties in honor of himself, Pat, and Johnson.

6. Alfred Knopf's diary, AAKI, 621:1, HRC.

7. Alfred Knopf's unpublished memoir, page 124, AAKI, 610:2, HRC.

8. Housing contracts. AAKI, 595:4, HRC.

9. Alfred Knopf's unpublished memoir, page 187, AAKI, 610:3, HRC.

10. Blanche Knopf to Alfred Knopf, undated but with contextual evidence of chronology, AAKI, 561:1, HRC.

11. Alfred Knopf's unpublished memoir, page 132, AAKI, 610:2, HRC.

12. A note on methodology: These figures are derived from my inventory of books published by Knopf from 1915 through 1929, based on bibliographies featured in *The Borzoi 1920* and *The Borzoi 1925* as well as listings in *The Publishers' Trade List Annual* from 1926 through 1929. Occasionally, the *Borzoi* and *PTLA* listings don't match; most noteworthy is Knopf's inclusion of Claude Bragdon's *Four-Dimensional Vistas* in his *PTLA* description of inaugural 1915 books, while *The Borzoi 1920* lists the publication year as 1916. Because the *Borzoi* listings reflect after-the-fact reporting, I opted to rely on their data for compiling release dates for the company's first decade. When using *PTLA* listings for the subsequent years, I included only authors who were featured under the heading Trade Books, excluding educational books and special series. If the Knopfs chose to cross-list one of these titles within the trade book section, I included it in the tabulations. Despite these vagaries, the trend for the company's first three years is confirmed in Geoffrey Hellman's "Publisher: Flair Is the Word," *New Yorker*, 27 November 1948, 44.

13. Blanche Knopf to Stephen Haden Guest, 2 July 1928, AAKI, 1516:1, HRC.

14. Alfred Knopf, "Russian Literature," *New York Times Review of Books*, 16 April 1916. Note: the publication name changed to the *New York Times Book Review* in 1920.

15. The Reminiscences of Bennett Cerf (1967–1968), pages 517–19, session 12, in the Columbia Center for Oral History Collection. See also Michael Meyer, "About That Book Advance . . . ," *New York Times Book Review*, 12 April 2009.

16. Other changes included a new fee for registering the book with the American copyright office, and the requirement that the proper notice appear near the title page. The renewal term remained unchanged, maintaining an 1831 statute that set the initial term at 28 years and the renewal term at 14 years. However, under the 1891 law, renewal was available only if the applicant complied with all requirements within six months before the first

term was scheduled to expire. *Copyright Enactments: Laws Passed in the United States Since 1783*. Copyright Office Bulletin No. 3, Revised (Washington: Copyright Office, Library of Congress, 1973), 49–54.

17. Ibid., 67–73.

18. Ibid., 93.

19. For the effects of these international copyright enactments, see "ABC of Copyright" in *The Author's Annual 1929*, ed. Henry W. Lanier (n.p.: Payson & Clarke, 1929), 205; Frederick H. Hitchcock, "Copyrighting," in *The Building of a Book*, 2nd ed. (New York: R. R. Bowker, 1929), 253; and Geoffrey Hellman, "Publisher: A Very Dignified Pavane," *New Yorker*, 20 November 1948, 48.

20. Ada Galsworthy to Alfred Knopf, 20 December 1915, AAKI, 501:8, HRC.

21. "P.E.N. History," P.E.N. American Center website, www.pen.org (history page no longer available).

22. Alfred Knopf's unpublished memoir, page 118, AAKI, 610:2, HRC.

23. Advertisement for *Green Mansions, New York Times*, 4 June 1916.

24. Advertisement for *Green Mansions, New York Times*, 2 April 1916.

25. The copyright page of Boni & Liveright's Modern Library edition, released in 1921, also includes the line "copyright 1916 by Alfred A. Knopf," presumably only because their book featured an unauthorized reprint of the Galsworthy foreword. Boni & Liveright did not rent plates from Knopf for their edition, which was pocket-sized. When Bennett Cerf and Donald Klopfer acquired the Modern Library, they compensated Knopf for the introduction by paying a modest fee.

26. Alfred Knopf's unpublished memoir, page 118, AAKI, 610:2, HRC.

27. "Ready August 1st," advertisement for *Green Mansions, New York Times*, 30 July 1904.

28. William Henry Hudson to Alfred Knopf, 12 January 1913, AAKI, 501.4, HRC.

29. William Henry Hudson to Alfred Knopf, 1 August 1913, AAKI, 501.4, HRC.

30. William Henry Hudson to Alfred Knopf, 28 October 1916, AAKI, 501.4, HRC.

31. William Henry Hudson to Alfred Knopf, 20 September 1916, AAKI, 501.4, HRC.

32. Knopf's diminished influence after *Green Mansions* proved to be a strong seller is evident in a search of the Online Computer Library Center's WorldCat database: Dutton released *A Crystal Age* and *Idle Days in Patagonia* in 1917; *Far Away and Long Ago* in 1918; *Birds in Town and Village* in 1919; *Birds of La Plata, Dead Man's Plack, A Shepherd's Life*, and *Adventures Among Birds* in 1920; *A Traveller in Little Things* and *Fan, the Story of a Young Girl's Life* in 1921; *The Naturalist in La Plata* in 1922; *Birds in London, A Hind in Richmond Park, Nature in Downland, Hampshire Days, The Collected Works of W. H. Hudson*, and *Rare, Vanishing & Lost British Birds* in 1923, the year after Hudson's death; and *A Hudson Anthology*, arranged by Edward Garnett, in 1924. The George H. Doran Company also took a small share of the Hudson properties, releasing *The Book of a Naturalist* in 1919, re-titled and reissued as *The Disappointed Squirrel, and Other Stories from "The Book of a Naturalist"* in 1925. Many of Hudson's books found multiple incarnations among American publishers during the 1920s. Boni & Liveright launched the Modern Library series in 1917 with an edition of *Green Mansions. Birds and Man* was published by Knopf in 1916 and by Dutton in 1923. *Afoot in England* was published by Knopf in 1922 and by Dutton in 1923. The Modern Library released *The Purple Land* in 1926, after Dutton had published it in 1916. *The Land's End* was issued by Dutton in 1923 and by Knopf 1927. *Tales of the Pampas* was released by Dutton under the title *El Ombú* in 1923, seven years after Theodore Roosevelt raved about the copy he received from Knopf. *A Little Boy Lost*, an illustrated collection of

wilderness tales for young adults, was published by Knopf as a children's book in 1917 and released by Dutton in 1923 in a collected edition, which contained *Ralph Herne,* published also by Knopf in 1923.

33. Alfred Knopf to William Henry Hudson, 25 July 1917, AAKI, 654:11, HRC.

34. William Henry Hudson, postscript to *Little Boy Lost* (New York: Knopf, 1918), 222.

35. Advertisement, *Dial* 73, no. 2 (August 1922), xiii.

36. Alfred Knopf to Mills & Boon Ltd., 5 July 1916, Private Collection of G. Thomas Tanselle.

37. Edward Garnett to Alfred Knopf, 23 July 1915, AAKI, 709:6, HRC.

38. Edward Garnett to Alfred Knopf, 13 December 1920, AAKI, 709:6, HRC.

39. Alfred Knopf to Edward Garnett, 27 February 1922, AAKI, 709:6, HRC.

40. Alfred Knopf to Edward Garnett, 12 May 1922, AAKI, 501:5, HRC.

41. James Hepburn, *The Author's Empty Purse and the Rise of the Literary Agent* (London: Oxford University Press, 1968), 57.

42. Mary Ann Gillies, *The Professional Literary Agent in Britain, 1880–1920* (Toronto: University of Toronto Press, 2007), 101.

43. Albert Curtis Brown, *Contacts* (London: Cassell, 1935), 2.

44. Alfred Knopf's unpublished memoir, page 172, AAKI, 610:3, HRC.

45. The award for outstanding picture went to *Wings,* a silent film also about World War I, with footage of stunt pilots portraying flyboys. Also recognized with an Oscar that year was the revolutionary talking picture *The Jazz Singer,* the story of a cantor's son who struggles with questions of Jewish-American assimilation.

46. Geoffrey T. Hellman, "Publisher: Flair Is the Word," *New Yorker,* 27 November 1948: 48.

47. Jacket copy, Warwick Deeping's *Sorrell and Son* (New York: Grosset & Dunlap, 1926).

48. Promotional copy appearing on the closing pages of Warwick Deeping's *Sorrell and Son* (New York: Knopf, 1927). The Garamont typeface was designed by Frederic Goudy in 1921.

49. Alfred Knopf's unpublished memoir, page 206, AAKI, 610:3, HRC.

50. William Aspenwall Bradley Literary Agency Collection, 85:6–11, HRC.

51. Blanche Knopf, speech delivered at a Hotel Astor banquet celebrating the house's fiftieth anniversary, 29 October 1965, AAKI, 675:2, HRC.

52. Alfred Knopf, interview by Jules Schwerin. Transcript, AAKI, 681:3, HRC.

53. Samuel Knopf to Saul Salzberg, 4 May 1932, AAKI, 1516:2, HRC.

54. Alfred Knopf's memoir, page 133, AAKI, 610:2, HRC.

55. Ibid., page 132.

56. A useful examination of the Knopfs' entry into Latin American publishing can be found in the 2007 master's thesis "House of Knopf: Publication, Persuasion, and the Public Opinion" by Mose James Buchele, housed in the University of Texas at Austin's Perry Castañeda Library.

57. Alfred A. Knopf, 1975, draft of "On Publishing Thomas Mann," an article scheduled for publication in P.E.N.'s *The American Pen,* Volume 7, Number 3, AAKI, 661:9, HRC. In the article, Knopf also attributes his interest in German literature to Joel Spingarn, who returned from the Great War impressed by Teutonic literature.

58. Alfred Knopf to Helen Lowe-Porter, ca. 1927. William A. Koshland Files, 2:1, HRC. See also Cathy Henderson and Richard Oram, *Dictionary of Literary Biography,* vol. 355: *The House of Knopf, 1915–1960* (Farmington Hills, MI: Gale Cengage, 2010), 316.

59. Alfred A. Knopf, draft of "On Publishing Thomas Mann," manuscript page 2.

60. Henderson and Oram, *Dictionary of Literary Biography*, vol. 355: *The House of Knopf, 1915–1960*, 316.

61. Helen Lowe-Porter to Alfred Knopf, 29 June 1928. William A. Koshland Files, 2:1, HRC.

62. Catherine Turner, *Marketing Modernism between the Two World Wars* (Amherst: University of Massachusetts Press, 2003), 99–110.

63. Alfred Knopf to Helen Lowe-Porter, 15 December 1927. William A. Koshland Files, 2:1, HRC. For information on the fee arrangement between Secker and Knopf, see various correspondence between Knopf and Lowe-Porter, ca. 1935, when Secker was nearing liquidation. Knopf advised Lowe-Porter to retain a lawyer to elicit payment from Secker.

64. Thomas Mann to Blanche Knopf, 6 July 1928, AAKI, 693:9, HRC.

65. Alfred Knopf's unpublished memoir, page 152, AAKI, 610:3, HRC.

66. Pat Conroy, *My Reading Life* (New York: Nan A. Talese / Doubleday, 2010), 163–64.

67. James F. English, *The Economy of Prestige: Prizes, Awards, and the Circulation of Cultural Value* (Cambridge: Harvard University Press, 2005), 55.

68. Julie Bosman, "Publishing Is Cranky over Snub by Pulitzers," *New York Times*, 18 April 2012.

69. Promotional copy, Svend Fleuron, *Grim: The Story of a Pike* (New York: Knopf, 1921).

70. Hellman, "Publisher: A Very Dignified Pavane," 56.

71. Michael Mikoś and David Mulroy, "Reymont's *The Peasants:* A Probable Influence on *Desire Under the Elms*," *The Eugene O'Neill Newsletter* 10, no. 1 (Spring 1986), www.eoneill.com/library/newsletter/x-1/x-1b.htm.

72. Clipping from the *Saturday Review of Literature*, 19 May 1928, AAKI, 595:5, HRC.

73. "In the West Indies," *New York Times*, 6 December 1925.

74. Lloyd Morris, "The Nō Plays of Japan," *New York Times Book Review*, 7 May 1922.

75. Radically exalting German culture during the Great War, Richardson's *Pointed Roofs* is listed in the 1916 PTLA as the first volume in a trilogy, though it would in fact spur a much longer, thirteen-volume stream-of-consciousness *Pilgrimage* series, in which the female protagonist pursues a quest for her own authentic identity.

76. Alfred Knopf to Joseph Lesser, n.d., 1967, AAKI, 656:7, HRC. Lesser was hired as the firm's office manager in 1920 and succeeded Samuel Knopf as treasurer.

77. Guy Chapman to Alfred Knopf, 1 September 1925, AAKI, 595:5, HRC.

78. Guy Chapman to Samuel Knopf, 28 June 1927, AAKI, 1516:5, HRC. Alfred A. Knopf Ltd. was not formally dissolved until January 1950, though the publishing assets of the London office were liquidated in 1932. The long-term lease prevented Knopf Ltd. from ceasing operations sooner. Throughout those final years, the firm managed tenants in the building, making real estate—not publishing—the primary business of Knopf Ltd. for most of its existence. Much of Britain's commercial and residential real estate has been concentrated for generations in the hands of the few gentry. Therefore, such long-term leases are not uncommon and in many ways approximate ownership. Knopf's building was located in a heavily developed urban area but was nonetheless part of the Duke of Bedford's estate.

79. Royalty statement for *The Lovely Ship*, AAKI, 692:1, HRC.

80. R. Le Clerc Phillips, "English Novelist Discusses Woman," *New York Times*, 24 January 1926.

81. Alfred Knopf to Joseph Lesser, ca. 1967, AAKI, 656:7, HRC.

82. Paul Reynolds to Alfred Knopf, 2 December 1920, AAKI, 595:5, HRC; and interview transcript, undated but filed with materials related to the Knopfs' documentary

endeavor with Jules Schwerin, which spanned the early 1960s, AAKI, 679:5, HRC. Paul Revere Reynolds's son (1905–1988), who bore the same name, succeeded his father in the business.

83. Alfred Knopf to A. S. Lowy, 3 July 1928, AAKI, 1516:1, HRC.

84. A. S. Lowy to Blanche Knopf, 5 July 1928, AAKI, 1516:1, HRC.

85. Correspondence between Blanche Knopf and Stephen Haden Guest, ca. 1928, AAKI, 1516:1, HRC.

86. Samuel Knopf to Guy Chapman, 15 August 1927, AAKI, 1516:5, HRC.

87. Samuel Knopf to Guy Chapman, 28 June 1927, AAKI, 1516:5, HRC.

88. Handwritten bid, Thos. H Martin & Co., April 1928, AAKI, 1516:6, HRC.

89. Samuel Knopf to Saul Salzberg, 4 May 1932, AAKI, 1516:2, HRC.

90. Pamphlet of Borzoi survey, n.d. AAKI, 1515:5, HRC.

91. Accounting records ca. 1931, AAKI, 1514:10, HRC.

92. Report, unsigned and undated, presumably prepared by Joseph Lesser in response to Alfred's November 1959 request for a financial summary of Alfred A. Knopf Ltd., AAKI, 1514:9, HRC.

93. Alfred Knopf's unpublished memoir, page 174, AAKI, 610:3, HRC.

94. Alfred Knopf's unpublished memoir, page 199, AAKI, 610:3, HRC.

95. Stephen Haden Guest to Blanche Knopf, n.d., AAKI, 1516:1, HRC.

96. "Pio Baroja," *Times Literary Supplement*, 5 August 1926.

97. "Catherine the Great," *Times Literary Supplement*, 1 September 1927.

98. "An Ex-Coloured Man," *Times Literary Supplement*, 22 March 1928.

99. "Come to Harlem and See Life in the Raw," advertisement, *Times Literary Supplement*, 14 October 1926.

100. "Alfred A. Knopf Christmas Gifts," *Times Literary Supplement*, 16 December 1926.

101. Kenneth Burke, *A Grammar of Motives* (Berkeley: University of California Press, 1969), 314. First published in New York: Prentice-Hall, 1949.

102. Ibid., 341.

4. Producing American Literature

1. Grosset & Dunlap immediately issued a cheap edition by arrangement with Knopf.

2. Joseph Hergesheimer to Blanche Knopf, 17 October 1927, AAKI, 691:10, HRC.

3. H. L. Mencken, *Treatise on the Gods* (New York: Knopf, 1930), 345–46. Throughout the book, Mencken makes disparaging comments about people of all faiths.

4. George H. Douglas, *The Golden Age of the Newspaper* (Westport, CT: Greenwood Publishing Group, 1999), 202.

5. Alfred Knopf's unpublished memoir, supplemental draft, page 104, AAKI, 619:8, HRC.

6. Ibid., page 12, AAKI, 619:1, HRC. Knopf and Mencken shared a birthday, September 12, frequently citing this as evidence of their tremendous compatibility.

7. Ibid., page 24A, AAKI, 618:6, HRC.

8. Emigrating from Ireland in 1914, Boyd was a Knopf translator and author, publishing a short biography of Mencken as a Borzoi Book.

9. Ernest Boyd, "Aesthete: Model 1924," *The American Mercury* 1, no. 1 (January 1924): 54.

10. Jack Selzer, *Kenneth Burke in Greenwich Village: Conversing with the Moderns, 1915–1931* (Madison: University of Wisconsin Press, 1996), 48–50. Also see page 129, which features a photograph of Burke in costume as a mock professor.

11. Malcolm Cowley, *Exile's Return* (New York: Penguin, 1994), 192. First published New York: W. W. Norton, 1934.

12. H. Alan Wycherley, "Mencken and Knopf: The Editor and His Publisher," *American Quarterly* 16, no. 3 (Autumn 1964): 464–5.

13. Alfred Knopf's unpublished memoir, supplemental draft, page 45, AAKI, 618:7, HRC.

14. Alvin Josephy, *A Walk toward Oregon* (New York: Knopf, 2000), 14.

15. "Borzoiana," advertisement for assorted Knopf titles, *New York Times*, 20 September, 1925.

16. Blanche Knopf, speech delivered at a Hotel Astor banquet celebrating the house's fiftieth anniversary, 29 October 1965, AAKI, 675:2, HRC.

17. Alfred Knopf's unpublished memoir, supplemental unnumbered pages, AAKI, 618: 5, HRC.

18. Jason Epstein, *Book Business: Publishing Past, Present, and Future* (New York: Norton, 2002), 17–19.

19. Willa Cather to Ferris Greenslet, 19 May 1919, Andrew Jewell and Janis Stout, eds., *The Selected Letters of Willa Cather* (New York: Knopf, 2013), 274–77.

20. Willa Cather to Blanche and Alfred Knopf, 16 May 1923, ibid., 339.

21. Willa Cather to Blanche Knopf, 27 December 1921; Willa Cather to Blanche Knopf, 29 December 1922; Willa Cather to Blanche Knopf, 26 December 1931; Willa Cather to Blanche Knopf, ca. 1926, Andrew Jewell and Janis Stout, eds., *A Calendar of the Letters of Willa Cather*, University of Nebraska, http://cather.unl.edu/index.calendar.html.

22. Alfred Knopf's unpublished memoir, unnumbered supplemental pages, AAKI, 618:5, HRC.

23. Willa Cather to Alfred Knopf, 1 September 1921, Jewell and Stout, *The Selected Letters*, 305.

24. Carl Van Vechten to Alfred Knopf, 10 October 1923, AAKI, 728:9, HRC. Van Vechten composed his letters using green and purple typewriter ribbons, sometimes on letterhead printed in fuchsia.

25. The fabric sample is no longer attached to the letter, so it is not possible to determine whether the Knopfs complied. Subsequent correspondence indicates that "tall paper" editions were in fact produced for the book. Carl Van Vechten to Alfred Knopf, 18 March 1926, AAKI, 729:3, HRC.

26. "In the West Indies," *New York Times*, 6 December 1925. This news story quotes Knopf's promotional copy.

27. Diary entries typed on 17 February 1965, AAKI, 595:5, HRC.

28. Langston Hughes's autobiography, *The Big Sea*, reprinted in *The Collected Works of Langston Hughes*, vol. 13 (Columbia: University of Missouri Press, 2002), 169.

29. Randolph Lewis, "Prejudice in Publishing: Alfred A. Knopf and American Publishing, 1915–1935" (master's thesis, University of Texas at Austin, 1990), 63. Lewis's study describes Hughes's 1930s transformation into a writer who embraced communism and wished to be perceived as a political voice, rather than being defined by his ethnicity—a transition from which the Knopfs attempted to steer their lucrative author. Clearly, there were limits to the Knopfs' affinity for alternative voices.

30. James Danky, "Reading, Writing, and Resisting: African American Print Culture," in *A History of the Book in America*, vol. 4: *Print in Motion* (Chapel Hill: University of North Carolina Press, 2009), 354.

31. Assorted correspondence between Langston Hughes and Blanche Knopf, circa 1926, William A. Koshland Files, 1:5, HRC. The Koshland files were acquired after Randolph

Lewis completed his research. The fact that these files contain letters related to the publication of *The Weary Blues* is an indication of the book's status as a profitable classic; Koshland did not join the company until 1934, when he was hired as the business manager. He eventually became president of the firm in 1966 and at the time of his death in 1997 was chairman emeritus.

32. "W," an editorial staffer at Alfred A. Knopf, Inc., to Langston Hughes, 29 June 1926, William A. Koshland Files, 1:5. "W" could not refer to Koshland since he had not yet joined the company.

33. Randolph Lewis, "Prejudice in Publishing," 80.

34. Langston Hughes, *The Big Sea,* 202.

35. Ibid., 203.

36. Alfred Knopf's unpublished memoir, page 209, AAKI, 610:3, HRC.

37. Dashiell Hammett to Editorial Department, 15 February 1928, AAKI, 691:9, HRC.

38. Ibid., Dashiell Hammett to Blanche Knopf, 20 March 1928.

39. Ibid., Dashiell Hammett to Harry Block, 19 July 1929.

40. Ibid., Blanche Knopf to Dashiell Hammett, 2 April 1928.

41. Alfred Knopf's unpublished memoir, supplemental draft, page 84, AAKI, 619:1.

42. The Reminiscences of Bennett Cerf (1967–1968), page 521, session 12, in the Columbia Center for Oral History.

43. Carl Brandt, "Agents," in *The Building of a Book,* 2nd ed. (New York: R. R. Bowker, 1929), 12–20.

44. Alfred Knopf's unpublished memoir, page 126, AAKI, 610:2, HRC.

45. William Shehadi, ed., *Kahlil Gibran: A Prophet in the Making* (Beruit: The American University of Beruit, 1991), 152.

46. Joan Acocella, "Prophet Motive," *New Yorker,* 7 January 2008, 72.

47. William Aspenwall Bradley Agency Collection, 85:6–11, HRC.

48. Scott Fitzgerald to Blanche Wolf, 19 January 1928, AAKI, 690:5, HRC.

49. Blanche Wolf to Stephen Haden Guest, 2 July 1928, AAKI, 1516:1, HRC.

50. Alfred A. Knopf to William Aspenwall Bradley, 4 September 1924, William Aspenwall Bradley Agency Collection, 85:6, HRC.

51. Alfred Knopf's unpublished memoir, page 83, AAKI, 610:2, HRC.

52. Lewis was a Canadian-born Vorticist whose mother was English and whose father was American.

53. Alfred Knopf's unpublished memoir, page 137, AAKI, 610:2, HRC.

54. T. S. Eliot to John Quinn, March 1923, quoted in Tom Dardis's *Firebrand: The Life of Horace Liveright* (New York: Random House, 1995), 98.

55. Alfred Knopf's unpublished memoir, page 137, AAKI, 610:2, HRC.

56. Ibid., page 125.

57. Alfred Knopf to John Schwartz, 16 November 1956, AAKI, 1514.8, HRC.

58. Edith Stern, "A Man Who Was Unafraid," *The Saturday Review,* 28 June 1941, 10 and 14.

59. John Tebbel, *A History of Book Publishing in the United States,* vol. 3: *The Golden Age between Two Wars 1920–1940* (New York: R. R. Bowker, 1978), 131–32.

60. Alfred Knopf, review of *Editor to Author: The Letters of Maxwell E. Perkins,* originally printed in *New York Times Book Review,* 26 March 1950. Reprinted in *Portrait of a Publisher, 1915–1965,* vol. 1: *Reminiscences and Reflections* (New York: The Typophiles, 1965), 200.

61. Alfred Knopf, "Publishing Then and Now" in *Portrait of a Publisher, 1915–1965,* vol. 1, 45.

62. Tebbel, *A History of Book Publishing in the United States*, vol. 3, 52.

63. Judith Jones, *The Tenth Muse* (New York: Knopf, 2007), 53–55.

64. Ibid., 63–68.

65. "Special Report to Directors and Stockholders," 14 May 1940, AAKI, 656:7, HRC.

66. Tebbel, *A History of Book Publishing in the United States*, vol. 3, 670.

67. Ibid., 663 and 668.

68. Alfred Knopf's unpublished memoir, page 127, AAKI, 610:2, HRC.

69. "Financial Setup, Alfred A. Knopf, Inc.," undated report produced no earlier than 1946, AAKI, 656:7, HRC.

70. Josephy, *A Walk toward Oregon*. 110–11.

71. Untitled report, AAKI, 656:7, HRC.

72. Joseph Lesser to Alfred Knopf, 18 April 1933, AAKI, 656:7, HRC.

5. Distinctive by Design

1. George Salter, "There *Is* a Borzoi Style," in *Portrait of a Publisher, 1915–1965*, vol. 2: *Alfred A. Knopf and the Borzoi Imprint: Recollections and Appreciations* (New York: The Typophiles, 1965), 282.

2. Sidney Jacobs, "Alfred and Designers," in *Portrait of a Publisher, 1915–1965*, vol. 2, 286.

3. Alfred Knopf, "Some Random Recollections: An Informal Talk Made at the Grolier Club, New York, 21 October 1948," in *Portrait of a Publisher, 1915–1965*, vol. 1: *Reminiscences and Reflections* (New York: The Typophiles, 1965), 15.

4. Interview transcript, undated but connected to the Knopfs' documentary endeavor with Jules Schwerin, which spanned the early 1960s. AAKI, 681:3, HRC.

5. Knopf memoir, page 106, AAKI, 610:2, HRC. The assistant was Edward Booth, who became a Knopf author in 1945 with *God Made the Country*, an homage to rural life.

6. Both copies are now housed at the HRC.

7. Alfred Knopf, "Some Random Recollections," 14.

8. Jack W. C. Hagstrom, "Alfred A. Knopf's Borzoi Devices," 2005, BibSite, Bibliographical Society of America, www.bibsocamer.org/BibSite/contents.htm.

9. John Carter, *ABC for Book Collectors*, 7th ed., revised by Nicolas Barker (New Castle, DE: Oak Knoll, 1995), 77. Originally published in London by Rupert Hart-Davis, 1952.

10. G. Thomas Tanselle, "A System of Color Identification for Bibliographical Description," *Studies in Bibliography*, vol. 10 (1967; published annually).

11. Alfred Knopf, "Some Random Recollections," in *Portrait of a Publisher, 1915–1965*, vol. 1, 20.

12. Lurton Blassingame, "The Trinity—and a Dog," *New Yorker*, 21 August 1926, 15.

13. G. Thomas Tanselle, "Book-Jackets, Blurbs, and Bibliographers," *The Library* 26, no. 2 (June 1971): 97.

14. "The Knopf Archive at Texas" (Special Issue), *The Library Chronicle of the University of Texas at Austin* 22, no. 4 (1992): 32. The photograph also appears in the *Dictionary of Literary Biography*, vol. 355: *The House of Knopf*, 36.

15. Alfred Knopf, "Dwig and the Borzoi," in *Portrait of a Publisher, 1915–1965*, vol. 1, footnote on page 91.

16. Frank Comparato, *Books for the Millions* (Harrisburg, PA: Stackpole, 1971), 265.

17. *Chicago Daily News* clipping, n.d., AAKI, 588:4, HRC.

18. Knopf memoir, page 119, AAKI, 610:2, HRC.

19. Floyd Dell, *Moon-Calf,* jacket copy (New York: Knopf, 1920).

20. Claude Bragdon to Alfred Knopf, 15 February 1922, AAKI, 731:11, HRC.

21. Elmer Adler to Alfred Knopf, 16 April 1931, AAKI, 593:3, HRC.

22. Alfred Knopf to Claude Bragdon, multiple letters ca. 1922, AAKI, 731:10–11, HRC.

23. The English edition contained illustrations by James Affleck Shepherd, a prolific caricaturist.

24. "George Salter: Gallery of Selected Works," Wellesley College, Department of German, www.wellesley.edu/German/GeorgeSalter/Documents/image_gallery.html.

25. "Elmer Adler and the Graphic Arts Collection at Princeton University Library." Princeton University Library, www.princeton.edu/~rbsc/exhibitions/adler/index.html.

26. Elmer Adler to Alfred Knopf, 19 February 1934, AAKI, 593:3, HRC.

27. John Tebbel, *A History of Book Publishing in the United States,* vol. 3: *The Golden Age between Two Wars 1920–1940* (New York: R. R. Bowker, 1978), 303.

28. Ibid., 167.

29. Jay Satterfield, *The World's Best Books: Taste, Culture, and the Modern Library* (Amherst: University of Massachusetts Press, 2002), 95.

30. Tebbel, *A History of Book Publishing in the United States,* vol. 3, 343.

31. Bruce Rogers to Alfred Knopf, 18 July 1923, AAKI, 734:5, HRC.

32. Elmer Davis, "Joseph Hergesheimer Contemplating His Pious Youth," *New York Times,* 10 February 1924.

33. Sales representatives' samples, private collection of Michael Winship.

34. Harold E. Shaw, president of Holliston Mills, contributed a chapter on book cloths in Frederick Hitchcock's *The Building of a Book* (New York: Bowker, 1929), providing useful information regarding nomenclature. Shaw describes the many "linen" cloths that were being marketed at the time under the name "vellum," such as Rex Vellum, Vellum de Luxe, Aldine Vellum, and Art Vellum. He places "linen" in quotation marks because that too was a term fraught with vagaries in the book-binding business of the 1920s, when "linen" did not necessarily refer to flax-based cloth (202–3).

35. Cathy Henderson and Richard Oram, eds., *The Company They Kept: Alfred A. and Blanche W. Knopf, Publishers,* exhibition catalogue (Austin: HRC, 1995), 52.

36. Joan Crane, *Willa Cather: A Bibliography* (Lincoln: University of Nebraska Press, 1982), 102–3.

37. Michael Zinman to author, Email, 21 March 2012.

38. William Dwiggins to Alfred Knopf, 19 October 1926, AAKI, 700:6, HRC.

39. Willa Cather to Dorothy Canfield Fisher, ca. 1922, Andrew Jewell and Janis Stout, eds., *The Selected Letters of Willa Cather* (New York: Knopf, 2013), 320.

40. Sigrid Undset, *Jenny,* jacket copy (New York: Knopf, Pocket Books edition, 1929).

41. Advertisement for *My Mortal Enemy, New York Times,* 31 October 1926.

42. Elmer Adler to Alfred Knopf, 12 June 1931, AAKI, 593.3, HRC.

43. Correspondence between Alfred Knopf and William Addison Dwiggins, 1926 through 1927, AAKI, 732.7, HRC.

44. Willa Cather to Alfred Knopf, 17 July 1934, Andrew Jewell and Janis Stout, eds., *The Selected Letters of Willa Cather* (New York: Knopf, 2013), 499.

45. William G. Blair, "Two Who Are 'Super Supers,'" *New York Times,* 1 February 1981.

46. Tebbel, *A History of Book Publishing in the United States,* vol. 3, 379.

47. Ibid., 351.

48. "Good Book-Making," *Publishers' Weekly,* 25 February 1922, 496.

49. Alfred Pollard, *Fine Books* (New York: Cooper Square, 1964), 14.

50. Tebbel, *A History of Book Publishing in the United States,* vol. 3, 28–29.

51. Jane Williams, "The Reduction of Labor Turnover in the Plimpton Press," *Annals of the American Academy of Political and Social Science* 71, no. 1 (May 1917): 71–81.

52. Paul Shaw, "Tradition and Innovation: The Design Work of William Addison Dwiggins," in *Design History: An Anthology*, ed. Dennis Doordan (Cambridge: MIT Press, 1995), 32.

53. Paul Bennett, Introduction, *Portrait of a Publisher, 1915–1965*, vol. 2: *Alfred A. Knopf and the Borzoi Imprint: Recollections and Appreciations* (New York: The Typophiles, 1965), viii.

54. Katherine Anthony, *Catherine the Great*, colophon (New York: Knopf, 1925).

55. Philip Gaskell, *A New Introduction to Bibliography* (reprinted by Oak Knoll Press, New Castle, DE, 1995), 221–22.

56. Matthew Bruccoli, *The Fortunes of Mitchell Kennerley, Bookman* (New York: Harcourt Brace Jovanovich, 1986), 6.

57. Megan Benton, *Beauty and the Book* (New Haven, CT: Yale University Press, 2000), 36.

58. Margaret Stetz and Mark Samuels Lasner, *England in the 1890s: Literary Publishing at the Bodley Head* (Washington, DC: Georgetown University Press, 1990), viii–ix. See also J. W. Lambert and Michael Ratcliffe, *The Bodley Head 1887–1987* (London: Bodley Head, 1987), 31–32.

59. William Morris, *The Ideal Book: Essays and Lectures on the Arts of the Book*, ed. William Peterson (Berkeley: University of California Press, 1982), 67.

60. Alfred Knopf to William Aspenwall Bradley, 8 September 1924, William Aspenwall Bradley Agency Collection, 85:6, HRC.

61. *New York Times* editorial quoted in Tebbel, *A History of Book Publishing in the United States*, vol. 3, 63.

62. Tebbel, vol. 3, 62–63.

63. Alfred Knopf, *The Borzoi 1920*, postscript (New York: Knopf, 1920), 134.

64. Alfred Knopf to Kahlil Gibran, 7 December 1927, AAKI, 709:9, HRC.

65. Quoted by Alfred Knopf in "Dwig and the Borzoi," in *Portrait of a Publisher 1915–1965*, vol. 1, 110. Knopf's homage to Dwiggins was originally published in *Esquire*, December 1959.

66. "Mrs. Blanche Wolf Knopf of Publishing Firm Dies," *New York Times*, 5 June 1966.

67. Kenneth Burke, *The Philosophy of Literary Form* (Berkeley: University of California Press, 1973), 299. Originally published in Baton Rouge: Louisiana State University Press, 1941.

6. Bookselling and the Borzoi

1. Advertisement, *New York Times*, 23 April 1922.

2. John Tebbel, *A History of Book Publishing in the United States*, vol. 3: *The Golden Age between Two Wars, 1920–1940* (New York: R. R. Bowker, 1978), 130.

3. "Books You Must Have," advertisement, *Publishers' Weekly*, 25 September 1915: 899. Four of the five titles featured in the ad were reprints, including *Ideals and Realities in Russian Literature*, which Knopf's copy describes with surprising candor as "a new and cheaper edition of a standard book that has long been out of print." *The Little Angel*, a collection of fifteen stories by L. N. Andreyev, was apparently the sole wholly original Knopf production featured in this ad.

4. Knopf's *New York Times* advertising did not feature the term "Borzoi Books" until April 1916, which is (perhaps coincidentally) when Alfred and Blanche were married.

5. Alfred Knopf, "Dwig and the Borzoi," in *Portrait of a Publisher, 1915–1965*, vol. 1: *Reminiscences and Reflections* (New York: The Typophiles, 1965), 121. Barron Collier owned a national advertising agency.

6. Ibid.

7. Quoted in Geoffrey T. Hellman, "Publisher: A Very Dignified Pavane," *New Yorker*, 20 November 1948: 46.

8. Ibid.

9. "Mr. Knopf Announces *The Borzoi 1920*," advertisement, *New York Times*, 17 October 1920.

10. Alfred Knopf, *The Borzoi 1920*, foreword (New York: Knopf, 1920).

11. Alfred Knopf's correspondence, AAKI, 595 (multiple folders), HRC.

12. Adolph Kroch, "To Alfred Knopf, from a Bookseller," in *Portrait of a Publisher, 1915–1965*, vol. 2 (New York: The Typophiles, 1965), 41.

13. Ibid.

14. Alfred Knopf's unpublished memoir, page 106, AAKI, 610:2, HRC.

15. Catherine Turner, *Marketing Modernism between the Two World Wars* (Amherst: University of Massachusetts Press, 2003), 83.

16. "Borzoiana," advertisement for assorted Knopf titles, *New York Times*, 20 September 1925.

17. Alfred Knopf to John Howell, promotional postcard, ca. 1932, private collection of G. Thomas Tanselle.

18. Seasonal listings, *Publishers' Weekly*, 9 February 1918: 432–33. The photo caption places the Mackenzie School in Monroe, New York, which reflects a relocation; as mentioned in the first chapter, Alfred completed his studies at the original campus, in Dobbs Ferry, New York.

19. Alfred Knopf's unpublished memoir, 106–7, AAKI, 610:2, HRC.

20. Alfred Knopf's unpublished memoir, supplemental draft, pages 17A–17AA, AAKI, 618:6, HRC.

21. Terry Teachout, *The Skeptic: A Life of H. L. Mencken* (New York: HarperPerennial, 2003), 228.

22. Alfred Knopf's unpublished memoir, supplemental draft, 17B, AAKI, 618:6, HRC.

23. Alfred Knopf to Joseph Hergesheimer, 2 March 1922, AAKI, 715:8, HRC.

24. Richard Fuller to Alfred Knopf, 18 February 1922, AAKI, 595:5, HRC.

25. John Tebbel, *A History of Book Publishing in the United States*, vol. 2: *The Expansion of an Industry, 1865–1919* (New York: R. R. Bowker, 1975), 63–79. See also Hellmut Lehmann-Haupt, *The Book in America*, 2nd ed. (New York: R. R. Bowker, 1952), 385.

26. "Macy & Co. Reply on Book Decision," *New York Times*, 7 December 1913.

27. Tebbel, *A History of Book Publishing in the United States*, vol. 3, 66.

28. Charles Madison, *Book Publishing in America* (New York: McGraw-Hill, 1966), 54.

29. Janice Radway, *A Feeling for Books: The Book-of-the-Month Club, Literary Taste, and Middle-Class Desire* (Chapel Hill: University of North Carolina Press, 1997), 154–55.

30. Robert Haas to Knopf employee Walter Tulley, 27 September 1926, AAKI, 564:8, HRC.

31. Alfred Knopf, "Publishing Then and Now," in *Portrait of a Publisher, 1915–1965*, vol. 1, 40. Knopf's Bowker Memorial Lecture was delivered 15 October 1964.

32. W. A. Lyle to Alfred Knopf, May 1922, AAKI, 595:5, HRC.

33. Ibid., William Caven to Alfred Knopf, 5 August 1922.

34. Ibid., Walter Kingsley to Alfred Knopf, October 1919.

35. Ibid., Carl Culpepper to Alfred Knopf, 29 December 1922.

36. Ibid., Carl Hull to Alfred Knopf, 14 February 1921.

37. Ibid., R. W. Pence to Alfred Knopf, 11 February 1921.

38. Ibid., Harry Dounce to Alfred Knopf, 3 January 1920.

39. Jason Epstein, *Book Business: Publishing Past, Present, and Future* (New York: Norton, 2002), 95–96.

40. Alfred Knopf's 1918 diary entries, AAKI, 621:1, HRC.

41. Promotional leaflet, 21 December 1921, AAKI, 595:5, HRC.

42. Lawrence Levine, *Highbrow/Lowbrow: The Emergence of Cultural Hierarchy in America* (Cambridge: Harvard University Press, 1990), 241.

43. Ellen Garvey, "Ambivalent Advertising," in David D. Hall, ed., *A History of the Book in America*, vol. 4: *Print in Motion* (Chapel Hill: University of North Carolina Press, 2009), 177.

44. Alfred Knopf's handwritten notes, n.d., AAKI, 595:5, HRC.

45. C. C. Eckhardt, Review of *The Genesis of the World War* by Harry Elmer Barnes, *Mississippi Valley Historical Review* 13, no. 3 (December 1926): 417–19.

46. Correspondence between Harry Barnes and Paul Thomas or Alfred Knopf, ca. 1924–1939, AAKI, 699 (multiple folders), HRC.

47. Harry Barnes to Alfred Knopf, 28 March 1927, AAKI, 699:2, HRC.

48. Joseph Lesser to Alfred Knopf, ca. 1967, AAKI, 595.6, HRC.

49. Alfred Knopf to Walter de la Mare, 3 September 1925, 721.1, HRC.

50. *The College Bookstore Association Bulletin* 1, no.1 (1928), NYPL.

51. Tebbel, *A History of Book Publishing in the United States*, vol. 2, 66–67.

52. Michael Winship, *American Literary Publishing in the Mid-Nineteenth Century* (New York: Cambridge University Press, 2002), 154–55. First published in 1995.

53. I have found no evidence that the many Knopf series were offered for sale through subscription, which is perhaps an indication of Knopf's wish to avoid competing with college retailers. Jackets for titles in the various series were used only to solicit subscriptions to the catalogs or to *The American Mercury*.

54. Paul Thomas to Joseph Lesser, 5 December 1928, AAKI, 572.3, HRC.

55. Promotional leaflet for the Text-book Department, ca. 1924, Private collection of G. Thomas Tanselle.

56. Promotional leaflet, 21 December 1921, 595.5, HRC.

57. Carl Kaestle and Janice Radway, "A Framework for the History of Publishing and Reading in the United States, 1880–1940," in *A History of the Book in America*, vol. 4, 7.

58. Alfred Knopf's unpublished memoir, pages 242–43, AAKI, 610:3, HRC.

59. Kenneth Burke, *A Rhetoric of Motives* (Berkeley: University of California Press, 1969), 43 and 64. First published in New York: Prentice-Hall, 1950.

7. A Majestic Brand

1. Geoffrey Hellman, "Publisher: A Very Dignified Pavane," *New Yorker*, 20 November 1948, 44 and 54.

2. John Tebbel, *A History of Book Publishing in the United States*, vol. 2: *The Expansion of an Industry, 1865–1919* (New York: R. R. Bowker, 1975), 167.

3. Frank Presbrey, *The History and Development of Advertising* (New York: Doubleday, 1929), i.

4. Michael Winship, "*Uncle Tom's Cabin:* History of the Book in the 19th-Century United States," essay derived from a presentation delivered in June 2007 at the *Uncle Tom's Cabin* in the Web of Culture conference. Institute for Advanced Technology in the Humanities, University of Virginia, www.iath.virginia.edu/utc/interpret/exhibits/winship /winship.html.

5. Susan Geary, "The Domestic Novel as a Commercial Commodity: Making a Best Seller in the 1850s," *Papers of the Bibliographical Society of America* 70 (1976): 388–89.

6. Richard Brodhead, "Veiled Ladies: Toward a History of Antebellum Entertainment," *American Literary History* 1, no. 2 (Summer 1989): 277.

7. Geary, "The Domestic Novel," 373.

8. Interview transcript, undated but corresponding to the Knopfs' documentary endeavor with Jules Schwerin, which spanned the early 1960s, AAKI, 679:5, HRC.

9. Emanuel Demby, "Psychographics Revisited: The Birth of a Technique," *Marketing Research* 6, no. 2 (Spring 1994): 27.

10. Arthur Judson Brewster and Herbert Hall Palmer, *Introduction to Advertising* (New York: McGraw-Hill, 1929), 220–21.

11. Ibid., 211–12.

12. Stuart Ewen, *Captains of Consciousness: Advertising and the Social Roots of the Consumer Culture* (New York: McGraw-Hill, 1976), 190.

13. Richard Ohmann, *Selling Culture: Magazines, Markets, and Class at the Turn of the Century* (London: Verso, 1996), 25.

14. The *Little Review* serialized James Joyce's *Ulysses* between 1918 and 1920 before censorship quashed the novel's US distribution.

15. Karen Leick, "Popular Modernism: Little Magazines and the American Daily Press," *Publications of the Modern Language Association* 123, no. 1 (2008): 125–39.

16. Catherine Turner. *Marketing Modernism between the Two World Wars* (Amherst: University of Massachusetts Press, 2003), 81.

17. Frank Irving Fletcher, *The Meaning of Borzoi: A Series of Advertisements and a Preface* (New York: Knopf, 1923), 2.

18. Alfred Knopf's unpublished memoir, page 206, AAKI, 610:3, HRC.

19. Jackson Lears, *Fables of Abundance: A Cultural History of Advertising in America* (New York: Basic Books, 1994).

20. Brewster and Palmer, *Introduction to Advertising*, 215.

21. Quoted in Turner, *Marketing Modernism*, 142.

22. William O'Barr, *Culture and the Ad* (Boulder, CO: Westview Press, 1994), 6.

23. John Tebbel, *A History of Book Publishing in the United States*, vol. 3: *The Golden Age between Two Wars, 1920–1940* (New York: R. R. Bowker, 1978), 320–321.

24. Max Weber, *Essays in Sociology* (New York: Routledge, 1998), 188. Originally published in 1948.

25. Turner, *Marketing Modernism*, 96.

26. Advertisement for *New York Herald Tribune* book review, *New Yorker*, 21 March 1925, 32.

27. Harold Ross to George Oppenheimer, 29 January 1925. AAKI, 595:5 HRC.

28. Advertisement for *Nigger Heaven*, *New Yorker*, 28 August 1926, 53.

29. Advertisement for *My Brother Jonathan*, *New Yorker*, 24 November 1928, 55.

30. "The Talk of the Town," *New Yorker*, 8 December 1928, 21.

31. Cartoon, *New Yorker,* 15 December 1928, 26.

32. Cartoon, *New Yorker,* 2 March 1929, 60.

33. Advertisement for the works of Knut Hamsun, *New York Times,* 8 November 1920.

34. Peter Gay, *Modernism: The Lure of Heresy* (New York: Norton, 2008), 191.

35. Advertisement for assorted Knopf titles, *New York Times,* 21 September 1958.

36. "For Just a Few Intelligent People," advertisement for Knopf titles, *New York Times,* 9 January 1921. Knopf used a similar headline, "For Just a Few Intelligent Readers," in *New York Times* advertising for Mencken's books the previous year.

37. Edward Nawotka, "Reviewing the State of Book Review Coverage," *Publishers Weekly,* 9 October 2006, 4.

38. Alfred Knopf, "My First Job," *Atlantic Monthly,* August 1958, 79–80.

39. Alfred Knopf's unpublished memoir, page 232, AAKI, 610:3, HRC.

40. Advertisements for *Homo Sapiens, New York Times,* 30 October 1915 and 31 October 1915.

41. Alfred Knopf, "Some Random Recollections" in *Portrait of a Publisher, 1915–1965,* vol. 1: *Reminiscences and Reflections* (New York: The Typophiles, 1965), 15.

42. Elmer Adler to Blanche Knopf, 16 June 1927, AAKI, 731:9, HRC.

43. Julie Melby, "Elmer Adler and the Little Gallery of the Pynson Printers," *Princeton University Library Chronicle* 73, no. 5 (Spring 2012): 393–96.

44. Advertisement, *New York Times,* 2 April 1916.

45. "Food Expert Arrested," *New York Times,* 7 July 1905, "Court Calendar / State Courts / Decisions," *New York Times,* 21 December 1907.

46. "The Deadly Virus: The Influenza Epidemic of 1918," National Archives, www .archives.gov/exhibits/influenza-epidemic/.

47. Alfred Knopf's unpublished memoir, page 129, AAKI, 610: 2, HRC.

48. Turner, *Marketing Modernism,* 99.

49. Advertisements, *New York Times,* 12 November 1916 and 10 December 1916.

50. Advertisement, *New York Times,* 30 September 1917.

51. Advertisement, *New York Times,* 20 September 1918.

52. Advertisement, *New York Times,* 24 November 1918.

53. Over two decades, Dunn had made a name for himself as a prolific commercial illustrator with numerous publishing clients.

54. Ellen Garvey, "Ambivalent Advertising," in *A History of the Book in America,* vol. 4: *Print in Motion* (Chapel Hill: University of North Carolina Press, 2009), 173.

55. Alfred A. Knopf, *Those Damned Reminiscences: Further Selections from the Memoirs of Alfred A. Knopf,* ed. Cathy Henderson (Austin: HRC, 1995), 6.

56. Warwick Deeping, *Kitty,* promotional copy bound into the closing pages (New York: Knopf, 1927).

57. "A Book for Every Father and Every Son," advertisement for *Sorrell and Son, New York Times,* 28 February 1926.

58. Advertisement, *New York Times,* 7 November 1920.

59. All Cather information in this paragraph is drawn from Erika Hamilton, "Advertising Cather During the Transition Years (1914–1922)," *Cather Studies* 7, no. 1 (2007): 13–26.

60. "History of a Publishing Season," advertisement, *New York Times,* 8 October 1922.

61. "Book Lineage," advertisement, *New York Times,* 16 March 1919.

62. "Landmarks of a Memorable Season," advertisement, *Washington Post,* 12 December 1926.

63. "Give Books for Valentines," advertisement, *Los Angeles Times,* 10 February 1924.

64. Tebbel, *A History of Book Publishing in the United States*, vol. 3, 33.

65. "Today's Radio Program," *New York Times*, 14 April 1922.

66. Joseph Hergesheimer to Blanche Knopf, 25 April 1930, AAKI, 691:10, HRC.

67. Joan Shelley Rubin, *The Making of Middlebrow Culture* (Chapel Hill: University of North Carolina Press, 1992), 270–71.

68. Ibid., 272.

69. Ibid., 278.

70. Felicia Pearson, "Moviegraphs," *Washington Post*, 6 November 1927.

71. "Literary Sandwich Men," *Publishers Weekly*, 14 April 1921, page 1422. See also Tebbel, *A History of Book Publishing in the United States*, vol. 3, 332.

72. Tebbel, *A History of Book Publishing in the United States*, vol. 3, 334.

73. Ibid.

74. Geoffrey T. Hellman, "Publisher: Flair Is the Word," *New Yorker*, 27 November 1948: 48.

75. The offer of free transit advertising was not exceptional. In an act that supported women's rights, or perhaps merely the attempt to appear progressive, Collier's Street Railways Advertising Company, based in New York but providing services in more than 700 cities, awarded $8,000 worth of complimentary advertising space to suffragists in New York City. Margaret Finnegan, *Selling Suffrage: Consumer Culture and Votes for Women* (New York: Columbia University Press, 1999), 63.

76. Tebbel, *A History of Book Publishing in the United States*, vol. 3, 334.

77. Spier was acquired by Warren Kremer Paino Advertising in 2006.

78. The HRC's Knopf archive contains Spier correspondence from 1921, 1922, and 1923 only. Spier launched his own advertising firm in 1929.

79. Edward Bernays, *Propaganda* (Brooklyn: Ig Publishing, 2004), 37. Originally published in New York: Horace Liveright, 1928.

80. Joseph Hergesheimer to Blanche Knopf, 25 April 1930, AAKI, 691:10, HRC.

81. Blanche Knopf to Kahlil Gibran, 16 January 1919, AAKI, 691:2, HRC.

82. For Knopf's early authors, publicists sometimes also carried the risk of being blamed if an author was denied royalties on a book that failed to sell more than 500 copies. Orrick Johns agreed to let Knopf publish his *Asphalt and Other Poems* under such an arrangement after Knopf explained to him the tremendous marketing efforts required to launch a work by a first-time author. Johns was also instructed to write his own jacket and catalog copy and submit it, along with the standard author photo and biography, to assist the publicists. Alfred Knopf to Orrick Johns, circa 1916, AAKI, 501:1, HRC.

83. Correspondence between Carl Van Vechten and Franklin Spier, August 1922, AAKI, 728:9, HRC.

84. Hellman, "Publisher: Flair Is the Word," 46.

85. Alfred Knopf's unpublished memoir, page 138, AAKI, 610:2, HRC.

Afterword

1. Saul Maloff, "Golden Anniversary," *Newsweek*, 17 May 1965, 106.

2. Jay Satterfield, *The World's Best Books: Taste, Culture, and the Modern Library* (Amherst: University of Massachusetts Press, 2002), 164.

3. "Borzoi at Random," *Time*, 9 May 1960.

4. Gene Smith, "RCA Confirms Random House Bid," *New York Times*, 11 January 1966. Gramophone stationery can be found in AAKI, 501:1, HRC.

5. Elizabeth Manus, "Sonny Mehta, Uneasy King of Knopf," *New York Observer,* 18 October 1999, www.observer.com/1999/10/sonny-mehta-uneasy-king-of-knopf/.

6. "Facts & Figures 2009," *Publishers Weekly,* 5 April 2010, www.publishersweekly .com/pw/by-topic/industry-news/financial-reporting/article/42695-facts--figures-2009 -revised.html.

7. Julie Bosman, "Penguin and Random House Merge, Saying Change Will Come Slowly," *New York Times,* 2 July 2013.

8. Leslie Kaufman, "At Random House, Employees Will Enjoy 5,000 Shades of Green," *New York Times,* 6 December, 2012, http://mediadecoder.blogs.nytimes.com. Employees of Random House UK (in the author's homeland) did not receive this benefit because they operate within a separate subsidiary of Bertelsmann.

9. Geoffrey Hellman, "Publisher: Flair Is the Word," *New Yorker,* 27 November 1948, 36.

10. "Borzoi," *Oxford English Dictionary,* 2nd ed., vol. 2 (New York: Oxford University Press, 1989).

11. Lewis Coser et al., *Books: The Culture and Commerce of Publishing* (Chicago: University of Chicago Press, 1982), 68.

12. *A Publisher Is Known by the Company He Keeps* (New York: Louis de Rochemont Associates, 1961), DVD from 16 mm film. AAKI, HRC.

13. "50 Years of the Borzoi," *Publishers' Weekly,* 1 February 1965, 49–50.

14. Katherine Hourigan, interview by author, 18 August 2008.

15. Harding Lemay, *Inside, Looking Out: A Personal Memoir* (New York: Harper's Magazine Press, 1971), 230–49.

16. Transcript, Robert Nathan's speech delivered at a banquet commemorating the 50th anniversary of the Knopf firm, 29 October 1965, AAKI, 690:4, HRC.

17. Henry Holt, "The Commercialization of Literature," *Atlantic Monthly,* November 1905, 599.

18. David Streitfeld, "Life at Random," *New York Magazine,* 5 August 1991, 39.

19. Matthew Flamm, "Publisher's New (Growth) Chapter," *Crain's New York Business,* 2 October 2011, www.crainsnewyork.com/article/20111002/SUB/310029979.

20. The Reminiscences of Bennett Cerf (1967–1968), pages 919–20, session 19, in the Columbia Center for Oral History Collection.

21. "Nina Bourne Is Dead at 93," *New York Times,* 14 April 2010; "Happy birthday CATCH-22," advertisement, *New York Times,* 15 October 1962.

22. "We Bombed in New Haven," advertisement, *New York Times,* 28 August 1968.

23. Nina Bourne, interview by author, 18 August 2008.

24. Harriet de Onís, "The Man in the Sulka Shirt," in *Portrait of a Publisher, 1915–1965,* vol. 2 (New York: The Typophiles, 1965), 204.

25. "Knopf Is Eulogized as 'Greatest Publisher' in U.S.," *New York Times,* 16 August 1984.

INDEX

AMY ROOT CLEMENTS is assistant professor of English writing and rhetoric at St. Edward's University in Austin, Texas. She formerly served in the marketing departments of several publishing houses. She earned a PhD in English at the University of Texas at Austin, with specializations in rhetoric and bibliography, and she holds an MFA in creative writing from The New School. Clements was named the 2009 Malkin New Scholar by the Bibliographical Society of America.